Fresh
Cooking

FRESH
Cooking

a year of recipes from the
Garrison Institute Kitchen

SHELLEY BORIS

foreword by
Rozanne Gold

photos by
Caroline Kasterine

Monkfish Book Publishing Company
Rhinebeck, New York

Fresh Cooking: A Year of Recipes from the Garrison Institute Kitchen
Copyright © 2014 by Shelley Boris

Photographs © 2014 Caroline Kasterine
Cover illustration: Spoon © 2004 Shelley Boris
Book and cover design by Danielle Ferrara

Library of Congress Cataloging-in-Publication Data

Boris, Shelley.
  Fresh cooking : a year of recipes from the Garrison Institute kitchen / by Shelley Boris ; photographs by Caroline Kasterine.
     pages cm
  Includes index.
  ISBN 978-1-939681-15-7 (hardcover)
  1. Seasonal cooking. 2. Cooking, International. I. Garrison Institute (Garrison, N.Y.) II. Title.
  TX714.B6424 2014
  641.5'64--dc23
                          2013050909

ISBN: 978-1-939681-15-7
E-book: 978-1-939681-16-4

Printed in the United States of America

Monkfish Book Publishing
22 E. Market St., Suite 304
Rhinebeck, NY 12572
www.monkfishpublishing.com

For Peter.

And in memory of my parents,
Ruth Nitkin Boris and
Phillip Leonard Boris.

ACKNOWLEDGMENTS

I have tremendous gratitude for the help and support so many people have given me throughout my education, career, and during the time I have spent writing this book.

In particular, I would first like to thank my husband Peter Lewis for his incredible patience, intelligence, love, and help; and my sons Matt and Phillip for their love, patience, and opinions. My deepest thanks go to Diana and Jonathan Rose, and all the staff of the Garrison Institute, to name a few: Robyn Brentano, Jane Kolleeny, Linda (and her late husband Tim) Downey, Jeanne Johnson, Dennis Stobinski, and Rob Gabriel. A huge "thank you very much" to everyone at Monkfish Publishing for taking on this project, and for truly outstanding work: Paul Cohen, publisher; Anastasia McGhee, editor; and Danielle Ferrara, designer. I could not have done this book without the friendship, advice, and support of Rozanne Gold. A giant thank you to Caroline Kasterine for her beautiful photographs and to her husband Dmitri Kasterine for his counsel and good company during our Sunday photo shoots.

Thank you so very much to my business partner and friend, Kimball Gell, and to an amazing kitchen staff over the years, to name a few: baker Cree LeFavour (who also graciously helped with editing and dessert recipes), chef de cuisine Paul Winberry Jr., sous chef Lauren Grace, James Basciani, Janet Murff, Kazumi Futagawa, Lachele Conix-Wiley, and Joanne McCauley, Olga Leon, and thank you to Chelsea Carlton, Elena Delamater, and Debby Dichter.

Numerous friends, family, colleagues, and employers have helped me so much along the way, to all of you, thank you, a few by name: Matt Lewis Thorne, John Thorne, Georgia Dent, Pam Sway, Vicky Abrash, Jamie Potenberg, Dale Boris-Kane, Butch Kane, Fred Sway, Phyllis Boris, Lisa Queen, Eleanor Jackson, Barbara Kafka, Chip Allemann, Peter Dent, Bruce R. Cliborne, John Beal, Maureen Higgins, Bob Hoebee, Mindy Heiferling, Jack Ceglic, Joel Dean, and Giorgio DeLuca.

MENUS

FOREWORD

Shelley Boris, who heads the kitchen at the Garrison Institute, is a very gifted chef. Never mind that she has cooked for His Holiness the Dalai Lama, Lou Reed, and Philip Glass, her intelligent and compassionate approach to food is keenly felt and enjoyed by everyone who visits. Always mindful of the communal table—which is how one eats in the massive, sunlit dining room—Shelley's food is elemental, and deeply connected to the earth from which it comes. Food is ritual here, three times a day, and in itself is a meditation.

One experiences a sense of awe when approaching the massive front doors of the Garrison Institute, a turn-of-the-century former Capuchin monastery overlooking the majestic Hudson River in upstate New York. Inside await endless possibilities and opportunities for self-exploration, friendship, and quiet pleasures. There are few places in life, after all, where one can throw caution to the wind and embrace the personal unknown.

Created ten years ago by inspired thinkers Jonathan and Diana Rose, the Institute has become a hub for the world's great spiritual and educational leaders. It has served as hearth and home to its many guests, providing nourishment in both tangible and intangible ways. If your idea of bliss includes meditation, contemplation, and community, then the Garrison Institute is a place of manifest satisfactions.

I will always remember my first visit—there have been dozens since—roaming the vast corridors of the building, with its spare beauty and Mission-style furniture; the expansive meditation hall and laughing golden Buddha; the resonating dinner gong beckoning hungry guests to its hallowed dining hall, and the delicious food that sustained us throughout the day. Whether eating in silence or engaged in conversation, I felt the intention of the kitchen and the grace that accompanied each meal. The food, wholesome and inviting, exquisitely integrated the values of contemporary and holistic cooking.

As executive chef of the Garrison Institute for the past ten years, Shelley has nurtured each guest who has dined at her table. Sharing a kindred approach to cooking, we both came of age during New York's culinary heyday. In the late 1970s, when I was first chef to Mayor Ed Koch of New York and later consulting chef to the Rainbow Room and Windows on the

World, Shelley was the fresh-food manager at Dean & Deluca and then chef at Exile restaurant and Peter Dent Catering, where she wowed upscale New Yorkers with luxurious things to eat. But she also embodies a more rustic, countrified sensibility that better describes the food at the Garrison Institute. From her large kitchen with windows overlooking a spacious herb garden, Shelley delights in the planning of her menus, each a short story revealing something immediate in nature. January brings her comforting Onion Soup with Sprout Creek Cheese and Sour Rye Toast, followed by Winter Root Salad drizzled with a sherry-hazelnut dressing, baked white beans, and crimson quince blanketed in phyllo. May is expansive and spontaneous—Braised Lamb and Rhubarb Chutney, Rice with Sorrel, Garlic Chives and Mustard Greens; and Rhubarb Shortcakes.

Shelley would say that her menus and recipes are eccentric, personal, and idealistic. Although not strictly vegetarian, her repertoire is rich in vegetables yet still friendly to meat-eaters. "Here, we flip the typical equation," she explains. "Rather than cutting back on meat, these recipes help you think about where you might want to add meat and fish to your diet." Nice. Family-style and practical, Shelley's approach and that of the Garrison Institute is to embrace the diversity of the tastes and needs of their guests. Shelley's recipes follow suit and are organized into menus that alert the cook to the undulating poetry of the seasons. I find her ideas inspiring. Whether adding a bit of ground juniper to roasted cauliflower, showering slivers of fresh mint into a pasta dish packed with tomatoes, mozzarella, and capers, or simply roasting local pears to accompany a main course, the outcome is always fresh cooking—in thought and in technique.

Shelley is an artist, both in and out of the kitchen. She also is a wife, mother, and entrepreneur who is held in high esteem in the Hudson Valley. Her catering firm, Fresh Company, embraces cooking styles and ingredients from around the world—I too love imported ingredients and think they crack the world wide open for all of us—yet Shelley also is a *bodhisattva* of local agriculture, championing the efforts of neighboring farms, food producers, and culinary artisans.

Twenty-five years ago, I created the concept of "Hudson River cuisine" for a three-star restaurant, the Hudson River Club, located in New York's World Financial Center, predicting that the Hudson Valley would one day become our own

Napa Valley, a notion dear to my heart. I encouraged New Yorkers to eat locally—as intimately as "in our own zip code"—at the time when farmers' markets were beginning to emerge throughout the region. As the Garrison Institute just celebrated its tenth year, the Hudson Valley has indeed emerged as an important and thriving center of gastronomy. It is bursting with farms, wineries, artisanal cheese makers, bread bakers, game raisers, distillers, and brewers, dozens of them representing the sustainable types of businesses with whom Shelley has developed lasting relationships.

For those of you who know the area, she buys produce from Blooming Hill Farm, and much of her meat and eggs from Padgett Farm, Four Winds Farm, and Glynwood Farm. A board member emerita of Cold Spring's Farmers' Market, Shelley supports the people who take care of the land and do the hard work. As she does.

Shelley brings that same dedication to her kitchen at Garrison Institute. Cooking for hundreds every day and creating special events *is* hard work. It takes determination, and a conscious point of view. Shelley gets rid of the clutter, extra steps, and superfluous ingredients in her recipes in order to focus on the essence of each dish. Like the mantra of the Institute itself, she brings "inspired thinking and thoughtful action" to every menu. Working within a limited budget also became a driving force of creativity for her and resulted in recipes that were inexpensive to produce. This is exactly what a home cook desires and why Shelley decided to write the book in the first place. Perhaps it will sit nestled next to like-minded tomes like the *Chez Panisse Menu Cookbook*, the *Greens* cookbook, Perla Meyers' *The Seasonal Kitchen*, and the Moosewood cookbooks—all game-changers in the way that people connect to food and cooking in a larger context—where taste and ethics are not at odds.

More than a cookbook, *Fresh Cooking* is a celebration of community. Thousands of Institute guests have indulged in Shelley's generous food over the last decade—sometimes in silence, but always together. In Shelley's kitchen, the food always speaks for itself.

—Rozanne Gold

INTRODUCTION

In 2002 I landed at the Garrison Institute to start up and run the kitchen. Broadly speaking, the Institute's initiatives use meditation to help people focus and, in turn, work on important problems of our day like peace, poverty, and the environment. Many outside groups also come for retreats—to wrestle with ideas, to search, reflect, and practice—scientists, rinpoches, Zen archers, teachers, doctors, students, and the general public. The Garrison Institute is housed in what used to be a Capuchin friary. The atmosphere is distinctly linked to the building's history. It is a big, old, red-brick structure overlooking the Hudson River and West Point, set on a quiet ten-acre campus with gardens, a long bed of lavender full of bees, apple trees, old stone walls, and an array of outbuildings. My office is the old bakery. The ratskeller is a classroom. The sanctuary is now the meditation hall. There are rooms for 165 guests and a great wooden dining hall. The kitchen—spacious and sunny, with four ovens and a twelve-burner stovetop—hasn't changed much from the days when the monks cooked there.

How did I get here?

I grew up in urban, and then suburban, New Jersey in the 1960s and '70s. My family was "Jewish by food." That meant on Jewish holidays we ate traditional foods such as handmade kreplach, gefilte fish, chopped liver, horseradish, matzo brei, and my dad's ongefrishteh matzo (matzo steamed on a wire rack over boiling water, brushed with chicken fat and sprinkled with coarse salt). The remainder of the time we had a predilection for Italian food, though experimentation dominated my mother's kitchen. She was a fearless shopper, willing to try anything. At a time when American food was dumbing down, she bought rose hips and pigeon. When she prepared goat for Thanksgiving in 1968 it was quite unusual. The goat was overcooked that time, and I didn't try it again until 2013. I was also encouraged to try everything—coerced at times (mostly by my father) and bribed (also by my father). I could get him to buy me a record album for a bite of mushroom. But as I am a fussy eater by nature, there were times I stubbornly sat in front of a meal until it was cold and nasty, unable (though my parents thought unwilling) to take a bite.

My mother lived her last seventeen years in suburbia and never learned to drive. By bike or by bus, she shopped at the markets in Paterson; most were Italian, some Eastern European Jewish, a few German and Middle Eastern. In those days, there was a live-poultry market, a fish market, a butcher, a produce market, a coffee roaster, and even a store dedicated to roasting peanuts. We consumed great quantities of Chinese food. My dad, with maybe my sister in tow, would drive to the city for roast pork, duck, pickles (my son Phillip makes these now), and bialys.

Fortunately, my mother was actually a great cook, and I loved her suppers—we ate crabs, artichokes, clams, and whole fish. She combined a good palate with an open mind and could usually pick a recipe that would work or she could work with. That was how I was first introduced to pesto. My mother read a recipe for a typical pasta sauce from Genoa, Italy. Pesto was a great excuse to use the new-to-all-of-us Cuisinart food processor, and it was a revelation of flavor. Often she learned from Italian friends, who lived near my dad's business in Paterson, or she experimented based on dishes we tried at restaurants or saw in magazines, and she was a faithful watcher of the original Julia Child television series. She was very critical of herself and thoughtfully worked to make every meal as good as it could be. She trusted her palate and her eye and never stopped being curious. This made her a generous cook, as success meant that we, her family, needed to be pleased. And she thought of each of us individually, including herself.

In 1979, I moved to New York City and entered the second phase of my culinary education. There, among other jobs I held over the course of twenty years, I worked in the cheese department at the original Dean & DeLuca (D&D) on Prince Street. I loved that part of my job was getting to experience exotic ingredients from all over the world. We had olive oil at home, but I hadn't heard of extra-virgin olive oil from the first cold pressing. My dad had introduced me to Brie (originally a cheese bribe) and sourdough bread from a small cheese shop in Ridgewood, New Jersey, but Giorgio DeLuca showed me cheeses like Vacherin Mont d'Or made with unpasteurized milk wrapped in spruce bark or Livarot that arrived with hard cider packed inside the box.

At D&D I met my future sister-in-law, Matt Lewis, who introduced me to the cookbooks of Paula Wolfert, Richard Olney, Elizabeth David, Marcella Hazan, Edna Lewis, John Thorne (Matt's future husband), Barbara Tropp, Barbara Kafka, and Madeleine Kamman. The list goes on. From these great books I added a depth of technical knowledge to my intuitive manner of cooking—my "cooking school" years.

I also learned a lot about cooking from pros. After D&D I got my first job as a cook with a very talented chef named Bruce Cliborne. On the night I tried out he dropped a copper pot of hot polenta on the floor in front of me. The napalm-like porridge spattered and burned my arm, and because of his guilt, I landed a position right on the line. Bruce was talented but feckless, so I was soon (absurdly) promoted to chef, as the owners knew I would continue to learn from Bruce—and they could count on me to be sure the ingredients, and Bruce, would show up.

I ate in places I couldn't afford. Chanterelle was our neighborhood restaurant and then Bouley.

And I traveled, first for art, museums, and architecture—the temples and cathedrals of Europe—then for food. In Italy, I was lucky to visit a great vineyard in Florence and stay with friends in Bologna. I spent a summer eating and taking pictures in Morocco and drove across the Pyrenees eating trout, cèpes, and gâteau Basque. Twenty-five years ago in Northern Michigan I was introduced to ramps growing alongside black morels one day and white morels two days later.

My third food phase is a work in progress here at the Garrison Institute. I am still part student, but also part teacher. This phase began when the oldest of my two sons, Matt, was nearly two years old. That was the year my husband Peter coaxed me from the city to a small house on an old dirt road in Garrison, a hamlet in the Hudson River Valley. Abruptly, I went from being an urban creature in a bustling environment of eclectic tastes and cultures to a more quiet existence, cooking and living in the countryside while raising a family.

By the time I arrived at the Garrison Institute in 2002 I had a lot of restaurant and catering experience, so I wasn't unprepared for feeding large groups of people. Before I became a cook, I was that art student who loved traveling to religious sites and ruins, so landing a job at a monastery didn't seem totally outlandish. From the start, I tried to mesh the food I made at home with the food I needed and wanted to make at the Institute.

Quiet contemplation, deep listening, and meditation are such primary activities at the Institute that, from the beginning, Diana and Jonathan Rose, the Institute's founders, believed a mostly vegetarian diet was conducive to the work being done.

And it is their goal for the work at the Institute to help find ways to live light on the land. I wanted to develop menus for these largely vegetarian meals that were fun and flavorful, while suiting the half-grand and half-ascetic setting.

I like to cook to bring people together and thought home cooking should be the focus of the Institute meals. This also made sense because at the Institute everyone eats together around long tables under the tall windows of the inviting dining hall—cooks, shift workers, and guests alike are all invited to partake.

My love of cooking and my love of cookbooks, combined with my experience at the Institute and cooking with my friends, and for my family, is what prompted me to write this book. For many years we have had lots of requests from our guests for a cookbook. I knew a book would be great for my staff, as I can be loath to write down recipes; my interests are a moving target. And as my sons grew up they continued to take an interest in eating in a more and more thoughtful way, and both to some degree enjoy cooking or perhaps, like me, would often rather eat their own food. I started to think about how a cookbook would represent the food our guests eat so as to be a souvenir, and at the same time reflect the way I think about food and cooking in general for home cooks, especially those starting out. When my sons or my friends call me for advice or a recipe, I explain the way I think they will best make the dish they are interested in, at the time they are calling. What is available to them? What is their patience level, the ingredients they are likely to find, and the tools in their kitchen? Who are they cooking for, and what do I think they will like?

When I thought about the structure of the book I realized I think in terms of menus. Maybe that is the restaurant cook in me. (To be a little less controlling, I augment meals with hot sauce, herbs, cheese, and other condiments served on the side so everyone can dress their own dish.) So I decided to create a menu cookbook.

Menus are themselves like recipes, in this case, a framework for meals that can be made throughout the year in different versions. The menus here are organized by month to provide clear examples of what seasonality in cooking really is. The term may be overused, but a perfect, ripe peach is not only delicious but is available in the Hudson Valley for only about three weeks in August. A potato, while a great vegetable to store, is never so good as in September and October, and it is worth experiencing that ephemeral flavor if you can. Each month's menus are an example of a way to make that recipe at that time, in that place, but many can be adapted to any season or location—a Moroccan stew might have zucchini in the summer, replaced by butternut squash in October. For some people, and I understand this feeling, a constant local and organic emphasis can be off-putting, as it may be unavailable and unaffordable. I know delicious meals can be made from the ingredients at any supermarket anywhere in the United States. I have tried in this book to provide detailed recipes that may also be tweaked and twisted to your desire and budget. One family, or family member, might like lamb, another chicken, another might be vegan; the basic recipe is a starting place.

My cooking style is primarily Italian in spirit and technique, but my largely savory, European-centered palate also tends toward Asian influences. I am a product of metro-New York, but I am open to experimenting with new combinations, techniques, ingredients, and textures.

I find at the Institute a philosophy that doesn't dictate answers but asks you to pay attention to what you are doing, a lot like being back at art school. Even if it is a shortcut you are after, be aware of what's working, be honest and deliberate. Observe and taste along the way. If the fresh tomatoes you used are very ripe and your stew looks watery, cut back on the rest of the liquid or decide that a soupier stew is light and refreshing in the summer and go with it. If you don't have time to chop garlic finely, use extra cloves and add big pieces and enjoy eating them as they soften and become sweet. Stay as focused as you can, and when you lose your focus, as we all do, simply start paying attention again.

I've loved vegetables since I was a child, an inclination that has served me well at the Institute, where vegetables are so central to our menus. New Jersey, the Garden State, produced terrific corn, tomatoes, melon, and peaches when I was growing up.

And though the focus at the Institute is on vegetarian meals, I find that most people enjoy meat after a few days of going without. I offer groups what I call a small-meat meal— that is, meals that remain mostly vegetarian, but with a light complement of meat for flavor and variety. At your home, you may prepare lots more meat or none at all. At my home we like to use a charcoal Weber grill to cook steak and chicken. We all love seafood, and while sometimes we eat main courses of meat and fish, often we add small amounts of rare steak or pan-fried fish to noodles and broth, salad, tacos, or bowls of rice. The recipes in the book provide plenty of suggestions for adding meat in small or large quantities to the vegetarian recipes. Of the thirty-six menus here, eighteen are vegetarian with suggestions for adding meat or fish in modest amounts, sixteen use meat or fish as flavoring with suggestions for a vegetarian option, and two are straight-up meat recipes.

I think of our relatively limited budget as a creative force rather than as an impediment. I use the best ingredients that my budget allows, but most of us have to allocate our resources carefully, and often spending more on something really good and pairing it with ingredients that cost much less is a good way to achieve flavor and satisfaction.

I tend to spend a lot on salad greens, chocolate, we buy local maple syrup and honey about half the time, and local eggs all the time. I try never to sacrifice freshness and sustainability (to the extent I know), when it comes to fish and meat. In winter, I splurge on my favorite French toasted hazelnut oil, and in summer I mostly use local (often organic) fruits and vegetables. I try to make up for this extravagant spending by supplementing the menus with plenty of cabbage, root vegetables, onions, beans, and grains. These items are always high quality but not, of themselves, particularly expensive. I have included a chapter describing my idea of a simple well-stocked pantry with information on the ingredients I like to keep on hand.

The goal: satisfaction and pleasure, nourishment, timeliness, and a sense of plenty. And what is so engaging at the Institute is a lot like what is engaging and challenging for all home cooks—I have restrictions. In my case, the amount of meat I can use, keeping an awareness of the latest science regarding the environment, and a somewhat limited budget. Many guests have dietary restrictions or have made choices that limit what they will eat. I have to work on tolerance. Our guests are here for many days and for many of their meals. I have to think about menus over a span of a week or sometimes more. No matter how long I have been cooking, I must dig deep in order to be creative, in order to make menus and food I am proud to serve and want to eat.

Cooking is an art people can share on many levels. I hope this book serves as an example more than a prescription and therefore is an inspiration, especially for young cooks. My sons and husband have been my muses. When I think about pleasing them as I plan meals, I know folks at the Institute will be happy, too. I love when we eat together—new Chinese dishes in Flushing or pickling string beans and comparing brands of prosciutto with Phillip (my new favorite is from Iowa). My son Matt texted me a picture of a supper from his kitchen at college: rice seasoned with soy and sesame oil, sautéed Napa cabbage on top along with a few slices of bacon, a fried egg, and hot sauce. He and his friends are cooking in their house, and these aren't cooking guys per se. They just want to eat decent food and be together. I am very optimistic about this generation and love to feed them. I love their energy and their music and art and their desire to appreciate the moment. They enjoy food, but in a way that isn't too fussy, or as Phillip says, "Food that doesn't try too hard." It is a subtle message. All good things appreciated and shared but in balance, in perspective, generous, but chill.

I have been fortunate that throughout my life I have been able to eat around a table filled with good food and lots of people. I've watched my mother prepare a holiday table that extended past the dining room across the base of the staircase and into our living room. For years in the city, my friends and I did the same, my sister and I continue this tradition to this day, adjusting furniture and borrowing chairs to cook for crowds.

Right before a meal at the Institute one of us gets to ring a big gong to call everyone to the buffet. Each cook has a different ring. Some do jazz; I am opinionated, but fundamentally shy. I can't sing happy birthday in a dark room. So I thought of a structured way to ring the gong. I ring it three times, going from soft to loud. I know when and how to start and when to stop.

I am very grateful for the opportunity to cook at the Garrison Institute. Collecting my work in this book has afforded me a tangible way to contribute something back. Though no two meals I make are ever the same, one of the things I'm most grateful I've done for myself over the course of the last ten years is to write down these recipes, which I am pleased to be able to share.

A plate from Menu 3 with Stilton

JANUARY MENUS

01

ONION SOUP WITH SPROUT CREEK CHEESE AND SOUR RYE TOAST 2
WINTER ROOT VEGETABLE SALAD WITH SHERRY-HAZELNUT DRESSING 4
BAKED WHITE BEANS 5
LEMON, BALSAMIC, AND GRAPE SEED OIL VINAIGRETTE 6
QUINCE IN PHYLLO 6

02

TOFU STROGANOFF WITH BUTTERED NOODLES 8
ROASTED CELERY WITH LEMON AND THYME 9
SHIITAKE VINAIGRETTE 10
COLESLAW VINAIGRETTE 10
RICOTTA CHEESECAKE 11

03

COTTAGE PIE (MEAT AND MUSHROOM) WITH WINTER
   ROOT VEGETABLES 12
SWEET AND SOUR CABBAGE 13
ROASTED PEARS 14
BLUE CHEESE DRESSING 15
LEMON CURD WITH THYME–SEA SALT COOKIES 16

ONION SOUP WITH SPROUT CREEK CHEESE AND SOUR RYE TOAST

Whether we're cooking with meat or not, onions are like a roux for many of our dishes—the foundation for what follows. This recipe showcases the onions. Growing up, I remember sautéed onions browned quickly in a hot skillet, still firm, potent, and a bit spicy. I ate them ambivalently. Later, when my mother started watching Julia Child on television and reading her books, she learned to caramelize onions slowly for a supersweet flavor. That same flavor is the key to classic onion soup. It takes a lot of onions and some patience to make, especially a big pot, but it's so well liked that we find it worth the effort. Because we can't possibly put individual crocks under a broiler, we melt cheese on top of toast—I like sourdough or rye—and serve it on the side. Everyone can then submerge the toast in their bowl or dip it, as they like. **SERVES 8**

3 tbsp. unsalted butter or vegetable oil
8 Spanish onions, cut into ¼-in. slices
3 thyme sprigs
Salt & black pepper
½ cup white wine, Riesling is good (optional)
3 tbsp. Cognac or Armagnac (optional)
1 bay leaf

2 qt. water, beef, chicken, or vegetable stock
2 oz. firm cow's milk cheese, shredded (we like to use Sprout Creek Farm Toussaint or Gruyère, but your favorite melting cheese is fine)
8 slices sour rye bread, with or without caraway seeds, or sourdough

Melt the butter in a soup pot set over medium heat, add the onions, cover, and cook until they have released lots of water, about 10 to 12 minutes. Remove the cover, add the thyme, salt, and pepper, and reduce the heat to low. Cook, stirring often, until the onions are very soft, sweet, and dark golden, about 25 to 30 minutes. Add the wine, cognac, and bay leaf, and cook for 1 minute to burn off the alcohol. Add the water or stock, and cook over low heat, partially covered, for 15 to 20 minutes. Taste and adjust the salt and pepper. Remove bay leaf.

Shred the cheese in a separate bowl or container.

Preheat oven to 400 F or, if using the broiler, set to high. Lightly toast the bread and cut each slice in half.

Menu 1, onion soup

To make cheese toast: Spread the bread out on baking sheet. Cover each piece with shredded cheese and bake until the cheese is melted and lightly browned. (I like to grind a little black pepper on top, too.) If you're using a broiler to brown the cheese in the traditional manner, portion the soup into ovenproof tureens, top with a slice of toast, sprinkle with cheese, and set under the broiler until the top is bubbling and lightly browned.

NOTES AND VARIATIONS

For a one-pot, hearty meal, add cooked white beans right to the soup (along with some of the bean broth). Even heartier, add beef shanks or short ribs right from the start.

WINTER ROOT VEGETABLE SALAD WITH SHERRY-HAZELNUT DRESSING

Often we roast vegetables individually, but an extravagant mix of colorful root vegetables—celery root, carrots, parsnips, beets, turnips, rutabagas, yams, and potatoes—is pretty and delicious. Toss together any combination and, though not strictly roots in the same sense, onions and leeks make flavorful additions, as does winter squash. Be sure to keep any leftovers for a soup or frittata. **SERVES 8**

FOR THE VEGETABLES

8 cups mixed root vegetables, peeled and diced (about 1½-in. pieces)

3 tbsp. vegetable oil (grape seed oil is good)
Salt & black pepper

Preheat oven to 400 F. Each vegetable will cook at its own pace, so if you want them perfectly done, cook the different vegetables separately and then combine them. I don't mind some vegetables slightly more done than the rest as long as they're all tender. Toss the vegetables with a light coating of vegetable oil, salt, and pepper, and roast them together in a ceramic baking dish or a sheet pan lined with parchment for 20 to 25 minutes. Check your vegetables after 15 minutes, as cooking time varies depending on your preferred doneness.

FOR THE DRESSING

¼ cup sherry vinegar
1 tbsp. Dijon mustard
Salt & black pepper
3 tbsp. toasted hazelnut oil

(substitute walnut oil, another
good-quality toasted nut oil, or
olive oil)

Whisk together the vinegar, mustard, salt, and pepper. Slowly whisk in the oil until emulsified. Toss with the roasted vegetables and serve.

BAKED WHITE BEANS

This vegetarian version of Tuscan baked white beans is a staple at the Institute. Traditionally, the dish includes pancetta or another fatty cut of pork. I like the dish with or without pork. You can make it either way. **SERVES 8**

½ lb. dried cannellini beans, any
dried bean is fine (see Notes and
Variations below)
Water or stock to cover beans,
about 2 to 3 quarts
¼ cup olive oil plus 3 tbsp. for
finishing (optional)
6 to 10 garlic cloves, sliced
6 sprigs parsley
4 sprigs sage or thyme or 1 sprig

rosemary
1 onion, chopped
1 cup tomatoes, chopped
(canned are fine, drain most of
the juice, fresh plum tomatoes
when in season are good)
1 bay leaf
Salt & black pepper
½ cup chopped parsley
(optional)

Soak the beans overnight. Drain, discard any stones or debris.

Preheat oven to 350 F. Place the beans in a deep baking dish or an ovenproof casserole dish or pot. (You may also cook on the stovetop using a pot, but the oven method produces a nice crust as the olive oil and vegetables float to the top.) Cover with water or stock so that the liquid is 2 inches to 3 inches above the level of the beans. Add the olive oil, garlic, parsley, sage, onions, tomatoes, bay leaf, salt, and pepper. Bake uncovered, stirring every 30 minutes for 2 to 2½ hours. The cooking time will depend on the age and condition of the beans. When you stir the beans, be gentle as they're prone to fall apart. Collapse and stir in the brown bubbling topping each time.

After about 2 hours, taste the beans. I like them fully tender and creamy and don't mind if they're beginning to fall apart. If too much liquid evaporates, add a little water. Remove bay leaf. Serve with the broth or, if you like a thicker consistency, remove the liquid to a saucepan, reduce the broth, then add it back to the beans. Adjust the salt and black pepper. A tasty touch is drizzled olive oil on top along with chopped parsley.

NOTES AND VARIATIONS

Add a ¼ lb. piece of pancetta to the beans when you start cooking them. Other meat flavorings include pork shoulder, a lamb shank, a smoked ham hock, or beef marrowbones. You might also make the dish a main meal by adding cooked sausages at the end or serving them on the side with a salad. And any bean would be good. Experiment with pinto, great northern, kidney beans, or some of the more unusual varieties such as flageolets, Jacob's cattle beans, cranberry beans, or scarlet runners.

LEMON, BALSAMIC, AND GRAPE SEED OIL VINAIGRETTE

This is a simple, broken (not emulsified) dressing, light on oil. The lemon cuts the sweetness of the balsamic vinegar. For information on greens and instructions on dressing a salad, see page 229. Makes ¾ cup. **SERVES 4–6**

¼ cup grape seed oil
3 tbsp. balsamic vinegar

Juice of 1 lemon
Salt & black pepper

Mix the oil, vinegar, and lemon juice. Add a pinch of salt and pepper. Toss with salad greens.

QUINCE IN PHYLLO

Quince isn't easy to come by, but when you do find it, try it. It is inedible raw—sort of spongy, sour, and bitter at the same time. Cooked, it transforms into a buttery textured, tangy fruit that mingles with any sweetener. I like my desserts on the not-very-sweet side, so quince is a perfect choice for me. Combine quince with apples, pears, or both, as you like. They all complement one another. **SERVES 6**

3 quince, peeled, cored, and cut into ½-in. chunks, about 3 cups
1 cup white wine, any kind will work, or water
2 tbsp. raw sugar, maple syrup, or honey, plus ¼ cup raw sugar (to sprinkle on top of the pastry)
Juice of 1 lemon
5 to 8 sheets of soft, defrosted phyllo dough
½ cup clarified butter, melted (substitute melted coconut oil or grape seed oil)

Preheat oven to 350 F. Combine the quinces, white wine, raw sugar, maple syrup, or honey, and lemon juice in a saucepan over medium-low heat. Simmer until the quince is tender enough for a paring knife to cut through it easily, about 8 to 10 minutes. Drain the quince, reserving the liquid, and return the liquid to the pan. Reduce liquid to a syrup until about ⅓ of the volume remains, and set aside.

Form the dessert right on a parchment-lined baking sheet by arranging 3 sheets of dough equidistant from each other. Brush the dough with a very light coating of butter or oil. (If you like desserts a bit sweeter, you can sprinkle sugar between each layer.) Pile a portion of the quince in the middle of each of the 3 phyllo sheets. Spread the quince so that there is a 1-inch to 2-inch border of phyllo on all sides. Cover each of the 3 pastries with another sheet of phyllo, and brush them with butter. Next, in turns, fold the border of each up to hold the quince securely in. Gently cover the whole pastry with one or two more sheets of phyllo, tucking them under so that each feels secure. Finally, brush the top layer of phyllo with butter and sprinkle with sugar, using as little or as much as you like, depending on your taste. Bake for about 10 minutes before lowering the temperature to 300 F. Bake for an additional 20 to 25 minutes. The phyllo will be golden and the quince bubbling hot inside. Serve the reduced syrup on the side. Each pastry serves 2.

TOFU STROGANOFF
WITH BUTTERED NOODLES

This recipe was suggested to me by Rob Gabriel, the first director of the Garrison Institute. He was not a big fan of tofu, but the sour cream and mushrooms in this rich winter recipe made it all good. **SERVES 4–6**

1 oz. dried mushrooms (porcini, shiitake, or Polish mushrooms)
½ cup vegetable oil, divided
2 large Spanish onions, sliced into thin half circles or cut into ½-in. dice
3 garlic cloves, sliced or chopped
6 cups cremini mushrooms, rinsed and dried (substitute any variety of fresh mushrooms)
Salt & black pepper
2 lb. firm tofu, cut into 1-in. cubes
2 tbsp. soy sauce

1 lb. egg noodles (substitute rice or potatoes, diced)
2 tbsp. unsalted butter (optional)
3 cups hot water or white wine to soak mushrooms (a mixture of the two works as well)
1 cup sour cream (substitute plain yogurt or heavy cream)
6 sprigs of dill, minced (substitute chives or parsley)

Preheat oven to 400 F. Reconstitute the dried mushrooms in 3 cups hot water for at least 30 minutes. Drain and reserve the liquid, letting any grit fall to the bottom.

Sauté the onions in 2 tablespoons of the vegetable oil over medium-high heat in a pan large enough to hold all your ingredients. Stir occasionally until the onions are brown, 8 to 10 minutes, before adding the garlic. Stir and turn off the heat.

Depending on your taste and the size of the creminis, leave them whole or slice or quarter them. Toss them in a bowl with 4 tablespoons of the vegetable oil, salt, and pepper. Spread on a baking sheet and roast (a convection oven comes in handy here) until golden brown, about 10 to 12 minutes. Set aside, reserving the juice that's released on the baking sheet.

In a mixing bowl, toss the tofu with the remaining 2 tablespoons of the vegetable oil, soy sauce, salt, and pepper. Spread out on a baking sheet and roast until golden brown, about 10 to 12 minutes, or less if you like your tofu tender. (Fried tofu would work well in this recipe as well.)

Cook the noodles until just tender according to the package directions (unless you're very ambitious and make your own).

One pound of pasta will be plenty for up to eight people. Toss in butter and keep covered and warm.

Reheat the onions. Add the mushroom-soaking liquid and boil until it's reduced by half. Add all the mushrooms and the tofu. Turn off the heat and stir in the sour cream. Don't boil as the sour cream is likely to break. (If you're substituting heavy cream boil the mixture for 2 to 3 minutes until it thickens slightly.) Add the dill and spoon over the buttered noodles.

ROASTED CELERY WITH LEMON AND THYME

In the winter we look for affordable vegetables that taste good when stored. Celery fits the bill. When roasted, celery takes on both a sweet and pleasantly astringent taste. It's so full of water, however, that you have to start with a lot more than you might think, as it shrinks dramatically. Celery is naturally high in salt, which will concentrate as it roasts, so don't add salt until you taste it fully cooked. **SERVES 6-8**

4 sprigs of fresh thyme, or use ¼ tsp. dried oregano or another fresh herb (optional)	2 tbsp. vegetable oil
	Juice of ½ lemon
2 heads celery, rinsed and trimmed	Hot sauce or crushed red chiles (optional)
	Salt & black pepper

Preheat oven to 400 F. Pull the leaves from the thyme branches. I don't mind eating the tender branch tips, but the main branches can be bitter and tough. Set aside. Slice the whole head of celery on a slight diagonal about ½-inch thick and toss with oil. Roast on a baking sheet lined with parchment until lightly browned and tender, about 12 to 15 minutes. Lower the oven temperature if the celery is browning too fast but is still firm. Toss with thyme and squeeze some lemon juice on top. Serve with the optional hot sauce or crushed red pepper flakes, salt, and pepper. This can be eaten warm, room temperature, or cold.

NOTES AND VARIATIONS

When we serve roasted celery in a menu that doesn't feature mushrooms, we serve it with the following vinaigrette made with dried and soaked shiitakes, red chiles, and sesame oil.

SHIITAKE VINAIGRETTE

SERVES 8-10

4 to 6 dried shiitakes, soaked in
1 cup hot water for at least 10
minutes (reserve the liquid)
½ cup grape seed oil (any
vegetable oil will do)
¼ cup toasted sesame oil
¼ cup lemon juice

2 tbsp. minced scallions
1 tsp. Sambal Oelek or 1 dried or
1 fresh hot chile, red or green
1 garlic clove, minced
¼ tsp. peeled and minced fresh
ginger
Salt & black pepper

In a small mixing bowl combine the pre-soaked shiitakes, ¼ cup of the soaking liquid, oils, lemon juice, scallions, chile, garlic, ginger, salt, and pepper. Cook the celery as directed, but leave out the seasoning and toss with the vinaigrette instead.

COLESLAW VINAIGRETTE

This vinaigrette is made with seasonings I associate with coleslaw but in this case no mayonnaise. For information on greens and instructions on dressing a salad, see page 229. Makes about 1¼ cup. **SERVES 10-12**

¼ cup rice vinegar
¼ cup lemon juice
2 tbsp. dill seed
2 tsp. Dijon mustard

1 tbsp. peeled and minced fresh
ginger
¾ cup vegetable oil
Salt & black pepper

In a small bowl, whisk together the vinegar, lemon juice, dill seed, mustard, and ginger. Whisk in the oil until emulsified. Add a pinch of salt and freshly ground black pepper.

RICOTTA CHEESECAKE

This is a very simple recipe. It's great served plain or with fruit on the side. In winter, try cooked pears or apples; in spring, rhubarb; and in summer, any kind of berry. **SERVES 10-12**

2 lb. whole milk ricotta cheese
¾ cup sugar
Pinch of salt
5 eggs, beaten
¼ cup all-purpose, unbleached flour

1 tbsp. vanilla extract
1 tsp. lemon zest
Pinch freshly grated nutmeg

Preheat oven to 275 F. Butter a 9-inch springform pan.

Pulse the ricotta in a food processor to break down the curd for a creamier cake. With a paddle attachment on a stand mixer or a wooden spoon in a mixing bowl combine the ricotta, sugar, and salt before adding the eggs, flour, vanilla, lemon zest, and nutmeg. Pour mixture into the springform pan and bake until a knife comes out clean when inserted into the center of the cake and the top is golden brown, about 75 to 85 minutes.

Ricotta cheesecake from Menu 2, made in the spring with rhubarb sauce on the side

COTTAGE PIE (MEAT AND MUSHROOM) WITH WINTER ROOT VEGETABLES

Cottage pie is shepherd's pie made with beef in place of the lamb. It's a one-dish meal that's slightly more complicated, by Institute standards, than the recipes we usually prepare, so allow yourself a little extra time. This version uses more vegetables mixed with the meat filling than is typical of either shepherd's or cottage pie. You may make a fully vegetarian version using ground mushrooms in place of the meat. For a good springtime take on this wintery dish, add lots of peas to the meat in place of the root vegetables and mix cooked root vegetables such as turnips or parsnips with the potatoes before mashing them and putting them on top. Light, tangy side dishes are a welcome contrast, as the pie is rich.

SERVES 6–8

3 cups assorted root vegetables (carrots, celery root, turnips, and parsnips), cut into ½-in. dice
¼ cup vegetable oil, divided
Salt & black pepper
3 lb. potatoes, peeled and cut into large chunks (I like russets, which cook up dry and flaky for mashing, but any potato will do)
1½ to 2 cups whole milk or heavy cream
10 tbsp. to 12 tbsp. unsalted butter
2 cups Spanish onions, cut into ¼-in. dice

2 lb. ground beef or 3 lb. button mushrooms (ground raw in a food processor)
2 cups water, white wine, beef or vegetable stock (or any combination)
1 cup canned tomatoes, pureed
3 sprigs fresh thyme
1 bay leaf
¼ cup chopped parsley
3 garlic cloves, minced
Pinch ground mace (substitute nutmeg)

Preheat oven to 400 F. Toss the vegetables with 2 tablespoons of the vegetable oil. Add a pinch of salt and fresh black pepper. Spread the vegetables out on a baking sheet and roast until golden brown and just tender, about 20 to 25 minutes.

Put the potatoes in a pot, cover with cold, salted water. Bring to a boil over high heat and cook until very tender, about 15 to 18 minutes. Drain and mash with milk and butter. Add salt and pepper, taste, adjust, and set aside.

In a saucepan set over medium heat, sauté the onions in the remaining 2 tablespoons vegetable oil, stirring frequently, until soft, 4 to 6 minutes. (Cook until golden brown, if you prefer.)

IF USING MEAT

Add the beef to the onions, and cook over medium-high heat for 5 to 10 minutes, stirring until the meat is cooked through. Tilt the pan and pour out or spoon off the excess fat as it renders. Add the water, tomatoes, thyme, and bay leaf, and simmer uncovered over medium heat until the liquid is reduced and the meat is tender, about 1 hour. Add water as needed. Add salt and pepper, taste, and adjust.

IF USING MUSHROOMS

Add ground raw mushrooms to the onions and cook over high heat for about 5 minutes, stirring. Add water, tomatoes, thyme, and bay leaf, and simmer. The mushrooms will release a lot of liquid. Cook, uncovered, until the liquid is mostly reduced, about 30 minutes. Add salt and pepper, taste, and adjust.

FOR MEAT OR MUSHROOMS

In a mixing bowl, toss the meat (or mushroom mixture) with the vegetables, parsley, garlic, and mace. Remove thyme branches and bay leaf. Taste and adjust the salt and pepper.

Place the meat and vegetables in an ovenproof dish in a layer about 2 inches deep. Top with the mashed potatoes in an even layer and bake until the potatoes are golden brown on top and the mixture below is bubbling around the edges, about 30 to 40 minutes. Serve right from the baking dish.

SWEET AND SOUR CABBAGE

This recipe makes plenty, but if you have leftovers it holds well for few days in the refrigerator. Sometimes I add seeds that can be left in the salad, such as caraway or coriander. If I want more of the essence of the spices, I add the spices whole but pick them out before serving. **SERVES 8-10**

1 head red cabbage
2 tbsp. vegetable oil
1 onion, cut into ¼-in. dice
¼ cup water
¼ cup red wine vinegar
1-in.-long piece cinnamon stick
2 to 6 juniper berries, cardamom pods, allspice, or a combination of all three

2 whole cloves
1 garlic clove, sliced (optional)
1-in. piece fresh ginger, peeled and sliced (optional)
1 bay leaf
2 tbsp. raw sugar, maple syrup, or honey (optional)
Salt & black pepper

Cut the cabbage into wedges about 2 inches wide and then thinly slice the whole head. In a large saucepan, heat the oil over low heat until it's just hot. Add the onions and sauté gently until soft but not brown. Add the cabbage, water, and vinegar, and the whole spices you're using.

Cook partially covered, 12 to 15 minutes, stirring occasionally. Uncover and add the garlic and ginger (if using either), add bay leaf, and cook until the cabbage is soft and the liquid has mostly evaporated. Taste and add sugar, salt, and pepper. Serve warm, room temperature, or cold.

NOTES AND VARIATIONS

The addition of good-quality toasted nut oil—hazelnut, walnut, sesame, or almond—makes a tasty, rich condiment. In fall, chopped roasted chestnuts are also delicious mixed in.

ROASTED PEARS

Pears alone, roasted as they are here with nothing more than a little salt, pepper, and lemon, make a perfect side dish for the cottage pie. The rich potatoes on top and the presence of so many root vegetables demands a light, bright side dish. Bosc pears will retain their shape when cooked; Bartletts may be mushier. Either tastes good. If you're not serving the pears with cottage pie, combine the pears with roasted parsnips for a heartier, more savory side dish. **SERVES 6-8**

6 ripe pears, either soft, juicy Bartletts or firm but ripe Boscs
Juice of 1 lemon, divided

2 tsp. vegetable oil
Salt & black pepper

Preheat oven to 375 F. Peel the pears, cut them into approximately 2-inch chunks, tossing them as you work in a mixing bowl with half of the lemon juice. Add the oil, toss to coat, and spread the fruit on a parchment-covered baking sheet. Roast until soft and slightly brown on the edges, 10 to 15 minutes. If you are cooking parsnips, prepare them the same way as the pears, but know they will take longer to cook, about 20 to 25 minutes.

Gently transfer the pears to a serving platter and drizzle the remaining lemon juice over the top. Taste, add salt and pepper, and adjust. Serve warm or cold.

BLUE CHEESE DRESSING

Sheep's-milk blue cheeses like Roquefort or our New York State's Old Chatham Ewe's Blue are deliciously assertive and hold up well in a dressing, as does a basic, less expensive Danish blue. Stilton is my favorite blue cheese and makes a milder dressing. For information on greens and instructions on dressing a salad, see page 229. Makes about 2 cups. **SERVES 10-12**

¾ cup mayonnaise
½ cup grape seed oil
½ cup red wine vinegar
Juice of 1 lemon

1 tbsp. Worcestershire sauce (optional)
4 oz. blue cheese, crumbled
Salt & black pepper

Thoroughly blend the mayonnaise, oil, vinegar, lemon juice, and Worcestershire together in a bowl. Stir in the blue cheese, a pinch of salt, and bit of black pepper, taste and adjust the seasoning.

LEMON CURD
WITH THYME–SEA SALT COOKIES

This already extravagant meal deserves a special two-part dessert. Tangy, rich lemon curd benefits from the addition of a crisp cookie. This fancy butter shortbread with herbs is one of the many varieties of small cookies we make to welcome our guests when they first arrive at the Institute. If you don't have time, serve a store-bought shortbread, waffle cookie, wafer, or even a graham cracker.

LEMON CURD

In summer this lemon curd recipe makes a good parfait. Simply whip a bowl of heavy cream, take half the curd and fold the whipped cream into it. In individual glasses or a parfait bowl, alternate plain curd with the cream-curd combination. Add a few fresh raw berries, then curd, finishing with a dollop of plain whipped cream. The curd can also be spread in a thin layer in a baked tart shell for an easy dessert. Makes about 3 cups.

SERVES 8-10 WITH COOKIES OR ENOUGH TO FILL A 9-INCH TO 10-INCH TART SHELL

8 egg yolks	1 cup sugar
4 whole eggs	8 tbsp. (1 stick) unsalted butter
1⅓ cups lemon juice	Zest from 2 lemons

Combine the yolks, whole eggs, lemon juice, sugar, butter, and zest in the top of double boiler (or a metal bowl set on top of a pot of water). Whisk frequently until thick and the custard reaches 162 F on an instant-read thermometer. Strain through a sieve, cover with plastic wrap right up against the custard, and cool completely.

THYME-SEA SALT COOKIES

In place of thyme, experiment with herbs of your choice. I recommend hearty-leafed herbs such as rosemary, savory, lavender, or even sage. **MAKES ABOUT 36 COOKIES**

1¾ cups all-purpose, unbleached flour
Pinch of sea salt for baking plus a few pinches to sprinkle on top of cookies

1 cup (2 sticks) unsalted butter
¼ cup sugar plus 2 tbsp. (optional, for sprinkling)
1 tsp. fresh thyme leaves

Preheat oven to 325 F.

Mix the flour and the salt, set aside. Cream the butter and ¼ cup sugar in a mixing bowl using a paddle attachment with a stand mixer or a wooden spoon if working by hand. Beat until the butter is creamy and fluffy. Add the flour mixture in three batches before adding the thyme. Gather the dough into a ball then divide it into 4. Roll the dough into logs, using a little extra flour on the counter if necessary to keep the dough from sticking. Roll the logs in plastic wrap and freeze for at least 30 minutes until ready to bake.

Slice the logs into ¼-in. rounds and place 1 inch apart on a parchment-lined baking sheet. Sprinkle each cookie with a little sea salt (or raw sugar if you prefer). Bake until the cookies just begin to turn golden at the edges, about 15 to 18 minutes.

Menu 5, noodles with peanut sauce

FEBRUARY MENUS

04

BLACK BEAN SOUP 20
CORN TORTILLA QUESADILLA OR TORTILLA CASSEROLE 22, 23
AVOCADO, RED ONION, AND ORANGE SALAD 24
CARROT-LIME VINAIGRETTE 24
RICE PUDDING CAKE 25

05

TOFU OR NOODLES WITH PEANUT SAUCE 26
SAUTÉED BOK CHOY 29
OVEN-FRIED RICE 29
PEAR, BEET JUICE, AND OLIVE OIL VINAIGRETTE 31
APPLE CRISP 32

06

BRAISED SPICY LAMB WITH APPLES 32
RICE NOODLES 33
BEET SLAW 34
GINGER-GRAPEFRUIT VINAIGRETTE 34
BREAD PUDDING WITH PEARS 35

BLACK BEAN SOUP

Beans are a staple at the Institute, and black beans are the most popular variety. This soup may be served like chili by reducing the broth to thicken the consistency. Serve plain or over rice made yellow with the addition of annatto or turmeric. You may also make a simpler, less Mexican, more Spanish, version by omitting the dried chiles. Sometimes I salt the beans as they cook and sometimes at the end of the preparation, as in this recipe. If you salt the beans early in the process the bean will absorb more salt. I think the age of the dried beans you are using has more to do with how quickly they cook than if you salt or even soak the beans first. Taste as you go, and leave extra time so that your beans are tender. **SERVES 6-8**

FOR THE CHILE PUREE

2 tsp. vegetable oil (to toast the chiles)

3 dried ancho chiles or a combination of dried chiles, such as chipotle, guajillo, pasilla, or mulato

½ cup water (to reconstitute the chiles)

1 cup cilantro leaves

Heat the vegetable oil in a saucepan over medium heat. Add the chiles and toast briefly on each side. They will soften and puff up while darkening on the outside. Be careful not to burn them. (If you prefer, put the chiles in a hot oven for a few minutes to toast them, but watch them carefully, as they burn quickly.) Put the chiles in a bowl and cover with boiling water. Poke a few holes in the peppers so that they don't float to the top, and/or cover the bowl with a plate so that the chiles stay completely submerged in the water. When they're soft, after about 30 minutes, drain them, reserving the water. Remove the seeds and stems and place them in a blender or food processor. Add ½ cup of the soaking water and the cilantro leaves. Process to a smooth paste, adding water as needed.

FOR THE SOUP

2 tbsp. vegetable oil
1 Spanish onion, cut into
½-in dice
3 tbsp. chopped cilantro stems
3 to 6 garlic cloves, minced
1 tsp. cumin seeds, toasted
and ground
1 jalapeño, chopped with seeds
(or without seeds for a less
spicy soup)
4 cups any combination
of water, vegetable stock,
chile-soaking water, or bean-
cooking liquid
2 cups dried black beans,
soaked overnight (or use the
quick-soak method, see Notes
and Variations below)
2 cups fresh or canned
tomatoes, peeled and seeded
(optional)
1-in. or 2-in.-long piece
cinnamon stick (optional)
1 bay leaf
¼ cup fresh lemon juice
1 tsp. dried oregano
Salt & black pepper
Optional garnishes: lime
wedges, chopped cilantro, hot
sauce, sour cream

In a large stock pot, sauté the onions in the oil until soft, about 8 to 10 minutes. Add the cilantro stems, garlic, cumin, and jalapeño, and sauté another 2 to 3 minutes. Add the presoaked beans, water, tomatoes (if using), cinnamon stick, and bay leaf. Stir and simmer until the beans are tender, about 1 to 3 hours. (Yes, the beans might cook in 1 hour or 3, depending on how fresh they are, and there isn't really any way to tell unless you get them from the farm where they were grown. Allow ample time or prepare the beans a day ahead.)

When the beans are tender, remove the cinnamon stick and bay leaf, add the chile purée, and cook for another 12 to 15 minutes. For a thicker soup, purée a cup of the beans and add them back to the pot. Add lemon juice, oregano, salt, and pepper. Taste and adjust the salt and pepper. Serve hot with optional garnishes.

NOTES AND VARIATIONS

If dried beans haven't been soaked, use this quick soak method. Bring them to a boil in about 4 to 5 times as much water and drain. Doing this twice will help speed their cooking, but the beans might break up a bit.

If you aren't serving the black bean soup with corn tortillas, add a little masa harina to the soup at the end as a thickener and to add a subtle corn taste.

CORN TORTILLA QUESADILLA

Corn or flour tortillas filled with cheese and whatever else you like or have on hand are what we in the United States call quesadillas. Served on the side with black bean soup, the simplest plain cheese variety is a great vehicle for dipping. **SERVES 4-6**

16 6-in. round corn tortillas (we use white corn tortillas from Harbar in Boston, but any variety will do)
2 cups shredded cheese (we often use New York State cheddar, but any cheese you like will work)

Salt
2 tbsp. to 3 tbsp. vegetable oil (optional)

Sprinkle 8 of the tortillas with enough cheese to cover. Sprinkle a little salt on top of the cheese and any other filling (see Notes and Variations below) you might be using. Top each tortilla with the remaining 8 tortillas.

Place the tortillas in a large skillet or griddle over medium heat. I use a dry pan and wait for the tortillas to brown in spots and for the cheese to melt before I flip them over to lightly brown the other side. If you add vegetable oil to the pan the tortillas will get crispier and will be a little oily but very tasty. Sometimes I sprinkle a little sea salt on top of the tortillas.

NOTES AND VARIATIONS

Some delicious additions on their own or in any combination include: chopped fresh cilantro, Tabasco, sliced green chiles with or without the seeds, crumbled cooked chorizo, roasted sweet potato or winter squash, chopped fresh tomato, beans (whole or refried, if you aren't serving the beans in this menu), chopped pork shoulder, duck, organ meats, scrambled egg, onions, shrimp, roasted poblano chiles, chicken, turkey, leftover stewed meat, such as chicken cooked in red chiles and lime juice.

TORTILLA CASSEROLE

Making tortilla casserole involves layering corn tortillas between various fillings and then baking the dish like lasagna. The corn tortillas soften and absorb the sauce and the result tastes almost like a tamale. We make vegetarian and meat versions with pork, beef, chicken, or fish. While the casserole is tasty with different fillings, a very simple casserole of beans, green chiles, and cheese is quite nice and very easy. **SERVES 6-8**

4 cups fresh tomato sauce or the equivalent quantity of tomatillos, lightly stewed
¼ cup vegetable oil (optional)
16 corn tortillas
3 cups cooked black beans (pinto beans or any other bean variety works as well)
4 cups shredded firm cheese such as cheddar, or fresh cheese, loosened with a fork (reserve 1½ cups to sprinkle on top)
½ cup chopped cilantro
¼ cup chopped jalapeño (substitute roasted poblano or any green chile you like)

Flavorings such as: chipotle chile, ancho chile paste, dried oregano, chopped garlic (optional)
Chopped or small seasonal vegetables such as: red onion, corn kernels, summer squash, okra, or kale (optional)
Salt & black pepper
3 cups bean-cooking liquid (if you're using canned beans, replace this with tomato or tomatillo sauce mixed with water since canned-bean liquid is not very tasty)

If you want to take the time, you can sauté the tortillas in a pan with a little oil to crisp them before forming your casserole. This adds a rich, toasty flavor to the dish, but it isn't necessary.

Preheat oven to 350 F. Use a 13 x 9 or equivalent baking dish that holds about 3 quarts. Spread one cup of tomato sauce on the bottom. Lay down 4 to 6 corn tortillas to cover the surface. (It's fine if they overlap.) The more tortillas, the more liquid you will need to add and the more tamale-like the casserole will be. Over the tortillas, spread half of the beans, a third of the cheese, half the cilantro, half the green chiles, and half of any flavorings and seasonal vegetables you're using. Sprinkle salt and pepper on each layer. Add another cup of tomato sauce. Lay down another layer of tortillas and repeat with the remaining fillings. Place a third layer of tortillas on top and fill the baking dish with bean broth and the remaining tomato sauce so that the liquid just covers the top layer. Cover with parchment and then foil. (If you put foil on top of the tomato sauce it may disintegrate into the casserole.)

Bake until the casserole is bubbling hot throughout, 45 to 60 minutes. Remove the covering and sprinkle the remaining 1½ cups cheese on top. Bake for a few more minutes uncovered or until the cheese is melted and golden brown. Let the casserole stand for a few minutes before you cut and serve it.

AVOCADO, RED ONION, AND ORANGE SALAD

This is a refreshing salad to serve with winter soups and stews when there is very little good local produce at the market. Winter is as good a time as any buy to avocados, mangos, citrus, and pineapples. There are many possible additions and substitutions to this salad including olives, mint, cilantro, green chiles, and parsley. **SERVES 8**

4 large, juicy oranges, grapefruit, tangerines, or blood oranges	1 red onion, thinly sliced
2 ripe Hass avocadoes, sliced (substitute mango or pineapple or any combination)	3 tbsp. olive oil (optional)
	2 tbsp. red wine vinegar (optional)
	Salt & black pepper

Peel the oranges and cut into supremes—that means use a paring knife on either side of the membrane to slip the sections of fruit out so that they're completely peeled. If you can't be bothered, a simpler method is to cut the whole peeled orange into chunks or wagon wheels, membrane and all. Add the avocado, onions, oil, and vinegar (if using). Add salt and pepper, taste, and adjust the seasoning.

CARROT-LIME VINAIGRETTE

If you don't have a juicer to make fresh carrot juice, substitute orange or tomato juice for the carrot juice. For information on greens and instructions on dressing a salad, see page 229. **SERVES 6-8**

3 tbsp. lime juice	6 tbsp. grape seed oil
3 tbsp. fresh carrot juice	1 garlic clove, minced
1 tsp. Dijon mustard	Salt & black pepper

Whisk together the lime juice, carrot juice, and mustard in a small mixing bowl. Whisk in the oil until emulsified, then add the garlic, salt, and pepper.

RICE PUDDING CAKE

There are many ways to make rice pudding. Ours is not as rich as many others and is baked rather than cooked on the stovetop. At the Institute, where we serve rice with so many meals, making pudding is a good way to use leftovers. Many people like to put raisins in rice pudding, plain or plumped with rum or whiskey; I like my rice pudding plain. Follow your own preference. This recipe is pretty simple, although I recommend baking the custard submerged in a water bath for an even texture. The result is a pudding that has the consistency of cheesecake. It's sliceable and easy to serve a modest portion with fruit on the side. Feel free to add any flavoring, extracts, syrups, or fresh or dried fruits you like. For an exotic and pretty version, season your rice with saffron or turmeric. For a savory pudding, add a cup of cheese in place of the sugar, a pinch of salt, and serve plain or topped with salsa or slaw. **SERVES 8-10**

2 large eggs
2 large egg yolks
⅔ cup raw sugar or the sweetener of your choice
2 cups whole milk
1 vanilla bean, split (optional)
1 tsp. vanilla extract
½ tsp. ground cinnamon
¼ tsp. freshly ground nutmeg
4 cups cooked rice (jasmine works well, but any rice will do)
2 tbsp. unsalted butter, cut into chunks

In a medium-size mixing bowl, whisk together the eggs, egg yolks, and sugar.

In a small saucepan, warm the milk and split vanilla bean (if using) over medium heat until steaming. Set aside until the milk is warm, not hot. Remove vanilla bean, scrape the inside of the split pods with a dull knife and add to the milk.

Gradually whisk the warm milk into the egg mixture. If the milk is too hot the egg will curdle, but if it is warm it will help the custard form. Add the vanilla extract if you didn't use a vanilla bean, cinnamon, and nutmeg.

Add the rice and let it soak for up to an hour if you have time so that the rice becomes soft and absorbs some custard.

Preheat oven to 350 F. Lightly butter a 3-quart soufflé dish, or any ovenproof dish will do. Pour in the rice-custard mixture.

To create a water bath, which allows the custard to bake evenly. Set the soufflé dish in a larger baking pan on the oven rack. Add enough boiling water to reach halfway up the sides of the soufflé dish. Bake until an instant-read thermometer inserted in the center reaches 165 to 170 F, about 90 minutes to 2 hours.

Serve this pudding right from the baking dish, adding a pinch of cinnamon on top or fruit on the side.

NOTES AND VARIATIONS

Add 1 cup of fresh ricotta cheese to the rice mixture. Add dried cherries before baking.

MENU 05

TOFU OR NOODLES WITH PEANUT SAUCE

Thick, with lots of peanut butter, this sauce is good as a dip or a topping. When made thinner it's great on cold noodles, thinner still for salad, kale, watercress, or spinach. This easy and very popular recipe uses natural peanut butter as the base, as opposed to many classic Asian sauces that are traditionally made with sesame paste. We use various wheat and rice noodles. **SERVES 6-8**

FOR THE PEANUT SAUCE

1 small bunch cilantro, roughly chopped

3 scallions, minced

2 garlic cloves, chopped

1 or 2 green chiles, serrano or jalapeño, depending on desired heat (optional)

1-in. piece fresh ginger, peeled and chopped

2 cups natural, smooth peanut butter

1 tbsp. toasted sesame oil

1 tbsp. soy sauce

Salt

¼ to ½ cup water (optional)

Begin by mixing the cilantro, scallions, garlic, chiles (if using), and ginger in the bowl of a food processor. When you have a smooth paste, add the peanut butter and blend until smooth but very thick. Add the sesame oil and soy sauce. Taste the sauce as you go. Add salt if needed. Add the water at the end to achieve the consistency and intensity of flavor you want.

FOR THE TOFU

2 lb. firm tofu, cut into
2-in. x 3-in. rectangular blocks
¼ cup vegetable oil
Salt & black pepper
16 cilantro sprigs (optional)

6 raw red or green chiles puréed with vinegar and optional garlic to serve on the side, or use premade sauce (such as Sambal Oelek)

To serve peanut sauce with noodles, cook about 1 pound of any variety or shape of noodle you like according to package directions, rinse with cool water, drain, and toss with thinned peanut sauce. Top with cilantro sprigs and crunchy vegetables such as carrots, cucumbers, sprouts, or roasted onions. Add extra spice, such as chopped fresh chiles, to taste.

To serve peanut sauce with tofu, preheat oven to 450 F. Drain tofu. Brush the tofu with oil, and sprinkle with salt and pepper. Spread on a baking sheet covered with parchment paper, and roast until the tofu just begins to turn golden brown, about 10 to 12 minutes.

Place the hot tofu on a platter and top each piece with a generous quantity of peanut sauce. Garnish with cilantro sprigs and serve optional hot sauce on the side.

NOTES AND VARIATIONS

For Thai flavor, add ½ cup unsweetened coconut milk and about ¼ cup lime juice, substituting Asian fish sauce (nam pla) for the soy sauce. For a version that tastes like a peanut version of the Japanese sauce in goma-ae, keep the sauce very simple: peanut butter, sesame oil, soy sauce, mirin (Japanese sweet cooking wine), and water, with no fresh ingredients (see page 117).

To serve peanut sauce with greens like goma-ae, toss sauce with blanched and chopped greens such as spinach or kale. Top with toasted sesame seeds.

A plate from Menu 6 with lamb and medium wide rice noodles

SAUTÉED BOK CHOY

This is a very simple basic recipe for sautéed bok choy that's good served plain or as an ingredient in other dishes. **SERVES 4**

1 large bunch bok choy or 8 small heads baby or Shanghai bok choy
¼ cup vegetable oil

4 to 6 garlic cloves, sliced
Salt & black pepper
Oyster sauce (optional)
Lemon wedges (optional)

Cut and rinse the large bok choy into 1-inch pieces, or cut the small heads lengthwise into quarters or eighths depending on their size. Heat the oil and garlic over low heat until the garlic is just tender but not brown. Add the greens and toss to cook over medium heat for about 2 minutes. Sprinkle with salt and pepper, if desired, and serve. Serve with oyster sauce or lemon wedges on the side for extra flavor.

NOTES AND VARIATIONS

I like almost all greens. At the Institute we often prepare kale, a mix of braising greens from Blooming Hill Farm they call mess o' greens, broccoli rabe, turnip greens, escarole, bok choy, dandelion, pea shoots, kohlrabi greens, and chard. I also love spinach and cook it often at home, but it cooks down so much that it isn't practical for large groups. We frequently serve greens as a side dish on their own, but we also mix them in with beans, pasta, noodles, rice, in a frittata, curry, soup, or pan quiche.

OVEN-FRIED RICE

Roasting rice in the oven is a lot easier and faster than actually frying rice in a pan, especially when cooking a large quantity. Leftover cold rice of any variety is best. Serve this as a side dish or add extra vegetables, meat, fish, or tofu and serve as a main dish. **SERVES 4-6**

4 cups cooked, cold jasmine rice (any kind of rice will do)

4 tbsp. to 5 tbsp. vegetable oil

6 scallions, white part minced, green part cut into ½-in. pieces

3 garlic cloves, minced

1-in. piece fresh ginger, peeled and minced

1 large onion, cut into ¼-in. dice

2 eggs (optional)

2 tsp. to 3 tsp. toasted sesame oil

1 cup mung bean sprouts (optional)

½ cup frozen or fresh peas, if in season (optional)

3 tbsp. chopped cilantro (optional)

1 tbsp. to 4 tbsp. soy sauce (optional)

Salt

1 lemon, cut into wedges (optional)

Hot sauce (optional)

Fresh chiles, chopped (optional)

Preheat oven to 375 F. Toss the cold rice in a mixing bowl with 2 tablespoons vegetable oil and spread the rice on a baking sheet. I use a sheet of parchment to prevent sticking. Set aside.

Heat 2 tablespoons vegetable oil in a saucepan over medium heat until hot. Add the white part of the scallions, garlic, and ginger, and stir constantly for about 1 minute. With a slotted spoon, remove the scallions, garlic, and ginger to a mixing bowl. In the same pan, add a little more vegetable oil if necessary, and sauté the onions over medium heat until soft and lightly brown. Add the onions to the bowl with the garlic mixture, and set aside.

Mix the eggs (if you're using them) with 1 teaspoon of the toasted sesame oil. Add a little more vegetable oil to same pan the onions were cooked in and set over medium heat until quite hot. The result you're looking for is a cross between scrambled eggs and a pan frittata. Add the eggs and, as they cook, use a rubber spatula to lift the edges so that when you tip the pan the raw egg runs to the edge of the pan. Continue lifting and cooking until the egg is just barely cooked. Remove the eggs from the pan and set aside.

Add the scallion greens and the optional sprouts, peas, and cilantro to the mixing bowl with the onion-garlic mixture.

Bake the rice until very hot and a little crispy on top, about 5 to 10 minutes. Add it to the bowl with the vegetables and toss it together with the eggs. You can also season with soy sauce (if using), but start with a small quantity (you can always add more). Taste and adjust the salt. I like to serve lemon wedges and hot sauce or fresh chiles on the side.

For the easiest possible version of this recipe for a large crowd, simply mix the rice, vegetable oil, scallions, garlic, ginger, onions, sesame oil, and soy sauce into a bowl, toss, lay out on baking sheets lined with parchment, and bake at 375 F until the rice begins to crisp on the edges of the pan, about 8 to 10 minutes. Toss with the separately cooked egg, sprouts, peas, and cilantro (if using), and serve.

Menu 6, braised spicy lamb with apples

PEAR, BEET JUICE, AND OLIVE OIL VINAIGRETTE

If you don't have a juicer, eliminate the beets and put the pears in a blender. For information on greens and instructions on dressing a salad, see page 229. Makes about 1 cup. **SERVES 6-8**

1 medium beet
1 pear, peeled and cut into chunks
3 tbsp. chopped parsley
1 tbsp. lemon juice
1 tsp. Dijon mustard

1 garlic clove, lightly smashed (optional)
Salt & black pepper
½ cup olive oil
3 tbsp. grape seed oil

Using a juicer, juice the beet and pear, set aside.

In a mixing bowl, whisk together the parsley, lemon juice, mustard, garlic, salt, and pepper. Slowly whisk in the oils until emulsified.

APPLE CRISP

This apple crisp recipe is simple and tasty. All it requires is a buttered dish, cut-up apples, raw sugar, butter, and flour. The sweet dough needs just enough flour to hold the crumb together, making this homiest of desserts so light and fragile that it ends up being delicate and fancy. You may also add oats, nuts, and spices. If you choose to mix in dried fruits, place them beneath the apples so they don't burn. **SERVES 6-8**

8 tbsp. (1 stick) unsalted, room-temperature butter, plus more to grease the baking dish
3 apples, peeled, quartered, and cut into ¼-in. slices (I prefer tart

apples, like Crispin and Granny Smith, but any will do)
¼ cup water
¾ cup all-purpose, unbleached flour
¼ cup raw sugar

Preheat oven to 375 F. Butter a 9 x 9 baking dish. Add the apples and water to the dish, and set aside.

In a mixing bowl add the butter, flour, and sugar. Using your hands, blend the ingredients until a very soft dough forms. Scatter the dough in small pieces over the top of the apples. Bake until the crumbs look dried out and golden, 55 to 65 minutes. Serve hot, warm, or cold, plain or with cream, ice cream, or yogurt.

MENU 06

BRAISED SPICY LAMB WITH APPLES

This recipe is inspired by Vietnamese pho. Try fresh shiitakes and tofu instead of lamb for a vegetarian version, using the dried-shiitake soaking liquid for the broth.

SERVES 4 FOR A MEATY MEAL OR 8 WITH MEAT AS A COMPLEMENT

4 lamb shanks (substitute beef shank, short ribs, or chuck steak)
Salt & black pepper
¼ cup vegetable oil (I like coconut oil in this recipe, but any vegetable frying oil is fine), divided
2 large onions, cut into ¼-in. slices
2 qt. water, white wine, beef broth or chicken broth (or any

combination)
8 dried shiitakes
4 garlic cloves, minced
1 tsp. fennel seeds
1-in. to 2-in. cinnamon stick
6 whole cloves
1 bay leaf
4 tart apples, peeled, cut into chunks and tossed with lemon or lime juice

8 scallions, cut into 1-in. pieces (use the green and white parts)
2 green chiles, serrano or jalapeño, sliced with seeds for extra heat
1 tbsp. Asian fish sauce (*nam pla* or substitute soy sauce)
1 tsp. toasted sesame oil

Juice of 1 lemon or lime (optional)
15 leggy cilantro sprigs, in a small serving bowl
10 to 20 sprigs of mint, in a small serving bowl
Lime wedges, in a small serving bowl
Hot sauce

Preheat oven to 350 F. Sprinkle meat with salt and pepper. Pour half the oil into a saucepan over high heat. When the oil is hot, put a few shanks in the pan and brown them on both sides. Transfer the browned meat to a deep baking dish or Dutch oven, and set aside. Add the remaining vegetable oil, and when it's hot, add the onions and cook at high heat, stirring frequently so that the onions get very brown, not necessarily soft and caramelized. Dark onions (not burnt) will produce a pleasant bittersweet flavor in the broth. Add the onions to the shanks along with the water, shiitakes, garlic, fennel seeds, cinnamon stick, cloves, and bay leaf. Cover and bake in the oven (or heat on the stovetop over low heat) for about 40 minutes. Check the liquid level occasionally, adding more water as needed. The lamb will still be tough. Add apples, scallions, and one sliced green chile. Bake (or cook on the stovetop) for between 20 and 30 minutes more or until the lamb is just tender. Test with a fork—I like braised meat to be fairly firm. (Very tender meat makes for a good sauce but tastes bland.) Remove from the oven or stovetop and skim any excess fat from the surface. Taste the liquid and season with the Asian fish sauce (nam pla) and sesame oil. Slowly add the lemon or lime juice (if using), tasting as you go. You may also want to add salt and black pepper. Remove bay leaf.

If you want a generous portion of meat, serve the shanks whole, one per person. If you are using the meat more as a flavoring, remove the shanks, take the meat off the bone, cut or break into large, bite-size pieces, and add back to the pot. Serve over rice noodles (see below) with cilantro, mint, lime wedges, and hot sauce on the side.

RICE NOODLES

Rice noodles are very simple vehicle for sauce. You can also use cello (mung bean) noodles or any other noodle or rice. **SERVES 4-6**

12 oz. package ¼-in.-wide rice noodles (any size is fine)

A dash sesame oil

Bring a pot of water to boil over high heat. Add the noodles and cook according to package directions. Drain, rinse with cool water, and toss with a small amount of sesame oil. Serve alone, with stews, toppings, or soup.

BEET SLAW

My mother cooked fresh beets in her not-so-trusty pressure cooker. (We always worried it was about to blow!) In those days I thought beets tasted like dirt. Now I am a fan of "earthy-tasting" beets. I eat them in hot or cold borscht, pickled, hot with butter, roasted, fried, grilled, or, as in this recipe, raw in a slaw. **SERVES 4–6**

4 large beets or the equivalent, peeled and grated
¼ cup rice vinegar

2 tbsp. fruity olive oil
½ tsp. anise seeds
Salt & black pepper

Place the beets in a mixing bowl. Toss with the vinegar, oil, and anise seeds. Season with salt and black pepper.

GINGER-GRAPEFRUIT VINAIGRETTE

For information on greens and instructions on dressing a salad, see page 229. Makes about 1 cup. **SERVES 6–8**

3 tbsp. freshly squeezed grapefruit juice
1 tbsp. sherry vinegar
1 tbsp. minced and peeled fresh ginger

Salt & black pepper
½ cup olive oil
3 tbsp. grape seed oil

Whisk together the grapefruit juice, sherry vinegar, ginger, salt, and pepper. Slowly whisk in the oils until emulsified.

BREAD PUDDING WITH PEARS

This recipe is a great way to use up stale bread. In this version I add caramelized pears. You can try fresh cranberries, apples, peaches, or cherries. You can even omit the sugar and make a savory version with cheese and vegetables. **SERVES 6-8**

3 tbsp. unsalted butter, cut into chunks, plus more for greasing the baking dish
3 large Bartlett pears (substitute any variety of pear)
Juice of 1 lemon
3 large eggs
3 large egg yolks
1 cup raw sugar, or your sweetener of choice, divided

2½ cups whole milk
1 tsp. vanilla extract
½ tsp. freshly ground nutmeg
¼ tsp. ground cinnamon
8 slices sourdough bread (any bread will do, but I like a dense, crusty loaf)
1 vanilla bean, split (optional)

Preheat oven to 350 F. Lightly butter a 1½-quart soufflé dish; any ovenproof dish will do. Peel, halve, core, and slice the pears into ½-in. pieces (crosswise or lengthwise) and toss with lemon juice to keep from browning. Set aside.

In a medium mixing bowl, whisk together the eggs, egg yolks, and half the sugar.

In a small saucepan, warm the milk over medium heat until steaming.

Gradually whisk the warm milk into the egg mixture. If the milk is too hot the egg will curdle, but if it is warm it will help the custard form. Add the vanilla extract if you didn't use a vanilla bean and cinnamon and nutmeg.

Add the bread and let it soak for up to 1 hour if you have time so that the bread is completely saturated with custard.

Scatter the butter in a medium saucepan. Sprinkle in remaining sugar. Add the vanilla bean (if using) and distribute the sliced pears evenly in the pan. Cook over medium heat until the sugar is bubbling and brown, 15 to 20 minutes. Watch the sugar carefully, taking care not to burn it. Swirl the pan around, but don't stir the pears or they will fall apart.

Place the pears in the bottom of the soufflé dish. You can arrange them in a pattern or just cover the bottom. Scrape the caramel into the dish over the pears. Scrape the inside of the vanilla bean (if using) and discard the pod.

Cover the pears with the soaked bread, and pour the remaining custard on top.

Set the soufflé dish in a larger baking pan and create a water bath, which allows the custard to bake evenly and protect it from breaking. Add enough boiling water to reach halfway up the side of the soufflé dish. Bake until a knife inserted in the center comes out clean, about 1 hour. Remove the bread pudding and let stand, if possible, for up to 20 minutes to cool and set.

While you can just serve this pudding right from the baking dish, if you turn it out of the pan, the pears and caramel will be very pretty on top. To release it, run a knife around the sides and invert onto a plate.

Bread pudding with pears from Menu 6

MARCH MENUS

07

FARRO SOUP WITH SAGE AND PARMESAN 38
ESCAROLE (WITH OR WITHOUT MEATBALLS) 39
MUSHROOM SLAW 40
LEMON–RED ONION VINAIGRETTE 41
INDIAN PUDDING 41

08

POSOLE WITH RED CHILES AND PORK 42
CHOPPED GREEN CABBAGE WITH LIME AND STAR ANISE 43
ROASTED SWEET POTATOES WITH SEA SALT AND LEMON 45
ORANGE-CUMIN VINAIGRETTE 45
VANILLA CUSTARD WITH ALMOND PRALINE 46

09

WHOLE WHEAT ORECCHIETTE AND ROASTED CHICKPEAS (WITH
    OR WITHOUT CLAMS) 47
FENNEL SLAW 49
ROASTED WINTER SQUASH CRESCENTS WITH VANILLA AND
    MAPLE SYRUP 49
CILANTRO VINAIGRETTE 50
BUTTERSCOTCH PUDDING 51

FARRO SOUP WITH SAGE AND PARMESAN

Farro is a form of wheat, related to spelt, that has a delicate, delicious flavor. The variety we typically buy is partially hulled, hence it's much softer and cooks faster than whole wheat berries. This recipe was inspired by Giorgio DeLuca. He didn't brown or even sauté the onions or garlic before adding them to the soup. The result is a sweet delicate flavor. For a meaty version, add a piece of pancetta, pork shoulder, or pieces of chicken on the bone.

SERVES 6–8

6 celery ribs, cut into ½-in.-thick slices

3 carrots, cut into ½-in.-thick slices (optional)

1 Spanish onion, cut into ¼-in. dice

1 fennel bulb, cut into ½-in. dice (optional)

8 garlic cloves, thinly sliced

1 bay leaf

2 cups farro

½ cup olive oil, plus more for finishing (a good oil for finishing is worth it here)

4 sprigs fresh sage

3 sprigs parsley

Salt & black pepper

1 cup grated Parmesan (substitute another hard cheese of your choice)

In a soup pot, combine 2 quarts water, celery, carrots (if using), onions, fennel (if using), garlic, and bay leaf. Set over high heat, bring the water to a boil and simmer for about 10 minutes. Skim off any scum that rises to the top. Add the farro, olive oil, sage, and parsley. Cook over medium heat until the farro is tender, 25 to 35 minutes. Remove bay leaf and add 1 or 2 pinches salt and black pepper before ladling into soup bowls. Drizzle a little extra olive oil on top along with a handful of cheese.

NOTES AND VARIATIONS

This recipe results in a very simple, soupy dish. By adding less water you'll end up with something closer to a risotto, and by adding more vegetables the result is more of a stew. If you add chickpeas or beans (about 2 cups) it will make a hearty meal all by itself.

In this recipe a few meatballs are tossed with a lot of escarole and are served beside or mixed into the farro soup (previous recipe). To serve escarole and meatballs on their own as a main course, add broth, crushed red pepper, and cooked beans. **SERVES 6-8**

FOR THE MEATBALLS

1 egg
1 slice sourdough bread, toasted (substitute any other kind of bread, unseasoned breadcrumbs, or matzo meal)
¼ cup milk or water
1 lb. ground beef
1 medium onion, minced
2 tbsp. vegetable oil

8 garlic cloves, chopped
Salt & black pepper
¼ cup olive oil (optional)
¼ cup currants (optional)
¼ cup pine nuts (optional)
3 tbsp. chopped parsley (optional)
2 tbsp. crushed red pepper (optional)

Preheat oven to 400 F.

Beat the egg in a mixing bowl.

In a separate bowl, soak the bread in the milk until soft. Squeeze out excess liquid and combine with the egg. Add the beef, onions, oil, garlic, and a pinch of salt and black pepper. (If using, also add the olive oil, currants, pine nuts, parsley and crushed red pepper.) Mix well without overmixing. Form meatballs, about the size of a ping-pong ball, roughly 2½ oz. each.

Place the formed meatballs onto a rimmed baking sheet until lightly browned on the outside, but still underdone inside, about 4 to 6 minutes. Set aside. (They will be finished after being added to the cooked escarole.) If you want to serve the meatballs separately from the escarole, cook them through until they're browned, 10 to 12 minutes more. Reserve the baking sheet.

FOR THE ESCAROLE

¼ cup vegetable oil
8 garlic cloves, sliced or chopped
1 large head escarole, washed and cut into 1-in. ribbons

Salt & black pepper
Lemon wedges (optional)
Pinch of Spanish saffron (optional)

Place a large skillet over medium heat. Add the oil and garlic, and cook until the garlic is lightly golden (or toasty brown if that's how you like it). Add the escarole and stir with tongs until all the greens are wilted, 2 to 3 minutes. Season with a pinch of salt and some black pepper, and optional saffron.

Combine the partially cooked meatballs with the escarole in the same pan. Pour off and discard the grease from the meatball baking sheet, but leave the meat juices. Scrape the pan, adding a few spoonfuls of the water released by the escarole to loosen the brown bits. Add the juices to the greens and meatballs. Gently mix and return the pan to the heat for a few minutes until the meatballs are cooked through. Serve on a platter with lemon wedges (optional).

MUSHROOM SLAW

I have come to really like raw mushrooms. Completely plain, the flavor of a mushroom is subtle and nutty with a pleasant aftertaste. In a salad, mushrooms act like sponges, soaking up generous quantities of lemon and olive oil to produce a very nice flavor. Mushroom slaw doesn't hold very well. As with cucumbers or Napa cabbage, after a short time, liquid starts to release and the slaw becomes watery. You can drain and roast any leftover slaw and use the water in the bottom of the bowl as a simple vegetable stock. **SERVES 6-8**

3 cups very fresh white button mushrooms, any size
½ cup good olive oil
Juice of 2 lemons
½ cup rough chopped flat-leaf parsley, mint, basil, or marjoram (optional)

½ cup shredded hard cheese, such as Parmesan or Gruyère
Salt & black pepper

So as not to be wasteful, cut off only the very end of the mushroom stem, where it's rough and dirty. Slice the mushrooms in your food processor or, if you prefer, slice them by hand as thin as you can. Put the mushrooms in a mixing bowl and toss with the olive oil, lemon juice, parsley (if using), cheese, a pinch of salt, and some black pepper.

LEMON-RED ONION VINAIGRETTE

For information on greens and instructions on dressing a salad, see page 229. **SERVES 4-6**

3 tbsp. lemon juice
¼ tsp. lemon zest
2 tbsp. minced red onion
2 tsp. Dijon mustard

Salt & black pepper
½ cup olive oil
3 tbsp. grape seed oil

Whisk together the lemon juice, zest, onions, mustard, and a pinch of salt and pepper. Whisk in the oils slowly, until emulsified. Taste the dressing and adjust the salt and pepper. If you like a thinner dressing, add a few drops of water.

INDIAN PUDDING

Typically, Indian pudding is sweetened with molasses. I like to substitute maple syrup. This pudding is a good for breakfast or dessert, plain or served with cold heavy cream, whipped cream, or ice cream. **SERVES 6-8**

1 cup yellow cornmeal (I prefer a coarse grind)
1 qt. whole milk
1 cup maple syrup (substitute a sweetener of your choice)
1 cup heavy cream (substitute whole milk)

⅛ tsp. freshly grated nutmeg (substitute your favorite spice: mace, cardamom, cinnamon, anise, etc.)

Preheat oven to 275 F.

Lightly butter a 2½-quart soufflé dish; any deep-sided ovenproof dish will work.

In a medium saucepan, whisk together the cornmeal and milk over medium-high heat until the mixture blends and begins to thicken, 5 to 7 minutes.

Remove the pan from the heat and stir in the maple syrup, cream, and nutmeg. Pour the mixture into the greased baking dish, and bake until the pudding is bubbling and brown on top, about 3½ to 4 hours. Allow the pudding to rest for a few minutes before serving plain or with cold heavy cream, whipped cream, yogurt, chopped nuts, or ice cream.

POSOLE WITH RED CHILES AND PORK

I order a small-kernel variety of posole, white or blue, from New Mexico. One source is loschileros.com. It cooks faster than the typical big kernels most often in found in stores around New York City, and it's much less starchy. Posole is very good when cooked as it typically is, with a fatty cut of pork such as shoulder, belly, or ribs. It's also tasty when cooked in water with red chiles and served with braised or roasted pork on the side, as in this recipe. Posole alone creates a delicate, sweet corn broth. Sliced or shredded cabbage is a typical posole topping, so if you don't make the slaw recipe included in this menu, try shredded cabbage or radish (or a mix) as a topping for your posole. **SERVES 6-8**

FOR THE POSOLE

3 to 6 dried Mexican chiles, either one variety or mixed such as: mild ancho, medium hot guajillo, and hot pasilla (substitute good-quality red chile powders of the same varieties)

2 tbsp. vegetable oil

1 Spanish onion, cut into 1-in. dice

12 garlic cloves, rough chopped or sliced

1 lb. dried whole posole (hominy), preferably the small New Mexican version, soaked overnight and drained

1 cup chopped cilantro stems

1 carrot, peeled and cut into 1-in. slices

1 tsp. cumin seeds, toasted and ground

1 tsp. coriander seeds, toasted and ground

1 bay leaf

Salt & black pepper

Prepare the chiles as on page 20.

In a soup pot set over medium heat, lightly sauté the onions and garlic in 2 tablespoons oil until onions are translucent, 3 to 5 minutes. Add the posole and 2 quarts of water and bring to a boil. Skim off any foam; add the cilantro stems, carrot, cumin, coriander, and bay leaf. Add the chile purée. If you want to cook the pork in with the posole, add the whole shoulder at this time. Lower the heat and simmer until the posole is tender, 1½ to 2 hours. Add salt and pepper as needed. Remove bay leaf. Serve as a soup with or without the pork.

NOTES AND VARIATIONS

If you choose not to make this whole menu, there is a tasty selection of garnishes for the posole: 2 cups rough chopped cilantro leaves, hot sauce or sliced fresh chiles, lime wedges, chunks of avocado, tortilla chips, sliced radishes, and/or cabbage.

FOR THE PORK

1 lb. or 2 lb. pork shoulder or belly	5 whole cloves or 3 allspice berries
1 Spanish onion, sliced	1 bay leaf
8 garlic cloves, roughly chopped or sliced	1 strip of orange zest
	Salt & black pepper

Preheat oven to 300 F. Place the pork in a Dutch oven with all the ingredients. Fill the pot ¼ of the way up with water and roast, turning the pork every 15 minutes until it reaches 160 F on an instant-read thermometer, about 45 minutes to 1 hour. Remove the liquid fat and bay leaf from the broth. Slice the pork and serve with the broth on the side of the posole or add the meat in chunks and the broth to the posole.

CHOPPED GREEN CABBAGE WITH LIME AND STAR ANISE

This is a refreshing cabbage slaw that can be eaten as a side salad or as a topping for the posole. **SERVES 6–8**

¼ cup freshly squeezed lime juice	2 to 4 whole star anise
2 tbsp. vegetable oil	3 cups green cabbage, cut into 1-in. pieces
1 tsp. to 3 tsp. maple syrup, honey, or unrefined sugar (optional)	Salt & black pepper

In a bowl, mix the lime juice, oil, maple syrup, and star anise, and set aside to steep for at least 1 hour to extract flavor from the spice.

You can dress the cabbage raw for the freshest, crunchiest slaw or blanch the cabbage in boiling water for 1 to 2 minutes and then rinse under ice-cold water. The cabbage will still be crunchy but more tender. (It will also hold longer once dressed since less water will be released from the blanched cabbage.) Put the cabbage in a mixing bowl and toss with the dressing. Add a pinch of salt and black pepper, taste, adjust, and serve.

Menu 8, posole with pork on the side

ROASTED SWEET POTATOES
WITH SEA SALT AND LEMON

Roasted sweet potatoes are very popular at the Institute. This is a basic side-dish recipe that can be adapted and used in many other recipes. These roasted sweet potatoes are excellent in stews, with beans, in a frittata, or tossed as a salad. You might consider seasoning the sweet potatoes with dried red chile powder before roasting or serve them with red chile mayonnaise on the side. There are many sweet potato varieties available these days, and they're all worth trying. At home, I like them baked whole until they're sticky and well done. I eat them plain, skin and all, hot or cold. The dark-red and dark-yellow fleshed varieties are like dessert. **SERVES 6-8**

4 large, or the equivalent, unpeeled, scrubbed sweet potatoes, any variety, cut into 1-in. to 2-in. pieces	½ cup cooking oil plus more for the baking sheet Salt & black pepper Juice of 2–3 lemons

Preheat oven to 400 F. Toss the sweet potato pieces in a bowl with the oil, a pinch of salt, and some black pepper. Spread them on a parchment-lined baking sheet or grease the sheet with a little oil. Roast until the sweet potatoes are brown and tender, 15 to 25 minutes, depending on your oven and how brown you like them. Toss with lemon juice. Serve hot, room temperature or cold, with additional seasoning if you wish.

ORANGE-CUMIN VINAIGRETTE

For information on greens and instructions on dressing a salad, see page 229. Makes about 1 cup. **SERVES 8-10**

3 tbsp. freshly squeezed orange juice 2 tsp. Dijon mustard ¼ tsp. ground cumin seeds, toasted	1 garlic clove, smashed (optional) Salt & black pepper ½ cup olive oil 3 tbsp. grape seed oil

In a large mixing bowl, whisk together the orange juice, mustard, cumin, garlic, a pinch of salt, and some pepper. Whisk in the oils slowly, until emulsified. Taste and adjust the salt and pepper. If you like a thinner dressing, add a few drops of water.

This custard is flavored simply with a few drops of vanilla extract. If you feel inclined, add up to 2 teaspoons per recipe of one or a combination of flavorings you like, such as: orange flower or rose water, cognac, rum steeped with spices like star anise or cinnamon stick, or fresh mint syrup. The butter fat in cream absorbs flavors more readily than water, so a little flavor goes a long way. If you are in the mood for simple custard you can forget about the praline, but it's a tasty, crunchy addition if you're up to it. This custard, which is cooked on top of the stove, is a little fussy and requires almost constant stirring. **SERVES 4**

FOR THE PRALINE

½ cup blanched or sliced almonds

½ cup white, granulated sugar

¼ cup water

1 tbsp. unsalted butter to grease baking sheet

Toast the almonds in a dry saucepan for 4 to 5 minutes, and set them aside to cool.

Lightly butter a baking sheet. Place sugar in a small saucepan and slowly and evenly add water to the pan, careful that the water doesn't splash over the sides. Cook over medium heat until the sugar and water become amber caramel, 5 to 6 minutes.

Remove the pan from the heat and stir in the almonds. Be careful, as the caramel is very hot. While it's hot, pour the nut mixture onto the buttered baking sheet and let it cool until firm, at least 30 minutes. Crack the brittle into 1-inch pieces and place in a food processor. Pulse until it's the texture of coarse salt. You can make the praline in advance and store it for weeks in an airtight container placed in a cool spot.

FOR THE CUSTARD

1½ cups heavy cream

1 vanilla bean, split lengthwise (optional) or substitute 1 tsp. vanilla extract

2 strips of lemon zest, each about 2 in. long

6 large egg yolks

¼ cup raw sugar

In a small saucepan, scald the cream with the vanilla bean (if using) and lemon zest. Turn off the heat, set aside to let the cream steep.

Whisk the egg yolks and sugar together in the top of a double boiler or in a metal mixing bowl set over a pot of boiling water. Remove the lemon zest (and vanilla bean if using) from the cream, before slowly whisking the hot cream into the egg mixture. Add vanilla extract if you aren't using a bean. Stir constantly in the double boiler until the mixture reaches 162 to 165 F on an instant-read thermometer. If you are feeling fussy, pass the custard through a sieve to remove small bits of firm egg or eggshell that might have gotten into the mixture.

You may pour the custard into individual cups or one serving bowl. Cover with plastic wrap until chilled. (This can take up to 6 hours in the refrigerator.) Sprinkle with praline before serving. This simple custard also makes an excellent sauce for all kinds of fresh fruit.

MENU 09

WHOLE WHEAT ORECCHIETTE AND ROASTED CHICKPEAS (WITH OR WITHOUT CLAMS)

Linguine with white clam sauce has been a favorite meal of mine for as long as I can remember. This clam stew is based on my basic clam sauce recipe. Generally, I prefer unbleached white flour pasta, but if you buy a good brand of whole wheat pasta and make sure not to overcook it, the pasta has a nice, grainy texture and a rich wheat flavor. I especially like whole grain pasta when combined with other strong flavors and textures as it is prepared here. Clams have been become quite expensive, and the smaller they are, the more they cost. I love clams and don't mind mincing even chowder clams, though most folks will prefer littlenecks, cherrystones, or top necks. The flavor of a few clams goes a long way, so let your purse be your guide. For a vegetarian version, substitute diced roasted vegetables such as mushrooms, fennel, or red onions for the clams. **SERVES 4-6**

1 cup dried chickpeas, soaked overnight

2 cloves garlic, smashed

Aromatic vegetables such as 1 carrot, ½ onion, and 2 celery stalks (optional)

1 bay leaf

½ to 1 cup olive oil

Salt & black pepper

1 to 3 dozen cherrystone clams

½ cup water or dry white wine

4 to 8 cloves garlic, chopped

1 bunch flat-leaf parsley

1 lb. whole wheat orecchiette

Grated hard cheese, such as Parmesan (optional)

Crushed red pepper to serve on the side (optional)

Preheat oven to 375 F. Cover the chickpeas in a soup pot with 2 quarts water. Add garlic, aromatic vegetables (if using), and bay leaf. Cook over medium heat until the chickpeas are tender, about 1 hour. Drain and set aside to cool. Discard vegetables and bay leaf. In a mixing bowl, toss the chickpeas with ¼ cup of the olive oil before spreading them out on a baking sheet. Roast until the chickpeas are brown and crisp, 20 to 25 minutes, tossing frequently for even cooking. Sprinkle with salt and fresh black pepper, and set aside.

Wash the clams and discard any that are even slightly open. Put them in a big pot with the water (or white wine), cover, and bring to a boil over high heat. Pay close attention, the minute the clams pop open, even a crack, take them out of the pot. It will only take a few minutes before they open fully. Drain, reserving the cooking liquid.

When the clams are cool enough to handle, remove them from the shell, leaving behind both muscles (the tough parts on either side). Leave the clams whole or, if you prefer, cut each clam with scissors or a sharp knife into 3 to 4 pieces and set aside. A processor will make the clams mushy, but if you are making this dish for a huge group go ahead—it will still taste great. Set the clams aside.

Heat ½ cup of the olive oil and the garlic in a saucepan over medium heat, and sauté until the garlic just begins to color, 2 to 3 minutes. Add the parsley and cook for another minute. Add the reserved broth, taking care to leave behind the sand that has settled at the bottom of the bowl. Simmer for another 3 to 4 minutes, remove from the heat, and add the cut clams.

Cook pasta until al dente and drain. Toss the warm pasta with the clam sauce. Taste and adjust the salt and pepper. Transfer the pasta to a serving dish and top with the roasted chickpeas. Pass the cheese and crushed red pepper at the table, if you choose to use them.

Add cooked greens to the dish and/or replace the pasta with small pieces of boiled potatoes.

FENNEL SLAW

We serve many very simple, sparse dishes at the Institute involving one plain vegetable (such as chopped cabbage) lightly dressed and paired with the more powerful taste of a single spice such as brown mustard seeds. Other examples of this kind of streamlined preparation are beets with anise and jasmine rice with sesame seeds. The pleasure of these dishes is that the two flavors combine to form a new taste. This fennel slaw with black pepper works just that way. Be sure to use plenty of pepper and focus on its flavor when combined with the anise-scented fennel. If we're making slaw for a big group at the Institute, we slice the fennel bulbs in our food processor. At home, you can do the same or slice by hand, cutting the fennel as thin as possible. Use a mandoline if you have one. **SERVES 4-6**

3 fennel bulbs, thinly sliced
½ cup fruity olive oil

Juice of 2 lemons
Salt & black pepper

Toss the fennel with the olive oil and lemon juice. Sprinkle with salt and plenty of black pepper, taste, and adjust.

NOTES AND VARIATIONS

For variety, combine the fennel and mushroom slaw recipes.
I recently discovered that if I use a vegetable peeler on the outside of a fennel bulb I don't need to remove (and waste) the outer layer.

ROASTED WINTER SQUASH CRESCENTS
WITH VANILLA AND MAPLE SYRUP

I like small dark-green buttercup or kabocha squash, but any acorn squash–size winter squash will work in this recipe. Roast the squash until it's brown at the edges and then eat it whole—skin and all. This recipe calls for an added sweetener, but you can leave it out if you like. Likewise, leave out the vanilla for a pure squash flavor. **SERVES 6-8**

2 to 4 small winter squash
2 tbsp. butter or vegetable oil
1 tbsp. to 4 tbsp. maple syrup
(substitute raw or brown sugar
or no sweetener, depending on
your taste)

1 tsp. vanilla extract (optional)
Salt & black pepper

Preheat oven to 350 F. Cut the squash in half. If the squash is difficult to cut, you can begin by slicing off the stem. Then place the squash cut-side down on a cutting board and slice in half. Slice the halves into crescents ½-inch to 1-inch-thick.

Melt the butter, syrup, and vanilla together in a pot until mixed and warm. Place the squash in a baking dish, brush the maple-syrup mixture over the flesh side, sprinkle with salt and pepper, and bake for 5 minutes. Baste with additional maple syrup and repeat every 5 minutes or so until the squash are brown in spots and completely tender, about 20 to 25 minutes.

CILANTRO VINAIGRETTE

For information on greens and instructions on dressing a salad, see page 229. Makes about 1¼ cups. **SERVES 6-8**

3 tbsp. lemon juice
2 tsp. Dijon mustard
Salt & black pepper
3 tbsp. chopped fresh cilantro

2 garlic cloves, lightly smashed
½ cup fruity olive oil
3 tbsp. grape seed oil

Combine the lemon juice, mustard, a pinch of salt, black pepper, cilantro, and garlic in the bowl of a food processor or a good blender, and work until smooth. Slowly add the oils until emulsified. Thin with water if you like. Taste, and adjust the salt and pepper.

BUTTERSCOTCH PUDDING

This pudding is flavored with regular dark brown sugar for a classic old-fashioned butterscotch flavor. **SERVES 4**

6 egg yolks
1 cup heavy cream
⅓ cup (packed) dark brown sugar

3 tbsp. unsalted butter, cut into 3 pieces
¼ cup whole milk
½ teaspoon vanilla extract

In the top of a double boiler or a metal mixing bowl set over a pot of warm, simmering, not boiling, water, lightly whisk the eggs.

In a small saucepan, warm the cream until steaming. Turn off the heat, but leave the cream on a warm burner.

Cook the brown sugar and butter in a saucepan over medium-high heat, stirring with a wooden spoon, until melted and bubbling, about 2 minutes. Remove from the heat and stir in the cream until well blended. Let the mixture cool for 2 minutes before stirring in the milk.

Slowly pour and whisk the milk-butter-sugar mixture into the egg yolks, stir in the vanilla, and set the mixture over the simmering water. Cook over medium heat, stirring continually, until the pudding thickens slightly and reaches 165 to 170 F on an instant-read thermometer.

Strain the pudding through a sieve and pour into individual cups or a small serving bowl. Cover with plastic wrap and refrigerate for at least 2 hours. The pudding keeps in the refrigerator for 2 to 3 days.

Cutting a big batch of sweet potatoes at the Institute

Magnolia in bloom and bamboo at the Institute in late April

APRIL MENUS

10

CARROT-COCONUT SOUP 54
ASIAN NOODLES WITH WILD WATERCRESS, SPRING ONIONS,
    AND PEANUTS 55
DAIKON SALAD 56
HONEY-LEMON VINAIGRETTE 56
ZALETTI 57

11

MATZO BALL STEW WITH CHICKEN OR VEGETABLE BROTH 58
KASHA, RAMPS, AND ONIONS 60
RAW ASPARAGUS SALAD 62
CHERVIL VINAIGRETTE 62
COCONUT MACAROONS 63

12

MAC AND CHEESE 63
BRAISED LEEKS WITH LEMON AND MUSTARD 65
ROASTED TURNIPS WITH GINGER 66
CREAMY SHALLOT DRESSING 67
CREE'S COWGIRL COOKIES 68

CARROT-COCONUT SOUP

This simple, refreshing soup is excellent by itself or poured right over noodles. **SERVES 4–6**

2 tbsp. vegetable oil
1 large Spanish onion, cut into
½-in. dice
1 bunch cilantro, stems chopped
and leaves set aside separately
4 large or 8 medium carrots,
peeled and thinly sliced
2 cups cold water
3 dried hot red chiles, any kind
you like
1 stalk lemongrass, crushed
(substitute 1 tbsp. minced
ginger)

12 oz. unsweetened coconut
milk
Juice of 1 lime
4 scallions, green and white
parts, thinly sliced
1 tbsp. to 3 tbsp. Asian fish sauce
(nam pla) or soy sauce
Salt & black pepper
1 serrano chile, sliced
6 dried shiitake caps (optional)
2 tsp. sesame oil (optional)

Heat the oil in the bottom of a soup pot set over medium heat. Add the onions, cilantro stems, and carrots, and cook, stirring frequently, until the onions are tender and begin to brown. The carrots should be bright and still firm.

Stir in the water, chiles, and lemongrass, and simmer for 5 minutes before adding the coconut milk and the juice of 1 of the limes. Cook, stirring occasionally, until the carrots are tender, about 10 minutes. Add the scallions and then the Asian fish sauce (*nam pla*) 1 tablespoon at a time, tasting with each addition. Add salt and pepper if you wish, but taste first as the fish sauce is salty. Serve plain or over noodles with sliced green chiles on the side.

NOTES AND VARIATIONS

A few drops of toasted sesame oil works nicely in the soup or as a garnish. For a soup with a little more depth, add dried shiitakes when you add the water.

ASIAN NOODLES WITH WILD WATERCRESS, SPRING ONIONS, AND PEANUTS

Serve this simple noodle salad alone or topped with broth or the Carrot-Coconut Soup in this menu. Wild watercress is very leggy; if you find it, use the whole thing, not just the leaves. **SERVES 4-6**

1 tbsp. vegetable oil
4 spring onions, cut into ½-in. pieces (substitute any allium: onion, leek, scallion, ramp, Chinese chive, etc.)
Salt & black pepper
12 oz. rice noodles, cooked, rinsed in cold water and thoroughly drained (substitute cello noodles, fine egg noodles, or plain wheat noodles)
1 tbsp. toasted sesame oil

1 bunch wild watercress, cut into 1-in. pieces (use wild if you can find it, but cultivated is fine)
4 tbsp. chopped, roasted, unsalted peanuts (use a food processor for large quantities)
1 tbsp. Asian fish sauce (nam pla) or soy sauce (optional)
1 tbsp. rice vinegar, lemon juice, or lime juice (optional)
1 fresh chile, any variety, sliced (optional)

Heat the vegetable oil in a saucepan over medium heat, and sauté the spring onions until they're tender and as brown as you like them. Add a pinch of salt and pepper. Transfer to a mixing bowl, toss with the noodles and sesame oil. Add the watercress and peanuts along with the optional fish sauce, rice vinegar, and chile. Serve with Carrot-Coconut Soup.

NOTES AND VARIATIONS

If you would like to serve these noodles by themselves, do add the optional fish sauce or soy sauce, vinegar or citrus, and chiles. For a heartier main course, top with raw or cooked fish, tofu, or sliced steak.

Menu 10, carrot-coconut soup

DAIKON SALAD

This is a refreshing side dish or a good garnish for the Carrot-Coconut Soup and Asian Noodles in this menu. Shiso is a Japanese herb in the mint family that comes in a few varieties, green and purple (originally what gave pickled ginger its pretty pink color). I prefer Japanese varieties to Korean shiso, which in my experience, has big and beautiful leaves, but milder flavor. Shiso of all varieties grows very well in the Hudson Valley. **SERVES 6-8**

1 large daikon, peeled and thinly sliced or shredded (any radish variety is a fine substitute)
3 tbsp. rice vinegar
1 tbsp. vegetable oil

Salt & black pepper
¼ tsp. turmeric (optional)
¼ cup purple shiso, cut into ½-in. ribbons (in summer, optional)

Combine the radish, vinegar, oil, and a pinch of salt and pepper. Add the turmeric and shiso (if using). Toss and serve.

HONEY-LEMON VINAIGRETTE

For information on greens and instructions on dressing a salad, see page 229. **MAKES ABOUT 1 CUP. SERVES 4-6**

½ cup olive oil

3 tbsp. grape seed oil

3 tbsp. freshly squeezed lemon juice

2 tbsp. honey

Salt & black pepper

Whisk together the oils, lemon juice, honey, a pinch of salt, and a grind of black pepper in a bowl. This is not an emulsified vinaigrette.

ZALETTI

These not-very-sweet cornmeal cookies originated in Venice, Italy. Our version has additions that aren't traditional, including dried cranberries instead of raisins, but the recipe is a versatile classic to which you can add your favorite nuts, seeds, and fruit.

MAKES ABOUT 40 COOKIES

2 cups cornmeal

1 cup all-purpose, unbleached flour

1 tsp. baking powder

Pinch of salt

¾ cup (1½ sticks) unsalted, room-temperature butter

½ cup sugar

2 eggs, beaten

1 tbsp. vanilla extract

1 tsp. lemon zest

½ cup dried cranberries, roughly chopped

½ cup almonds, whole

1 tsp. fennel seeds

Preheat oven to 350 F. Combine the cornmeal, flour, baking powder, and salt in a mixing bowl, and set aside.

Cream the butter and sugar using the paddle attachment of a stand mixer or a wooden spoon in a separate mixing bowl until the butter is light and fluffy. Fully blend in the eggs before adding the vanilla and zest. Add the dry ingredients in three batches until mixed, and then add the cranberries, almonds, and fennel. Divide the dough into 4 pieces, and then roll each into a log about 1 inch in diameter. Create a square by gently pressing each log on four sides, and refrigerate until firm, about 1 hour. You can slice the cookies thinly for a crisp texture or thicker for a cake-like texture. Both are good, but pick one so that all the cookies bake evenly. Cornmeal tastes best when it's not too well browned. I like these cookies just done, still bright yellow, baked 12 to 15 minutes.

MATZO BALL STEW
WITH CHICKEN OR VEGETABLE BROTH

I call this matzo ball stew rather than soup because there's so much stuff in it. The chicken soup recipe is based on my mother's. She used only capons for the broth; the big, castrated birds weren't so expensive in those days. Her version was full of vegetables; I've added even more. If you don't eat meat, make Corncob Broth (see page 60). **SERVES 4 TO 6**

FOR THE MATZO BALLS

In my family we don't strive for light matzo balls. This recipe is based on the recipe on Streit's matzo meal box. If you're interested, there are blogs galore to explore the light versus heavy, firm matzo ball preference. **MAKES 10 TO 12 MATZO BALLS**

4 large eggs
¼ cup vegetable oil, or melted
duck or chicken fat
¼ cup water
¼ cup duck or chicken
cracklings, chopped (optional,
see Notes and Variations below)

1 tsp. salt
Black pepper
1¼ cups matzo meal

Beat the eggs in a mixing bowl before mixing in the oil, water, chopped cracklings (if using), salt, and pepper. Add the matzo meal and stir thoroughly. Refrigerate the mixture for 30 minutes to 60 minutes before forming balls.

Partially fill a large pot with salted water and bring it to a boil over high heat. Moisten your palms with cold water, and form the mixture into balls, about 1 inch in diameter. Drop the matzo balls into the salted boiling water. When all the balls are in the pot, reduce the heat to low and simmer, covered, for 20 minutes. Remove the balls with a slotted spoon to a large bowl and serve with stew.

NOTES AND VARIATIONS

To make cracklings, cut the chicken skin and fat into small pieces, add a few halved garlic cloves, place in a small saucepan, and cover with water. To render, cook uncovered over low heat until the water evaporates and the trimmings begin to brown. At this point add a little more water and let fat render further. Repeat this a few times until the remaining bits of skin are crisp and brown but not burned. Fish them out and set aside. Drain the fat into containers leaving behind the small quantity of broth in the bottom of the pot. (If you add the broth to the fat it will settle to the bottom of the container and if left for more than a few days will spoil. Be careful to save only the fat.) You may freeze the fat or store it in the refrigerator. The garlic and fat make your kitchen smell good.

WITH CHICKEN BROTH

FOR THE STEW

1 4 lb. chicken
4 carrots, peeled and cut into 1-in. to 2-in. chunks
4 to 6 celery ribs
1 onion, cut into ½-in. dice
1 bunch flat-leaf parsley, stem and all, cut into 1-in. pieces
1 bunch dill, stem and all, cut into 1-in. pieces (reserve several sprigs for garnish)
6 cloves garlic, sliced

Salt & black pepper
1 parsnip, peeled and cut into 1-in. chunks (optional)
1 parsley root, peeled and cut into 1-in. chunks (optional)
1 celery root, peeled and cut into 1-in. chunks (optional)
1 to 2 turnips, peeled and cut into 1-in. chunks (optional)
1 to 3 leeks, cleaned and cut into 1-in. chunks (optional)

If you would like to make cracklings, see page 58 before cooking the chicken. Place the chicken, carrots, celery, onions, parsley, dill, garlic, salt, and pepper into a soup pot. Also add the parsnip, parsley root, celery root, turnip, and leeks (if using). Cover with cold water, bring to a boil, then reduce the heat to low. Let the broth cook at an easy simmer, partially covered, for about 1 hour, skimming the fat and foam off the top as needed.

Gently remove the chicken from the soup. The meat will fall apart; don't worry, it's fine. Remove all the meat from the bones, discard the bones, and return the meat to the broth. Taste and adjust the salt and pepper. Add the cooked matzo balls (page 58) and serve with a sprig of dill on top.

NOTES AND VARIATIONS

Drain the broth and serve the vegetables and chicken and matzo balls on the side, family style, so everyone can take what they like. Garnish with dill.

Although I'd made corncob stock for use in various recipes, my friend Vicky introduced me to enjoying it as a broth. Corn broth is very sweet with tiny beads of corn oil that float to the top, which resemble the beads of chicken fat that float to top of chicken soup in a most satisfying way. Corn is not in season around Passover, when we make this meal, but frozen corn on the cob is fine for broth. **SERVES 4-6**

FOR THE STEW

12 oz. frozen corn or four ears fresh, raw corn

4 carrots, peeled and cut into 1-in. to 2-in. chunks

4 to 6 celery ribs

1 onion, cut into ½-in. dice

1 bunch flat-leaf parsley, stem and all, cut into 1-in. pieces

1 bunch dill, stem and all, cut into 1-in. pieces, reserving several sprigs for garnish

6 cloves garlic, sliced

Salt & black pepper

1 parsnip, peeled and cut into 1-in. chunks (optional)

1 celery root, peeled and cut into 1-in. chunks (optional)

1 parsley root, peeled and cut into 1-in. chunks (optional

1 to 2 turnips, peeled and cut into 1-in. chunks (optional)

1 to 3 leeks, cleaned and cut into 1-in. chunks (optional)

Place the corncobs, carrots, celery, onions, parsley, dill, garlic, salt, and pepper in a soup pot. Add the parsnip, celery root, parsley root, turnips, and leeks (if using). Cover the vegetables with water, and bring the liquid to a boil over high heat. Once the pot boils reduce the heat to low and simmer until the vegetables are tender, about 30 minutes. Skim the fat and foam off the top of the broth as it cooks. Taste and adjust the salt and pepper. Add the cooked matzo balls and serve garnished with a sprig of dill.

KASHA, RAMPS, AND ONIONS

Buckwheat, especially in the whole-groats form of kasha, is an acquired taste—at least it was for me. I first started to like buckwheat pancakes and crepes, both of which were a mix of white and buckwheat flours. Eventually, I worked up to enjoying kasha, though even now I like it best with other ingredients to contrast with the grain's soft texture. Add pasta to this recipe if you're not serving it with Matzo Ball Stew for a version of kasha varnishkes. Ramps are wild leeks and are one of the favorites of the foraged-wild food world. I think they deserve this status—they have a great taste. There is a push for the public to stop foraging so many, as the common practice of picking the whole plant eventually destroys the patch. The most sustainable way to harvest ramps is to harvest a few leaves from each plant, allowing the plant itself to remain and propagate. Disturbed beds in the wild take years to recover. I happen to like the leaves, but many people find the bulbs the most satisfying part. **SERVES 6–8**

1 cup whole buckwheat groats (kasha), roasted or raw
2 tbsp. or 3 tbsp. vegetable oil, chicken fat, duck fat or butter
1 cup cold water
1 large Spanish onion, cut into 1-in. dice

12 ramps, leaves or whole plant, cut into 1-in. pieces (substitute scallions, leeks, or additional onion)
Salt & black pepper

For an extra nutty taste or if you are using raw groats, heat the extra tablespoon of fat in a saucepan until medium hot. Cook the groats until they start to turn a darker gold color, 2 to 3 minutes.

I like to cook kasha in a rice cooker at a ratio of one cup groats to one cup water with as much salt as desired. The groats on the surface will be a little undercooked. Don't worry, just mix and fluff the kasha and the firmer, lightly cooked groats will add texture. If you don't have a rice cooker, combine the groats, water, and a pinch of salt in a saucepan set over low heat, cover, and cook until the groats are tender, about 10 to 12 minutes.

While the kasha is cooking, heat the remaining oil in a saucepan over medium heat. Add the onions, and sauté until they begin to brown, 10 to 12 minutes. Add the ramps along with a pinch of salt and black pepper, and cook until the ramps are wilted and tender, another 2 to 3 minutes. Toss the onion mixture together with the kasha and taste. Adjust the salt and pepper as needed and serve.

NOTES AND VARIATIONS

Put up a pot of salted boiling water and cook up to a pound of pasta while the kasha cooks. Add the drained hot pasta to the kasha, ramps, and onions in any amount you like. I like more pasta than kasha. Our annual Earth Day dinner at the Institute in 2013 featured pasta made from malted barley from a local brewery, to which we added kasha, ramps, and onions. I used the kasha more as a seasoning by tossing the cooked kasha with a little vegetable oil and roasting it on baking sheets so that it was dry and slightly brown. Wide egg noodles, bow-tie pasta, or even corn pasta work nicely as well.

RAW ASPARAGUS SALAD

We started an asparagus patch at the Institute a few years ago and that was when I learned that, like peas shelled straight out of the garden, I prefer freshly picked asparagus raw. We don't produce much asparagus, but it prompts me to order some from a local source as they are so good. **SERVES 4**

1 large bunch asparagus	Coarse sea salt
¼ cup grated Parmesan or	1 tsp. lemon zest
Gruyère cheese (any cheese will do)	1 tbsp. vinegar or lemon wedges
¼ cup fruity olive oil	(optional)

Snap off the tough end of each asparagus stalk. Slice the asparagus on a diagonal into ¼-inch slices. Toss with the cheese, olive oil, a pinch of salt, and lemon zest. The vinegar (if using) should be added at the last minute, as the asparagus will turn an olive green because of contact with the acid. If you prefer, simply serve lemon wedges on the side.

CHERVIL VINAIGRETTE

For information on greens and instructions on dressing a salad, see page 229. Makes about 1 cup. **SERVES 4-6**

½ cup olive oil	3 tbsp. white wine vinegar
3 tbsp. grape seed oil	Salt & black pepper
4 tbsp. chopped chervil	
(substitute tarragon or parsley	
for hard-to-find chervil)	

In a bowl, whisk together the oils, chervil, vinegar, and a pinch of salt and pepper. This is not an emulsified vinaigrette.

COCONUT MACAROONS

This macaroon is sweet and marshmallowy in the center, slightly crunchy on the outside, with wide flakes of unsweetened coconut. **MAKES 24 COOKIES**

1 cup egg whites (from about 6 eggs), room temperature
1 cup sugar
1 tbsp. vanilla extract

½ tsp. salt
8 cups large-flake unsweetened coconut, toasted until golden brown

Preheat oven to 275 F.

Using the whisk attachment of a stand mixer, electric beaters, or by hand with a whisk, beat egg whites and sugar until stiff and glossy. Using a machine on a medium fast speed, this should take 5 to 7 minutes, by hand closer to 10. But watch the egg whites carefully while you mix as temperature and speed will make a big difference. Mix in the vanilla and salt on a low speed. Fold in the coconut by hand.

With an ice cream scoop or serving spoon, form 24 balls, slightly smaller in size than tennis balls, spaced about 3 inches apart on a baking sheet lined with parchment paper.

Bake cookies until they just turn brown, 15 to 18 minutes. Cool before serving.

MENU 12

MAC AND CHEESE

I prefer macaroni and cheese baked until it's crunchy on top. My family prefers it creamy from the stovetop. At the Institute we make it somewhere in between by baking it in hotel pans with plenty of béchamel (white sauce) and taking it out of the oven when the top is golden, crunchy on the edges and creamy inside. Follow your preference. **SERVES 4-6**

FOR THE BÉCHAMEL (WHITE SAUCE)

6 cups milk
Salt & black pepper
1 shallot, halved
1 clove garlic, sliced
A few sprigs parsley

1 bay leaf
1 stick butter (substitute vegetable oil)
½ cup all-purpose, unbleached flour

Combine the milk in a saucepan with a pinch of salt, black pepper, shallot, garlic, parsley, and bay leaf. Set over low heat and simmer for 5 to 10 minutes. Stir frequently and make sure it doesn't boil over. Turn off the heat and set the mixture aside to steep as you work on the roux.

Melt the butter in another saucepan over medium heat. Add the flour. Cook, stirring continually, over medium-low heat, 3 to 5 minutes. The mixture should be foaming—if not, raise the heat, but not so much that roux colors. Strain the shallot, garlic, parsley, and bay leaf from the milk in the other saucepan, and pour the milk into the flour mixture, whisking constantly until fully incorporated. It will bubble up and thicken. Cook at a low simmer for 10 to 12 minutes, stirring frequently. The sauce will thicken, tending to stick to the bottom of the pot. Stirring helps to keep it from burning. If it's too thick, add a little extra milk; if it's too thin, cook a little longer.

FOR THE MAC AND CHEESE

1 lb. penne, cooked according to package directions and drained (any cut of pasta is fine)

2 cups grated cheddar (substitute a local, firm, sharp cow's-milk cheese)

1 cup grated Parmesan, (any aged, dry cow's-milk cheese is fine)

Salt & black pepper

Freshly grated nutmeg (optional)

1 cup grated cheddar and Parmesan, mixed, for topping (optional)

2 cups canned tomatoes, diced with juices (optional)

6 thick slices bacon, cooked as you like it, crispy or soft, and cut into ½-in. pieces (optional)

In a big bowl, thoroughly stir together the pasta with the warm béchamel and the grated cheese. You might use all the béchamel or as little as a quarter of it. The amount you use will determine how creamy and saucy the dish is. If you plan to bake the macaroni and cheese, add a little extra sauce so that it doesn't dry out and all the sauce if you want it brown on top and creamy inside. Taste and adjust the salt and pepper, and add the nutmeg (if using). Serve creamy from the pot or pour the mac and cheese into a buttered 13 x 9 ovenproof baking dish, top with the optional mixed cheese, and bake until bubbling and hot around the edges and golden on top, 30 to 35 minutes. (Bake longer if you want it crispy and brown.)

Menu 12, mac and cheese, white turnips and rutabaga, and braised leeks with carrots added

If you're using the tomatoes, heat them gently in their own juices and serve on the side of the baked macaroni and cheese, on top, or mixed right into the creamy stove-top version. Serve the bacon the same way (if using).

NOTES AND VARIATIONS

Béchamel holds for days in the refrigerator and may also be frozen, so it may be made in advance. After you defrost béchamel, it may look broken. Heat and stir after it defrosts to bring it back together.

BRAISED LEEKS WITH LEMON AND MUSTARD

To me, leeks are fancy onions that remain French no matter what I make. This is a recipe for classic braised leeks that makes a great side dish. You can also chop these leeks and mix them with a grain, other vegetables, salads, or into gratins. **SERVES 4-8**

4 to 8 leeks
3 tbsp. clarified butter or
vegetable oil
3 sprigs thyme
Salt & black pepper

1 cup dry white wine, vegetable
stock, poultry stock, or water
3 tbsp. olive oil
Juice of 1 lemon
4 tsp. Dijon mustard

Leeks are often so sandy that they need to be washed twice. Rinse the worst of the grit off the whole leek before trimming away the very dark top third. (Discard this part or set aside to use for stock.)

There are two ways I trim the leeks for this dish depending on how much time I have or how many people I am cooking for. One way is to trim just the very end of the root while leaving most of it intact and then cutting the leeks lengthwise, top to bottom. The leek still looks good, and there are a variety of textures you can achieve when they're left mostly intact, from caramelized to mildly soft to slightly firm at the center. The other, faster, way to cook them is to halve the leeks then cut each half into half moons. Cooked, the result is more of a topping, like sautéed onions (for instructions, see Notes and Variations below).

To cook in halves, heat the clarified butter in a large saucepan over medium heat. When the oil is hot but not smoking, add the leeks cut-side down and cook until browned. Toss in the thyme. Turn the leeks over onto the thyme branches and cook another minute. Add salt, pepper, and wine. Lower the heat and simmer until the leeks are tender, turning once or twice. (Try to keep the leeks intact.) When they're tender, remove them from the pan and place on a serving platter. If all the liquid has been reduced away to nothing, add a little water to deglaze the pan before adding the olive oil, lemon juice, and mustard. Taste and adjust the salt and pepper. Pour the sauce over the leeks and serve.

NOTES AND VARIATIONS

For the quicker, less fussy method, cut the leeks in half after you trim the roots, then cut the leeks into 1- or 2-inch pieces. Wash them in a bowl of cold water, lifting the cut leeks so that the sand falls to the bottom. Let them drain in a colander for a few minutes or give them a few shakes before sautéing.

ROASTED TURNIPS WITH GINGER

Turnips are not a very common (or popular) vegetable for Americans, especially when eaten on their own. But roasted turnips are sweet, mild, and consistently popular at the Institute. I learned to use ginger in place of garlic, as I do here, from Richard Olney's *Lulu's Provençal Table*. **SERVES 6–8**

2 lb. turnips (I like the medium-size purple-top variety, but the small white Japanese variety or big ones from the supermarket work as well)

¼ cup vegetable oil
Salt & black pepper
1 tsp. to 2 tsp. peeled and grated fresh ginger

Preheat oven to 400 F. Peel the turnips, unless you are using the small Japanese variety, which need only a quick scrub. Cut the turnips into bite-size pieces and toss them in a mixing bowl with the oil and a pinch of salt and black pepper. Spread on a baking sheet and roast until the pieces are golden brown and a knife goes through the center of the largest piece with ease, about 15 to 20 minutes. They should be tender and cooked through.

Depending on your taste, you can instead juice the ginger and use 1 to 2 teaspoons of the liquid. Put the ginger (or juice) in a mixing bowl, toss with the turnips, taste and adjust the salt and pepper. Serve warm or at room temperature.

CREAMY SHALLOT DRESSING

For information on greens and instructions on dressing a salad, see page 229. Makes a generous cup. **SERVES 6-8**

¼ cup red wine vinegar
2 tbsp. mayonnaise
2 tbsp. finely chopped shallot
2 tsp. Dijon mustard

Salt & black pepper
½ cup fruity olive oil (use half grape seed, if you prefer)

Whisk together the vinegar, mayonnaise, shallot, mustard, salt, and pepper in a mixing bowl. Slowly whisk in the oil until emulsified. Taste and adjust the salt and pepper. Thin slightly with water if desired.

This recipe is a cross between an oatmeal cookie and a granola bar, chockful of goodies. It was created by our incredible baker, Cree LeFavour. **MAKES 24 TO 30 COOKIES**

1½ cups all-purpose, unbleached flour	3 eggs
1¼ tsp. baking soda	2¼ cup rolled oats
1 tsp. salt	¾ cup walnuts
1 tsp. cinnamon	¾ cup raisins
1½ sticks unsalted, room-temperature butter	½ cup unsweetened, flaked coconut, toasted
¼ cup granulated sugar	2 tbsp. sesame seeds
	1 tbsp. vanilla

Preheat oven to 350 F. Line a baking sheet with parchment paper. Mix the flour, baking soda, salt, and cinnamon, and set aside.

Using a wooden spoon or the paddle attachment at a medium-high setting of a stand mixer, blend the butter and sugar until the butter is creamy and fluffy.

Add the eggs, and incorporate thoroughly. Lower the paddle speed and add the flour mixture, little by little, until well mixed. Add the rolled oats, then add walnuts, raisins, coconut, sesame seeds, and vanilla.

Scoop the batter into 1½-inch balls and place on the baking pan about 2 inches apart. Bake until golden brown, 18 to 20 minutes. Cool for 5 to 10 minutes before removing from the pan and cooling on a rack.

Chocolate chip and Cree's cowgirl cookies

MAY MENUS

13

WHOLE ROASTED CHICKEN WITH GREEN GARLIC AND SASSAFRAS 70
ROASTED MUSHROOMS AND JERUSALEM ARTICHOKES 71
POLENTA WITH SPINACH, SPRING ONIONS, AND CHEESE 72
YOGURT AND HERB VINAIGRETTE 75
BUCKWHEAT BANANA-PECAN CAKE 75

14

EGGS FOR DINNER THREE WAYS:
    FRITTATA WITH ASSORTED GREENS AND SPRING ONIONS 76
    PAN QUICHE WITH CAULIFLOWER AND CHEDDAR 78
    PIPÉRADE 79
BLACK-EYED PEAS AND THYME 80
ROASTED ASPARAGUS 81
HERB VINAIGRETTE 82
CHOCOLATE CHIP COOKIES 82

15

SPICY SPRING-VEGETABLE CURRY WITH BROWN CARDAMOM 83
BRAISED LAMB WITH RHUBARB SAUCE 85
SWEET INDIAN CURRY WITH CHICKEN AND PEAS 88
RICE WITH SORREL, GARLIC CHIVES, AND MUSTARD GREENS 90
LEMON AND OLIVE OIL DRESSING 91
RHUBARB SHORTCAKES 92

WHOLE ROASTED CHICKEN
WITH GREEN GARLIC AND SASSAFRAS

Many families, restaurant chefs, and cookbooks boast that they have the secret to the best roast chicken. Along with cooking eggs and making a tender pastry crust, how you roast a chicken is a sign of whether "you can really cook." I have cooked through many "best" ways, and suspect I will keep changing the way I roast a chicken. This method is one that I use because it's simple, versatile, and results in a great roast chicken with an easy sauce. Start with a high-quality, fresh chicken. Green garlic shoots are the earliest mild spring garlic; sassafras grows all over the Hudson Valley and lends an herby, root beer flavor to the chicken. **SERVES 4 EATEN ALONE, 8-10 AS PART OF A STEW OR CASSEROLE**

One large handful sassafras leaves and young thin stems
1 3 lb. to 4 lb. chicken (a genuinely free-range bird makes a difference; buy the best bird you can afford)
Salt & black pepper
1½ to 2 cups cold water
1 cup dry white wine
2 bunches very young garlic, rinsed, roots trimmed and cut into ½-in. pieces (substitute garlic scapes, 2 heads mature garlic, or 1 red onion, peeled and cut into wedges)
2 carrots, peeled and cut into 1-in. pieces
1 celery stalk, cut into 1-in. pieces
4 sprigs parsley

Preheat oven to 400 F. At home I like to roast in ceramic gratin-type pans. At the Institute, we generally use a stainless steel hotel pan. Either is fine.

Place the sassafras in the bottom of the roasting pan.

Sprinkle the chicken with salt and pepper inside and out, and place it breast-side up in a roasting pan that's not much bigger than the bird. Pour about 1½ cups of the water and the wine around the chicken.

Scatter the garlic, carrot, celery, and parsley around the bird in the liquid. Roast the chicken for 20 minutes or until the skin begins to brown, basting with the liquid in the pan every 10 minutes or so. Gently turn the chicken upside down so that the browned top is in the liquid. Continue roasting for another 20 minutes until the exposed chicken skin is golden brown. Turn the chicken over again gently so as not to tear the skin. Add the remaining ½ cup of water, as needed. Roast the chicken until an instant-read thermometer inserted into the thickest part of the thigh reaches 160 F, about 45 to 50 minutes.

When the bird is done, transfer it to a serving platter. You are left with well-done veggies and a flavorful sauce. Skim the fat from the sauce, taste, and adjust salt and pepper. Serve as is or remove the veggies and reduce the liquid in a saucepan until it reaches the desired concentration and consistency.

NOTES AND VARIATIONS

Toss any vegetables you like around the bird, stir, and baste as often as you like. Eat the vegetables on the side, purée or mash them and add them to the sauce as a thickener. A few sets of flavor variations I like: lime, honey, cilantro, garlic, scallions, and fresh chiles; mustard, thyme, leeks, and dried mushrooms; garlic, orange, and bay leaf.

ROASTED MUSHROOMS AND JERUSALEM ARTICHOKES

Button mushrooms and unpeeled, scrubbed Jerusalem artichokes are earthy and modestly priced. Of course you can use maitakes or chanterelles if you just happen to have some on hand. I avoided Jerusalem artichokes for a long time, thinking I preferred them peeled, an arduous job. The skin is thin and it turns out it tastes just fine left on, even when puréed in a soup. **SERVES 4-6**

2 cups Jerusalem artichokes, well scrubbed and cut into 1-in. pieces
¼ cup vegetable oil, divided
Salt & black pepper

1 lb. button mushrooms (any size or variety is fine), cut into bite-size pieces
2 to 8 garlic cloves, cut into chunks

Preheat oven to 400 F. Toss the Jerusalem artichokes into a mixing bowl with ⅛ cup (half) the vegetable oil, and a pinch of salt and pepper. Spread on a parchment-lined baking sheet or in a shallow baking dish and roast until fully tender, 25 to 30 minutes. Set aside, and raise the oven temperature to 450 F.

At the Institute we roast mushrooms whole, stem and all, trimming only the very rough (often dirty) end. If you prefer, remove the stems. (Whole small mushrooms are fine.) Toss them in a mixing bowl with the chunky garlic, remaining oil, some salt, and pepper. Spread on a parchment-lined baking sheet or in a roasting pan. Roast the mushrooms until they're brown, 6 to 8 minutes. Check the mushrooms frequently since your oven might have hot spots; if it does, be sure to rotate the pan.

In a bowl, toss together the mushrooms and Jerusalem artichokes and serve. You can reheat them together if the artichokes are cold. This is very good plain, but feel free to add rosemary branches, a drizzle of olive oil, lemon juice, grated cheese, or chopped parsley if you're serving this as the main starch instead of the polenta in this menu.

POLENTA WITH SPINACH, SPRING ONIONS, AND CHEESE

Though originally porridge made from a variety of grains, polenta has come to describe cooked cornmeal, served in a manner similar to pasta. Like macaroni and cheese, some people prefer creamy polenta, while others like it set up in blocks or in a casserole. You can roast, fry, or bake it—we do it all. Our latest effort was introduced to me by a friend. He spreads the polenta out in a thin layer on a baking sheet well coated with olive oil and adds lots of cheese on top so that the polenta is like a pizza or focaccia with toppings. (This dish is very popular with those who are avoiding gluten.) We buy a wide variety of cornmeal, including fine meal from Italy and a coarser grind from the Hudson Valley's Wild Hive Farm. Occasionally we buy dried, local corn that's so coarse-cut it benefits from soaking overnight before cooking. I often start polenta on the stove in cold water, a nontraditional method that works for me. Typically, fine polenta is very gradually added to hot water while carefully whisking to prevent lumps. **SERVES 6-8**

Cherry tree in bloom near the garden at the Institute

1½ cups polenta	8 garlic cloves, rough chopped
1½ to 2 qt. water	or sliced
2 tbsp. butter	1 large bunch spinach, washed
¼ cup heavy cream (optional)	and cut into 2-in. pieces (any
5 tbsp. vegetable oil	cooking green is fine)
1 to 2 cups spring onions, cut	Salt & black pepper
into 1-in. pieces (substitute red	½ cup grated Parmesan (substitute
onions or leeks)	any aged cow's-milk cheese)

You may choose to prepare the polenta in advance, let it set, cut it, brush with vegetable oil, and roast before serving. Or, prepare the polenta just before serving if you want to make it creamy style.

Four cups of water to one cup of polenta is a good ratio to begin with. It's easy to add more water as needed or cook the polenta a little longer to thicken it if there is too much water. Each variety of polenta is slightly different.

Combine the polenta and cold water in a saucepan over medium heat. Whisk regularly, especially as the mixture gets hot. It will take at least 5 minutes, depending on the heat source. Keep an eye on it—the meal will suddenly expand and thicken the mixture. It may boil a little, but lower the heat as it will spit bits of hot porridge onto your arm as you stir. (Hot polenta is like napalm, so be careful.) Simmer over low heat, whisking regularly.

After about 45 minutes the polenta should be soft, tender, and the consistency of a fine potato purée. Whisk in the butter and heavy cream (if using). Either serve from a bowl piping hot or pour the mixture into an ovenproof pan ready to bake. You may also chill the polenta. The finer varieties, especially, have a gelatinous quality that allows you to cut the cooked polenta into pieces that can be brushed with oil and baked or sautéed until golden brown and crunchy on the outside.

In a large saucepan combine the oil, onions, and garlic and cook over medium heat until onions begin to brown, 6 to 8 minutes. Add the spinach and a pinch of salt and pepper. Use tongs to turn the leaves in the pan until they begin to wilt. Remove the pan from the heat.

Place the soft polenta in a deep platter or bowl, or place the browned polenta squares on a platter. Top the polenta with the sautéed spinach and onions. (I also like to add the small quantity of broth released from the spinach.) Serve cheese on top or on the side, as you like.

If you want to experiment with a "pizza" polenta, cook the cornmeal until it's very thick. Spread a generous amount of olive oil on a baking sheet and spread the polenta in a layer about a ½ inch thick on top and finish by brushing the top of the polenta with oil. Bake at 400 F until golden, about 10 minutes. Remove from the oven, top with cheese and your favorite pizza toppings, and pop back into the oven until the cheese is melted. Cut and serve. Lining the baking sheet with a piece of parchment helps prevent sticking, but it will also prevent the polenta from browning nicely on the bottom. The sheet of polenta can also be made in advance, cut into pieces, and reheated with toppings just before serving.

YOGURT AND HERB VINAIGRETTE

For information on greens and instructions on dressing a salad, see page 229. Makes a generous cup. **SERVES 6-8**

3 tbsp. plain yogurt (I like whole milk yogurt, but any variety is fine)
1 tbsp. lemon juice or red wine vinegar
½ tsp. Dijon mustard
Salt & black pepper

3 tbsp. roughly chopped fresh herbs, such as chervil, tarragon, dill, basil, parsley
1 garlic clove, minced
½ cup olive oil
3 tbsp. grape seed oil
Salt & black pepper

Whisk together the yogurt, lemon juice, mustard, a pinch of salt, black pepper, herbs, and garlic in a bowl. If you have a food processor or a good blender use it to blend the ingredients until smooth. Slowly add the oils until emulsified. Thin with water if you like. Taste, and adjust the salt and pepper.

BUCKWHEAT BANANA-PECAN CAKE

The flavor combination of buckwheat, banana, and pecans is very comforting. The flavors seem to belong together and create a cake that is sweet, rich, and soft. I'd like to try replacing the banana in this recipe with mashed roasted winter squash, but I haven't gotten around to it. **SERVES 6-8**

1½ cups all-purpose, unbleached flour	½ cup sugar
1½ teaspoons baking soda	3 eggs, beaten
Pinch salt	1½ cups ripe mashed banana
1 stick unsalted, room-temperature butter	2 tsp. vanilla extract
	1¼ cups buckwheat flour
	¾ cup pecans, toasted

Preheat oven to 350 F. Grease a 9-inch-round cake pan.

In a mixing bowl, combine the flour, baking soda, and salt, and set aside.

Cream the butter and sugar with a wooden spoon in a mixing bowl or use the paddle attachment on a stand mixer until the butter is creamy and fluffy. Add the egg and mix well. Blend in the mashed banana and then the vanilla. Add the buckwheat flour until fully blended. Add the flour mixture in batches until fully blended. Finally, add the pecans. Spread the batter into the cake pan and bake until the center springs back when you gently press down or a knife comes out clean when inserted into the center, 15 to 18 minutes.

MENU 14

EGGS FOR DINNER THREE WAYS

FRITTATA WITH ASSORTED GREENS AND SPRING ONIONS

Frittatas are a staple at the Institute, where we serve them for lunch or supper, using seasonal produce, cheese, and sometimes leftovers. At the Institute, where a very small group is 12, we make our frittatas in big skillets. We fill the pans pretty full and, so as not to end up with densely baked eggs, we add lots of filling. These big frittatas are like Spanish omelets (tortilla Española), where the traditional filling of potatoes and onions make up more than half the dish. By combining the mixed raw egg with warm, cooked ingredients, the eggs thicken, and the filling won't separate and settle to the bottom. SERVES 8-12 (FOR ADDITIONAL OPTIONS ON SERVING SIZE, SEE NOTES AND VARIATIONS BELOW)

15 eggs, beaten	8 cups greens, such as broccoli
1½ tsp. salt	rabe, nettles, dandelion, and/or
1 tsp. black pepper	mustard greens, cut into
3 tbsp. vegetable oil	1-in. pieces
2 cups spring onions, cut into	3 cups shredded Gouda or
1-in. pieces (substitute red	Gruyère
onions or leeks)	4 tbsp. clarified butter or
2 garlic cloves, sliced (optional)	vegetable oil

FOR A LARGE FRITTATA

Preheat oven to 400 F. Season the eggs with salt and pepper. Heat the oil in a 10- to 12-inch skillet over medium heat, and sauté onions and garlic for 2 to 3 minutes. They should still have some body to them. Add the greens and sauté until just tender or as you like them. Taste, and adjust salt and pepper. Add the hot greens to the eggs in a mixing bowl and stir so the eggs thicken, like a custard sauce.

Place your cast iron, rolled steel, or nonstick skillet over medium-high heat and add the clarified butter. When it's hot add the egg and vegetable mixture. Don't stir, it should be bubbling hot along the edge. Cook on top of the stove for about 5 minutes, lowering the heat if you think it's too high. Sprinkle the cheese on top (don't worry, some of it will sink in). Place the skillet in the oven and bake until the egg is just set or until an instant-thermometer inserted in the center reaches 160 F, about 15 minutes. Set the pan on a counter and let the frittata set for 5 minutes before inverting it onto a large plate. Slice into wedges and serve warm or at room temperature.

NOTES AND VARIATIONS

When making a small frittata, add the greens right to the pan; when they're hot add the egg. Using a fork, like you're making an omelet, lift the sides of the set egg to allow the raw egg to slip under. Add the cheese as the eggs begin to set. When set enough to manage, flip the frittata over. If you don't have the flick-of-your-wrist technique down, invert the frittata onto a large pot lid or plate and then slide the raw side back into the pan. Cook for another minute or 2 until the frittata is fully set. Rather than flipping it or inverting, you may also finish the frittata in the oven and bake until the egg is just set or until an instant-thermometer inserted in the center reaches 160 F, about 15 minutes. Set the pan on a counter and let the frittata set for

5 minutes before inverting it onto a large plate. Slice into wedges and serve warm or at room temperature.

To serve 6 to 8 people, use an 8- to 10-inch skillet, 10 eggs, about 2 cups vegetables, and 1 cup cheese. For 4 people, use an 8-inch skillet, 6 eggs, about 1½ cups vegetables, and ½ cup cheese.

PAN QUICHE
WITH CAULIFLOWER AND CHEDDAR

Quiche filling is custard made with a bit more egg than you would for a dessert such as crème caramel. Actually, it isn't much different than the frittata other than the addition of milk or cream. We serve these crustless quiches right from the pan. Because the savory custard is baked in a dish, the fillings, usually vegetables, can be wetter and more generous than a typical quiche, and the custard can be softer because we scoop it out rather than cut it. I use Julia Child's quiche proportion: roughly 3 eggs to 1½ cups of cream or milk. Cauliflower and cheddar are great fillings, as the gentle taste and texture of the cauliflower, with all its nooks and crannies, mingles thoroughly with the cheese and custard, forming a soft, rich cake. **SERVES 4-6**

3 tbsp. to 4 tbsp. olive oil (substitute any vegetable oil or room-temperature butter), divided

3 cups cauliflower florets, about half a head of cauliflower

Salt & black pepper

3 leeks

4 cloves garlic, sliced

1½ cups heavy cream (or use all milk or all cream)

¾ cup whole milk

5 eggs

¼ tsp. freshly grated nutmeg

1 cup shredded cheddar

Preheat oven to 350 F. Using about 1 tablespoon oil (or butter), grease an ovenproof 2 or 2½ quart baking dish.

Boil the cauliflower florets in lightly salted water for five minutes, drain, and then toss with 1 tablespoon oil and a pinch of salt and pepper. Spread on a baking sheet and roast until tender, 10 to 25 minutes. (Cook longer if you like a more caramelized flavor.)

Clean the leeks by cutting in half lengthwise (see Braised Leeks with Lemon and Mustard, page 66, for complete cleaning instructions). Then slice them into half rings about ¼ inch thick. Sauté the leeks and garlic over medium heat in the remaining tablespoon of oil until soft.

In a mixing bowl, whisk together the cream, milk, eggs, nutmeg, salt, and pepper.

Evenly distribute the cauliflower, leeks, cheese, and garlic in the baking dish. Gently pour the egg mixture on top. Bake until the quiche is firm to the touch and an instant-read thermometer inserted in the center reaches 165 F, and the custard is set when you insert a paring knife, about 45 to 55 minutes.

Let the quiche set for a few minutes before cutting. Serve warm.

PIPÉRADE

Pipérade is traditionally from the Basque region of France. It's essentially soft scrambled eggs made with white onions, red tomatoes, and green peppers (like the Basque flag). There are other versions made in Gascony, and I ate something like pipérade in Morocco prepared with tomatoes, onions, cilantro, and parsley directly from a large, communal platter with bread as a scoop. At the Institute, we take liberties and call all the versions we make pipérade. We tend to prepare it for smaller groups as, unlike a fritatta, it must be served warm. **SERVES 4-6**

3 to 5 tbsp. of olive oil (substitute butter, pork or duck fat, which are delicious)
2 large Spanish onions, cut into ¼-in. dice
2 cloves garlic, chopped
1 green pepper, cored, seeded, and cut into full-length strips
1 red pepper, cored, seeded, and cut into full-length strips
1 small hot fresh chile (optional)
2 ripe, fresh tomatoes
2 sprigs of marjoram, leaves only, chopped
2 sprigs parsley, leaves only, chopped
8 eggs, beaten
Salt & black pepper

You can either cut the tomato into bite-size chunks, skin and seeds included, or, if you prefer, peel the tomato and remove the seeds. The tomato juice will result in soupier eggs, but to my mind, they're light and tasty.

Gently heat the olive oil in a saucepan over low heat. Add the onions, garlic, peppers, and chile (if using), and cook until tender, about 15 to 20 minutes. Add the tomatoes and cook until heated through before gently mixing in the marjoram and parsley. Add the eggs, stirring gently, and cook until the eggs are mostly set but still creamy. Transfer to a platter, add a pinch of salt and pepper, and serve.

BLACK-EYED PEAS AND THYME

Black-eyed peas are eaten all over the world. I'm pleasantly surprised by their distinctive mineral notes and mild sweetness. We keep the dried peas on hand, although they're available frozen, canned, and, in some areas, fresh. They're less starchy and often faster to cook than many other dried legumes. This is a very simple recipe. I use quite a bit of thyme to give the peas more fragrance and flavor; plenty of soft-cooked celery serves to lighten the dish. Rosemary in place of the thyme also provides a nice combination. As part of this menu, because the frittata is rich and the asparagus are roasted with oil, the peas are not dressed with oil. They are, of course, delicious when served warm with a little butter or chilled with olive oil and lemon. **SERVES 6-8**

8 sprigs fresh thyme
2 cups dried black-eyed peas
1 large Spanish onion, cut into
½-in. dice
1 bay leaf
2 cups diced celery

1 tsp. crushed red pepper
(optional or serve on the side)
2 tbsp. olive oil or butter
(optional)
Salt & black pepper

Using your thumb and index finger, scrape as many thyme leaves as you easily can off the sprigs and set aside. Save the stems that still have leaves attached to cook with the peas or chop the tender tips of the thyme, stem and all, and set aside and use the stalk ends to cook with the peas. The tip of thyme stem is tender enough to eat whole.

Rinse the peas and discard any debris you might find. It's not necessary to soak them. Add the peas, onions, thyme stems, and bay leaf to a soup pot with 5 or 6 cups of water. Salt the water if desired. Bring to a boil and then reduce the heat to simmer for 25 to 30 minutes. Add the celery and crushed red pepper (if using). Continue cooking for 30 to 60 minutes, depending on the age of the peas. They're done when tender, so start tasting them at about 30 minutes. Drain as much of the liquid off as you like. Pull out the thyme stems and bay leaf. (I like the flavor of the pea broth so I save it as a vegetable stock. You can also serve the peas in a small bowl on the side with the broth.) The addition of a little olive oil or butter is nice to finish, but not necessary. Sprinkle with salt, fresh black pepper, and the tender thyme leaves, and serve the celery-dotted peas hot, at room temperature, or cold.

ROASTED ASPARAGUS

Roasted asparagus are tasty barely cooked, bright green and snappy, or browned and caramelized. I don't mind mixing various thicknesses, which, if you buy them in season at a farmers' market, is how they're often sold. I like the variety of textures that results from cooking varying sizes. I usually stick to buying asparagus in season when they're tastier and less expensive. **SERVES 6**

36 to 48 asparagus stalks, 6 to 8 per person, depending on the size

2 tbsp. vegetable oil
Sea salt
Lemon wedges (optional)

Preheat oven to 400 F. Snap off the tough end of the asparagus stalk. (Reserve for stock if you like. I'm not fond of asparagus in vegetable stock but other people like to use it, so try it once and see what you think.)

Brush the asparagus with the vegetable oil and sprinkle with sea salt.

Spread the asparagus out in a single layer on a baking sheet and roast for 3 to 4 minutes before rotating the pan and roasting for another 2 minutes.

Remove the asparagus when they're still bright and slightly brown at the tips, or let them roast for another 3 to 5 minutes if you like them well done. Remove from the oven and serve hot with the lemon wedges on the side, or cool and serve at room temperature.

Asparagus from our garden

HERB VINAIGRETTE

For information on greens and instructions on dressing a salad, see page 229. Makes 1 cup. **SERVES 4-6**

3 tbsp. roughly chopped fresh herbs, such as chervil, tarragon, dill, basil, parsley
2 tbsp. white wine vinegar
1 tsp. mayonnaise

1 small shallot, minced
Salt & black pepper
½ cup olive oil
3 tbsp. grape seed oil

Mix the herbs, vinegar, mayonnaise, shallot, salt, and pepper in a bowl with a whisk or in a food processor or a good blender until smooth. Slowly add the oils until emulsified. Thin with water if you like. Taste, and adjust the salt and pepper.

CHOCOLATE CHIP COOKIES

This is a good basic recipe with a nice balance between crisp and chewy. **MAKES 24 TO 30 COOKIES**

2½ cups all-purpose, unbleached flour
1¼ tsp. baking soda
Pinch salt
1 cup (2 sticks) unsalted, room-temperature butter

⅔ cup sugar
⅔ cup brown sugar
2 eggs
1½ tsp. vanilla
12 oz. semisweet chocolate chips

Preheat oven to 350 F. Line a baking sheet with parchment paper.

Mix the flour, baking soda, and salt in a bowl, and set aside.

Use a wooden spoon or the paddle attachment on a standing mixer to blend the butter and sugars until creamy and fluffy.

Add the eggs and incorporate thoroughly. Lower the paddle speed and add the flour mixture, little by little, until well mixed. Add the vanilla and then the chocolate chips. Chill the batter. Scoop into balls about 1½ inches in diameter and place on the baking sheet about 2½ inches apart. Bake until the cookies have spread and are golden across the top, about 18 to 22 minutes. They will be soft until they cool.

Add nuts if you like, or make the cookies any size. You can scoop the dough into balls with an ice cream scoop and freeze them on a baking sheet before bagging them once fully frozen to bake fresh, a few at a time.

Menu 14 with frittata made with greens and mozzarella, and more greens and asparagus served on the side

MENU 15

SPICY SPRING-VEGETABLE CURRY WITH BROWN CARDAMOM

To please a large crowd with some folks who eat meat and some who don't, we make vegetarian curry and separately braise meat with similar flavorings to serve on the side. This is a spicy recipe, both in terms of depth of flavor and heat. If you prefer a milder dish, cut back on the green chiles or serve them on the side. Chard is available in the spring and is a nice choice for the curry as the stems cut from the leaves and into pieces are like a second vegetable. Feel free to add other seasonal vegetables such as asparagus, peas, spring onions, fiddlehead ferns, spinach, kale, mustard greens, and, if you have time, artichokes. In late summer and fall, cauliflower is a nice addition to this curry. **SERVES 6-8**

1 cup dried chickpeas
Assorted aromatic vegetables to flavor the chickpeas, such as:
1 carrot
1 celery stalk
1 quartered onion
4 cloves garlic, peeled but not chopped
1 bay leaf
Salt & black pepper
¼ cup vegetable oil
3 Spanish onions, sliced
1 tsp. cumin seeds, toasted and ground
2 to 6 small dried red chiles, depending on your spice preference, toasted and ground (optional)
1 tbsp. turmeric
1 tbsp. peeled and minced fresh ginger
1 tbsp. minced garlic
¾ cup coarsely chopped cilantro
2 to 4 small green Indian chiles such as jalapeño, serrano, or habanero, depending on the heat you desire (optional)
6 brown cardamom pods
1 cup canned puréed tomatoes
2 tsp. brown mustard seeds
1½ cups chard stems, cut into ½-in.-long pieces
3 cups chard leaves, cut into 2-in. strips
3 cups freshly cooked basmati rice
¼ cup plain yogurt (I like whole-milk yogurt, especially Greek style)
1 lemon, cut into wedges (for garnish)

Place the chickpeas in a pot and cover with water. (Soaking the chickpeas will speed their cooking a bit, but is not necessary.) Add the aromatics (if using), bay leaf, salt, and pepper. Cook over medium heat until tender but not mushy, about 50 to 60 minutes. Drain chickpeas, discard aromatics and bay leaf, reserving the broth, and set aside.

In a saucepan, heat the oil and sauté the onions until soft but not brown. Add the cumin, dried chiles, turmeric, ginger, garlic, 6 tablespoons of the cilantro, and fresh, green chiles. (If you want the curry slightly milder, leave the green chiles whole so that you can remove them. Thinly slice them for a hotter curry.) Add the cardamom pods. Continue cooking, stirring frequently, until the is medium brown. Add the tomatoes and brown mustard seeds and cook until the flavors meld, a few minutes. Taste, and adjust the salt and pepper. The mixture at this point should be spicier than you want the curry to be in the end. Add the chard stems and simmer for a few minutes before adding the chard leaves. Add the chickpea stock or water to your desired consistency, and simmer for 6 to 8 minutes. It will be quite thick. Add more liquid as needed. Add the chickpeas and reduce the curry to the final preferred thickness.

Use a rice cooker to prepare basmati rice. I use a 1 to 1 ratio for basmati.

Just before serving, remove the pot from the heat and stir in the yogurt (the yogurt will break if it gets too hot). The more yogurt you add, the milder the curry will be, so taste and adjust. Add more salt if necessary.

Serve with freshly, cooked Basmati rice, the remaining chopped cilantro, lemon wedges, and extra sliced fresh chiles on the side.

NOTES AND VARIATIONS

I buy the best quality spices I can, often from Penzey's in Wisconsin, but also from our conventional grocery supplier. I frequently buy whole spices and we grind them in the kitchen as we use them. This is very much worth the effort for most seeds, pods, bark, etc. Sometimes we toast our spices first, although this step is not always necessary. Raw fennel seed is sweeter and tastes more Italian to me, while toasted fennel tastes more Indian, with a sharper, more acidic note.

BRAISED LAMB WITH RHUBARB SAUCE

Locally raised lamb is widely available in the Hudson Valley. Cuts such as shoulders and shanks braise well. A great vegetarian curry will please everyone, so serving lamb on the side for those who really enjoy it works nicely. This is a very adaptable recipe. And if you're interested in a lamb curry for everyone, simply brown the meat on the bone or cubed and cook it along with the chickpeas as in the Spicy Vegetable Curry (see page 83). Rhubarb has a fairly short growing season and the thin stalks from the local plants are tangy, crisp, and delicious. The season is so short, I don't mind eating rhubarb twice in one meal as it's presented here, with the lamb in the main dish, and in the shortcakes for dessert. If stone fruit are in season, use plums, peaches, or nectarines to make chutney. **SERVES 4-8**

Menu 15 with spring vegetable curry using fiddleheads, and rhubarb chutney

FOR THE BRAISED LAMB

2 lb. to 4 lb. lamb shoulder or shanks, cut into 2-in. boneless cubes, or left on the bone

Salt & black pepper

4 tbsp. vegetable or olive oil, divided

1 large Spanish onion, cut into ½-in. dice

1 carrot, peeled and cut into 1-in. pieces

2 qt. vegetable stock, water, or chicken stock

½ cup roughly chopped cilantro stems

2 limes or lemons, cut in quarters

6 garlic cloves, slightly crushed

4 dried or fresh red or green chiles

4 thyme sprigs

1-in. to 2-in. piece cinnamon stick

1-in. piece fresh ginger, peeled and sliced

1 bay leaf

Preheat oven to 350 F. Working with the lamb in pieces or whole, season the meat with salt and pepper. In a saucepan, and sear meat in 2 tablespoons of the oil until medium brown. (You may skip this messy step altogether and proceed with the raw meat. The results will be milder, sweeter, less "brown" tasting. You may also roast the meat in a 475 F oven for 5 minutes. You will get some color and pan juices but not as much as if you sear the meat in a pan, turning it as it cooks.)

Pour off the excess fat from the saucepan and toss in the onions and carrots, cooking over medium heat until just browned, about 6 to 8 minutes.

Transfer the lamb, carrots, and onions to a deep, ovenproof baking dish or Dutch oven. Add a little water to the pan you seared the meat in to release the brown bits stuck to the bottom and add to the baking dish along with the vegetable stock, cilantro, citrus, garlic, chiles, thyme, cinnamon, ginger, and bay leaf. If you're using cubes of meat, they may be fully submerged. If you're working with meat on the bone, it may be only partially submerged. Either is fine.

Place meat and vegetables in the oven and roast until completely tender. Cubed meat will cook in 45 minutes or so; large pieces of meat on the bone will need to be turned and basted and may take up to 2 hours to become tender. I like to stop cooking lamb before it falls off the bone. Less tender equals more flavorful meat.

Remove the meat and skim the fat from the broth. (At this point, take the meat off the bone, if you haven't already.) Remove bay leaf and citrus. Reduce the broth, taste and adjust the salt and pepper, and add it to the meat. Serve the meat beside the curry for people to add as they wish.

RHUBARB SAUCE

This simple, chutney-like sauce is a refreshing accompaniment to meat. **SERVES 4-8**

1 tsp. vegetable oil
2 tbsp. minced shallot
(substitute red onion)
8 rhubarb stalks, sliced into 1-in.
pieces
1 sprig thyme

1 bay leaf
2 tbsp. cider vinegar
2 tbsp. raw sugar or maple syrup
4 whole cloves
Salt & black pepper

Heat the oil in a saucepan over medium heat and sauté the shallot for 2 to 3 minutes. Add the rhubarb and herbs, and toss to coat with the oil. Cook until just slightly softened, 2 to 3 minutes. Remove the bay leaf and spoon the rhubarb pieces into a bowl; you will be left with rhubarb juice in the pan. Add the vinegar, sugar, and cloves to the juice and cook until the mixture is syrupy, 2 to 3 minutes. Remove the cloves and add the liquid to the rhubarb. Taste, and adjust salt and pepper. I like to chill this sauce for about 30 minutes before serving.

SWEET INDIAN CURRY
WITH CHICKEN AND PEAS

This is my take on a mild and rich Indian dish that has long been a favorite of Indian restaurants in the U.K. and the U.S. Frequently, I cook with whole chickens, but in this recipe I use boneless thighs or breasts, which makes it accessible and easy for crowds. You can create a vegetarian version by substituting assorted vegetables such as green beans and mushrooms for the chicken. **SERVES 6-8**

FOR THE CHICKEN MARINADE

2 lb. boneless chicken thighs
(breasts are fine, if you prefer
them)
¼ cup plain yogurt
2 tsp. sweet paprika

2 tsp. sweet curry powder
1 tsp. cumin seeds, toasted and
ground
2 garlic cloves, minced
Juice of 1 lemon

Cut the chicken into bite-size pieces and toss in a bowl with the yogurt, paprika, curry powder, cumin, garlic, and lemon juice. Set aside for at least an hour or cover and refrigerate overnight.

FOR THE CURRY

2 tbsp. vegetable oil
2 Spanish onions, cut into ½-in. dice
Salt & black pepper
6 tbsp. chopped cilantro, plus ½
cup coarsely chopped cilantro
(for garnish)
1 tbsp. minced garlic
1 green chile, jalapeño, serrano,
or habanero, depending on the
heat you desire (optional)
1 tsp. peeled and minced
fresh ginger

2 cups puréed tomatoes, fresh
or canned
2 tbsp. sweet curry powder (see
Notes and Variations below)
3 brown cardamom pods
1 cup heavy cream
1 cup fresh or frozen peas
¼ cup plain yogurt (I like
whole-milk yogurt, especially
Greek style)

In a soup pot, heat the oil and sauté the onions over medium heat until soft, about 5 to 7 minutes. Add salt and pepper. Add the cilantro, garlic, green chile (if using), and ginger, and sauté until the onions are brown, 4 to 5 minutes more. Add the tomatoes, curry powder, and cardamom pods. Cook over medium heat, stirring frequently, for 8 to 10 minutes. The mixture will be thick and dense.

Add the chicken and cook for another 5 to 7 minutes. Add the cream and cook until the chicken is done. Breast meat will take 5 to 7 minutes more, dark meat 8 to 10 minutes more. Add the peas and cook for 1 to 2 minutes more. Turn off the heat, taste to adjust the salt and pepper, and stir in the yogurt. Garnish with the fresh cilantro and serve.

NOTES AND VARIATIONS

I list store-bought curry powder in this recipe as it is meant to be relatively quick and easy, so but you may replace the store-bought curry powder blend with a freshly toasted ground mixture of spices for a more powerful flavor. For a mild curry such as this, a good spice combination might include: cumin, turmeric, coriander seed, cinnamon, fennel seed, and clove. For a deeper blend, cut back on the cinnamon and clove, add extra cumin, fenugreek, cardamom, dried red chiles, and black pepper.

RICE WITH SORREL, GARLIC CHIVES, AND MUSTARD GREENS

We often serve big bowls of plain rice at the Institute, just as I do at home. Plain rice makes a perfect bed for curry or beans, among other things. Depending on what I'm cooking, I also like to toss rice with small quantities of flavorful ingredients. As the rice comes to room temperature the seasoning helps to keep it from clumping and the herbs, vegetables, nuts, or spices add brightness and texture. The ingredients I most often add are: cucumber, hijiki, toasted sesame seeds, mustard seeds, citrus zest, and in this case, a combination of three powerful greens that fall somewhere between herbs and vegetables. While any of them would be good, together they form a bold, spring-green flavor. Sorrel melts into very little the minute it's warmed, but it packs a pleasant sour punch. Garlic chives, also known as Chinese chives or Chinese leeks, are delicious whether you're using the flat, broad leaves or the flowering stalks. Mustard greens are peppery and bright, cooked or added raw. **SERVES 6-8**

1 large bunch Chinese chives, cut into 1-in. pieces (substitute leeks, scallions, or ramp leaves rather than regular fine chives in this case)
2 tsp. vegetable oil
1 bunch mustard greens, cut into 1-in. pieces (substitute dandelion greens or arugula)

1 cup fresh sorrel leaves, cut into ½-in. pieces
3 cups jasmine rice (any variety will work)
Salt & black pepper
2 tsp. coconut oil, grape seed oil, or olive oil (optional)

Sauté the chives in a saucepan with the oil over medium-high heat for 1 minute. Transfer to a mixing bowl. The mustard greens are good raw or cooked. Sauté the same way if you want a softer texture. (Quickly sauté the dandelion greens; if you're substituting arugula, leave it raw.) Add the sorrel to the mustard greens and combine both with the chives and set aside.

When the rice is cooked (see Notes and Variations below for instructions), toss it gently into the bowl of greens. Add the optional fat for a richer feel, taste and add salt and pepper, and serve.

NOTES AND VARIATIONS

I use a rice cooker for rice. With a rice cooker I am able to achieve the slightly sticky, chewy texture I like. And I can pay less attention. Generally, for white rice I follow a 1 cup rice to 1 cup water ratio, plus about 2 tablespoons of water with rice I rinse, such as haiga, and plus ¼ cup for rice I don't rinse, such as jasmine. When I use basmati I use a 1 to 1 ratio. I don't add salt or fat to the rice cooker, but it's fine if you prefer it that way. If you don't have a rice cooker, there are many ways to master cooking rice. I start my rice in cold water. I use 1 cup rice to 2 cups water ratio. I turn the heat to medium high and when the water boils, I reduce the heat to the lowest possible setting, cover the pot, and let the rice simmer for about 15 minutes. I don't add salt or fat. My mother used to boil rice like pasta, in salted water, testing along the way and draining it in a colander when it was the way she liked it. Rice takes practice, and each variety cooks a little differently. In general, white rice takes 18 to 20 minutes; brown rice, 30 to 35 minutes. Some folks like fluffy rice, others like slightly sticky. A cheap rice cooker does a great job if you don't yet have the knack.

LEMON AND OLIVE OIL DRESSING

For information on greens and instructions on dressing a salad, see page 229. Makes about 1 cup. **SERVES 4 TO 6**

Juice of 3 lemons   Salt & black pepper
½ cup olive oil

Squeeze the lemon juice right on your greens in a big mixing bowl. Drizzle with the olive oil, add a pinch of salt and some pepper, toss and serve. Alternatively, shake the lemon juice and olive oil together in a bottle with a tight lid and add the salt and black pepper directly to the greens.

RHUBARB SHORTCAKES

I especially like rhubarb when it's very lightly cooked and not very sweet, even for desserts. Barbara Kafka, the cookbook author and great cook, came to our kitchen once to cook with us, and we made rhubarb shortcakes with fresh cheese in the biscuits in place of whipped cream. She showed us a technique for cooking the rhubarb super fast with nothing but a little sugar. These shortcakes are made with part almond flour and served with whipped cream. Try this dessert with strawberries along with or instead of rhubarb. **SERVES 8-10**

FOR THE RHUBARB

3 cups rhubarb, cut into ½ -in. pieces	3 tbsp. sugar

Spread the sugar in a saucepan. Sprinkle the rhubarb on top.

Turn the heat to medium and cook, shaking the pan frequently, for 6 to 8 minutes. Avoid stirring or use a rubber spatula sparingly. The rhubarb remains whole in the pan but gets soft quickly. As the sugar melts and blends with the juice released from the rhubarb, the pieces wilt. When they looked relaxed in the pan, remove from the heat and pour the mixture into a shallow bowl. Place in the refrigerator right away to stop the cooking and to chill. You can make the rhubarb a day or two in advance, if necessary.

FOR THE SHORTCAKES

2¼ cups all-purpose, unbleached flour	Pinch salt
⅔ cup almond flour	6 tbsp. cold butter, cut into ½-in. pieces
1 cup sliced almonds, lightly toasted	1 cup heavy cream
1½ tbsp. sugar	1 egg, beaten
1 tbsp. baking powder	⅛ cup raw sugar (optional)

Preheat the oven to 350 F. Mix the flour, almond flour, almonds, sugar, baking powder, and salt, with a paddle attachment of a standing mixer on low speed.

Add the butter and mix until the mixture is crumbly.

Add the heavy cream and mix until the dough just begins to come together. Remove the dough, form a ball, then flatten.

Roll out the dough onto a lightly floured surface to 1¼ inches thick. Use a round cookie cutter to cut biscuits, getting as many as you can the first time. (The second roll doesn't come out baked as light and flaky as the first.)

Glaze the top with beaten egg (or use heavy cream for a lighter shine) and sprinkle with raw sugar (if using).

Bake until just barely golden, 15 to 25 minutes.

TO ASSEMBLE SHORTCAKES

1 cup heavy cream
1 to 3 tsp. granulated or confectioner's sugar (optional) (I like unsweetened whipped cream, but many folks prefer a little sugar)

1 tsp. vanilla extract (optional)

Chill a metal mixing bowl or the bowl of a standing mixer. Add the heavy cream and optional sugar and vanilla and whip by hand for about 3 minutes or in the machine with the whisk attachment for about 1 minute until it forms soft peaks.

Slice the shortcakes in half and place the bottom halves on individual plates or a platter. Divide the fruit evenly and place it on the cut biscuit. Pour the resulting fruit juice over the fruit so that the biscuit soaks up the liquid. Top with a spoonful or two of whipped cream and cover with the biscuit top and serve.

Rhubarb shortcake from Menu 15 with rhubarb from our garden

Menu 16, fusilli with peas, squash blossoms, cheese, and bronze fennel

JUNE MENUS

16

FUSILLI WITH PEAS, SQUASH BLOSSOMS, FRESH CHEESE,
AND BRONZE FENNEL 96
CARROT SLAW WITH DILL 98
DANDELION, BABY LEEKS, AND WHITE BEANS 98
OREGANO VINAIGRETTE 99
STRAWBERRIES 100

17

BAKED LENTIL SOUP WITH GARLIC SCAPES AND
(OPTIONAL) GARLIC SAUSAGE 100
CAULIFLOWER AND CARDOONS WITH SAFFRON, ONIONS, CURRANTS,
PINE NUTS, AND PARSLEY 102
SLICED SUMMER SQUASH WITH LEMON AND OLIVE OIL 103
ARUGULA SALAD WITH SHREDDED CHEESE 104
SWEET FOCACCIA WITH CHERRIES 104

18

SPAGHETTI WITH SPINACH, PINE NUTS, GARLIC, BROTH,
AND OLIVE OIL 105
GLAZED CARROTS 107
NAPA AND ENDIVE SALAD 107
GARDEN-PEA VINAIGRETTE 108
HONEY-COCOA CAKE 108

FUSILLI WITH PEAS, SQUASH BLOSSOMS, FRESH CHEESE, AND BRONZE FENNEL

I think of June as the height of spring, but really it is the beginning of summer. Squash blossoms are available as are a wider selection of herbs in our own garden. Because the early shoots are so flavorful, smaller quantities of early summer ingredients add a potent flavor, and an otherwise small garden can make a real difference in the kitchen, as it does at the Institute. Fresh cheese in this pasta dish combines and disperses the sweet, fragrant bronze fennel, one of our "big" crops. Sweet garden peas are often still around in June, but the job of shelling fresh peas is generally too labor intensive for the Institute kitchen. We buy fresh peas and fresh fava beans about once a year, because at the Institute, it's an all-day, one-person job to prepare enough for a single dish to feed a large group. At home it is worth it. The same is true if you see fresh fava beans in their pods at the market. Buy them at least once; they're delicious, raw or cooked, as an alternative to the peas in this recipe. SERVES 4-6

12 squash blossoms
1 lb. imported fusilli pasta, cooked according to the instructions on the package and drained (any shape will do)
2 cups fresh cheese, ricotta type, left out to reach room temperature (see Notes and Variations, page 97)
2 cups raw fresh garden peas (substitute defrosted frozen peas or raw sugar snap peas cut into ½-in. pieces, see Notes and Variations, page 97)

1 tablespoon chopped garlic
¼ cup chopped bronze fennel (substitute 1 teaspoon of freshly ground untoasted fennel seeds)
½ cup fruity olive oil
Salt & black pepper
½ cup grated Parmesan (optional)
2 tablespoons unsalted butter (optional)

Remove the stamen of the male blossoms by cutting off ⅛ inch of the flower from the stem end of the blossom. The stamen will easily slip out (to me, it's bitter). Cut the blossoms into 1-inch pieces.

If I have time, I whip fresh ricotta in a food processor to make it creamy and smooth, but it is not a necessary step. Experiment and see which texture you prefer.

Ingredients for Menu 16

In a bowl big enough to hold all the ingredients with room to stir, add blossoms and cheese, the peas, olive oil, Parmesan (if using), fennel, garlic, salt, and pepper.

My family loves butter on pasta; if you like butter, add it to the cooked pasta. Using a rubber spatula, toss the pasta gently but thoroughly with the fresh cheese mixture. Taste and adjust the salt, and add a good quantity of cracked black pepper. The squash blossoms should be soft and wilted.

NOTES AND VARIATIONS

We get a fresh cheese from a local dairy (Sprout Creek Farm) that is similar to ricotta. Whole milk ricotta, the fresher the better, is perfect.

When buying squash blossoms you may find female blossoms, attached to small squash, or male blossoms, attached to a stem. Both taste the same. If you are harvesting from your own garden, choose male blossoms. Only a few are needed to pollinate the plants so that they will bear squash. If you choose a female blossom you will miss out on that squash.

If you can't find fresh peas in the pod but can find tender raw pea greens, they make a good substitute. Chop a cup or two raw and add them to the cheese when you add the fennel. They will wilt when you add the hot pasta.

CARROT SLAW WITH DILL

Most any vegetable that's firm and tasty raw will serve as a slaw. I love a crunchy tangy side dish with almost every meal. Carrots are part of a big family of vegetables, many of which are used as herbs and their seeds as spices, including anise, caraway, celery seed, chervil, coriander, cumin, fennel, parsley, and in this case, dill. **SERVES 6-8**

6 large carrots, peeled and grated
3 tbsp. rice vinegar
2 tbsp. minced, fresh dill

1 tbsp. grape seed or olive oil (optional)
Salt & black pepper

In a large bowl, combine the carrots, vinegar, dill, oil (if using), and a pinch of salt and pepper. Mix and serve.

DANDELION, BABY LEEKS, AND WHITE BEANS

I see commercially grown dandelion leaves all the time in the supermarket. I love these greens when they're truly bitter, and I fear the commercial variety will get milder and tamer to suit the taste of most people. I used to blanch my dandelion leaves before sautéing to sweeten them a bit, but the new cultivated varieties are fine sautéed raw. In spring you can, of course, just go outside and dig. **SERVES 4-6**

FOR THE BEANS

1 cup dried white beans (substitute any dried bean you like or canned white beans, cannellini, giant white, or navy beans)

Assorted aromatic vegetables to flavor the beans, such as:
1 carrot
1 celery stalk
1 quartered onion
4 cloves garlic
1 bay leaf

I find dried beans benefit from an overnight soak. The next day, cook the beans in a pot with plenty of water over low heat for 1 to 2 hours. Add the aromatics you have on hand. Salt and a bay leaf are fine if that's all you have. Carrot, celery, onions, and garlic make a sweeter broth. The beans are done when they're fully tender. The amount of time beans take to cook varies a lot depending on their age, so check after 40 minutes. I like beans to be fully tender. Drain the beans, reserving the broth. Only a few tablespoons of broth are called for this dish, but save some for other soups or stews.

FOR THE GREENS

2 tbsp. vegetable oil
3 to 6 small young leeks, cleaned (see page 66) and cut into 1-in. pieces (see Notes and Variations below)
6 cloves garlic, sliced

3 dried red chiles (optional)
2 large bunches of dandelion greens, cut into 2-in. pieces
2 tbsp. olive oil (optional)
Salt & black pepper
Lemon wedges (optional)

In a saucepan, sauté the leeks, garlic, and red chiles (if using) in the oil over medium-high heat until lightly brown, about 3 to 5 minutes. Add the dandelion greens and sauté until wilted, about 2 to 5 minutes depending on the size and age of the greens. Turn off the heat, add the beans, a few tablespoons of the bean liquid and olive oil (if using). Taste and add salt and pepper, and serve with lemon wedges (if using) on the side.

NOTES AND VARIATIONS

Young leeks are often available at farmers' markets in June, but you can substitute two regular leeks, ramps, spring onions, or scallions.

OREGANO VINAIGRETTE

For information on greens and instructions on dressing a salad, see page 229. Makes a scant cup. SERVES 4–6

¼ cup red wine vinegar
2 tbsp. Dijon mustard
¼ teaspoon dry oregano

Salt & black pepper
½ cup olive oil

Whisk together the vinegar, mustard, oregano, salt, and pepper in a large bowl. Slowly whisk in oil until emulsified.

STRAWBERRIES

Really good strawberries are hard to come by. If it rains too much the berries are watery and flavorless, and the birds and bugs love them. Strawberries also spoil quickly. If you see small, local strawberries, buy them. If they're very pricey, instead of following this menu with other somewhat expensive items like squash blossoms, maybe you can have bean soup for dinner and strawberries for dessert. I love strawberries plain, and my boys like to dip them in sugar. I must admit the gritty sweet sugar is quite good on the juicy, tangy-sweet berries.

In-season local strawberries

MENU 17

BAKED LENTIL SOUP WITH GARLIC SCAPES AND (OPTIONAL) GARLIC SAUSAGE

The idea of baking soup came to me when we ran out of stove-top space on a particularly busy day in the kitchen; it was a happy accident. When soup is baked in the oven with olive oil poured on top, a tasty, thin brown crust forms on top that adds extra flavor. Garlic scapes are the flowering stem of the garlic, and they have a mild garlic flavor. Break off the woody end as you would with asparagus and eat as a vegetable. The touch of spring in the garlic scapes brings the lentils out of winter. This recipe calls for sliced sausage served on the side of the lentils, or see Notes and Variations below for poaching the meat along with the beans. **SERVES 6–8**

3 cups dried lentils (I like French green lentils a lot, but any variety is fine. The texture will vary depending on what you use)

2 qt. water, vegetable or chicken stock

1 cup coarsely chopped flat-leaf parsley

1 cup celery or fennel, cut into ½-in. pieces

½ cup olive oil

8 garlic scapes, cut into 1-in. pieces, substitute scallions, leeks, or Chinese chives

4 carrots, peeled and cut into ½-in. disks

4 sprigs thyme

1 bay leaf

Salt & black pepper

1 lb. saucisson (garlic sausage, optional), poached and sliced (see Notes and Variations below)

Preheat oven to 400 F. Place all ingredients except the sausage in an ovenproof 6- to 8-quart pot or casserole dish. Bake for 15 minutes, stir, and continue baking. Repeat this process, checking and stirring every 15 minutes, until the lentils are completely tender, about 50 to 60 minutes. Add water as needed, depending on the consistency you like. Remove the thyme branches and bay leaf from the lentils before serving.

While the lentils are cooking, poach the saucisson on top of the stove over a medium heat. Pierce the skin a few places and submerge in water and simmer until 160 F, about 30 to 35 minutes. Set aside to cool slightly, slice, cover to keep warm.

Serve with the poached sausage on the side for folks to put on top of lentils.

NOTES AND VARIATIONS

Saucisson is semi-cured garlicky pork sausage that is fatter in diameter than a typical sausage and can be found at specialty food stores. (Read label or ask at the shop as some saucisson are fully cooked and just need heating.) Any mild garlic or sweet Italian sausage will substitute, as would spicier sausages such as merguez, semi-cured chorizo, or spicy Italian sausage. Other good meat variations include poached pork, lamb shoulder, or duck legs.

If you want to poach sausages right in the lentils for added meat flavor, add saucisson after about 15 minutes; 30 minutes for thinner sausage. The sausages cook fairly quickly and become bland if you cook them too long, all the flavor goes into the broth. I don't mind the tender long-cooked sausage in leftovers but on the first night it is good to cook the sausage until just 160 F, which takes about 18 to 20 minutes tops.

If you bake the lentils until most of the water evaporates the results are a thicker lentil casserole that you can serve over rice or polenta or with toppings such as chopped parsley, olive oil, or toasted walnut oil. Lemon wedges on the side are good with lentils as is fresh cheese on top.

CAULIFLOWER AND CARDOONS WITH SAFFRON, ONIONS, CURRANTS, PINE NUTS, AND PARSLEY

Cardoons are in the artichoke family, and they taste and look like a cross between an artichoke heart and a celery stalk. Growing up, I never saw a raw cardoon, but an Italian family friend made cardoon fritters with breadcrumbs, egg, cheese, parsley, and garlic and fried the patties in olive oil. They were delicious—like vegetable meatballs. This recipe, which combines cauliflower and cardoons, uses a Sicilian-inspired ingredient combination. It's good as a side dish or over pasta. Try it with fregola, a Sardinian-style couscous, or grain of your choice. **SERVES 6-8**

½ cup water
¼ cup currants
Pinch saffron
1 head cardoon
1 head cauliflower, trimmed and cut into florets
¼ cup olive oil, divided (grape seed is a good substitute)
Salt & black pepper
1 Spanish onion, cut into ½-in. dice
3 cloves garlic, minced

½ cup pine nuts, lightly toasted
1 tbsp. to 2 tbsp. red wine vinegar (any vinegar or citrus juice would be good)
2 tbsp. chopped parsley (substitute bronze fennel)
½ tsp. freshly ground fennel seed (optional)
½ tsp. crushed red pepper (optional)
2 to 4 sardine fillets, fresh and cooked or canned (optional)

Preheat oven to 400 F. In a small saucepan combine the water, currants, and saffron. Heat until just boiling, and simmer over low heat until most of the water has evaporated, about 3 minutes. Remove from heat and set aside.

Peel the stalks of cardoon to remove the strings and any prickly outside skin. You might have to cut here and there to remove brown spots. Cut into in ¼-in. slices and boil in lightly salted water until tender, about 12 to 15 minutes. Drain and set aside.

Toss the cauliflower in a bowl with 2 tablespoons of the oil and a pinch of salt and pepper. Roast until golden brown and tender, 15 to 20 minutes. Set aside.

Heat the remaining 2 tablespoons oil in a saucepan over medium heat. Sauté the onions and garlic until soft and golden, about 3 minutes. In a large mixing bowl, toss the onions, garlic, cauliflower, cardoon, currants, and pine nuts. Season with olive oil, vinegar, parsley, and a pinch of salt and pepper. Add any optional ingredients, including fennel seed, crushed red pepper, and sardines. Serve warm or at room temperature.

SLICED SUMMER SQUASH WITH LEMON AND OLIVE OIL

The flavor of fresh summer squash, by which I mean all summer squash, including zucchini, for example, is so good yet so ephemeral. I tend to cook fresh squash hot and fast so that it still has a bite—the way I also like asparagus—keeping the sweet flavor intact. If the summer squash is out of season I cook it longer, looking for more caramel color to add sweetness to a vegetable that doesn't store or travel too well. **SERVES 4-6**

4 to 6 assorted summer squash, such as zucchini, ronde de Nice, golden zucchini, or patty pan, thinly sliced (use a mandoline if you have one)

1 tbsp. olive oil, grape seed oil, or clarified butter
Salt & black pepper
1 lemon, cut into wedges

Preheat oven to 450 F. Place the squash slices on a baking sheet and brush very lightly with oil (or clarified butter). Turn the slices over and brush the other side, and sprinkle with salt and pepper. Roast until the squash begins to sweat, 2 to 3 minutes. Transfer to a bowl and serve with lemon wedges on the side.

ARUGULA SALAD WITH SHREDDED CHEESE

For additional information on greens and instructions on dressing a salad, see page 229. **SERVES 4-6**

2 bunches arugula, rinsed and dried
½ cup shredded or shaved firm, sharp cheese, Gruyère or aged-Gouda style

2 tbsp. fruity olive oil
1 tbsp. sherry vinegar
Salt & black pepper

SWEET FOCACCIA WITH CHERRIES

This is a sweet pizza that's good for dessert, breakfast, or with butter melted on top. **SERVES 6-8**

1 cup dried or fresh pitted cherries
1 cup hot water
¼ cup red wine
2 tbsp. orange flower water
2 tsp. vanilla
1 cup almonds

⅓ cup pine nuts
3 tbsp. raw sugar
3 tbsp. fennel seeds
2 tbsp. orange zest
1 recipe pizza dough (see page 180) made with ¼ cup olive oil plus extra for brushing the pan

Soak the dried or fresh pitted cherries in the hot water, wine, orange flower water, and vanilla for about two hours or overnight in the refrigerator.

In the bowl of a food processor very briefly pulse and grind the almonds, pine nuts, sugar, fennel seeds, and zest so that the mixture is still coarse. It's fine if it's uneven in texture. Set aside.

Follow the recipe for pizza dough on page 180, but double the olive oil quantity. After the first rise, lay the stretched dough onto a baking sheet brushed with olive oil.

Preheat oven to 425 F. Cover the dough on the sheet with plastic wrap and allow it to rise again until puffy and nearly double in size, roughly 1 hour. Remove plastic wrap and bake for 12 to 18 minutes until the focaccia has risen and looks set and light golden. Remove the focaccia and top evenly with the cherries and some of the juice that clings to them along with the nut mixture. Bake until golden brown, an additional 10 to 12 minutes. If the nuts or cherries start to get too dark, lower the oven temperature to 350 F.

Bake until the bread is very springy when you press on it. (For an unnecessary but tasty treat, brush the hot bread with melted butter before serving.)

MENU 18

SPAGHETTI WITH SPINACH, PINE NUTS, GARLIC, BROTH, AND OLIVE OIL

Years ago I ate at a small restaurant in the Berkshires and was surprised by this subtle pasta dish. I am not sure how far I have veered from the original I tasted that day, and I'll never know because I can't even remember the name of the restaurant. What I remember was perfectly cooked spaghetti with a little broth at the bottom of the bowl and barely cooked spinach. It was so good I drank every bit of the liquid. Because it cooks down to nothing, spinach is hard to prepare for large groups at the Institute, except when served raw in a salad. In this dish we add hot pasta to raw spinach so that it doesn't completely wilt. **SERVES 4**

6 cloves garlic, sliced
¼ cup cold water
2 tbsp. olive oil, divided
1 lb. to 2 lb. raw spinach, thoroughly cleaned (I like a lot of spinach)
Salt & black pepper
1 lb. good-quality spaghetti (see Notes and Variations below)
3 tbsp. pine nuts, lightly toasted (toasted chopped walnuts are a good substitute)
1 cup grated Parmesan, or another firm grated cheese of your choice
1 tsp. crushed red pepper (optional)

Menu 18, spaghetti with spinach and pine nuts

Combine the garlic in a saucepan with water and 1 tablespoon of the olive oil. Simmer over low heat until the garlic is soft but not brown. Add a little extra water as needed so that it doesn't completely evaporate. There should be a few tablespoons of water left in the pan.

Add the garlic, oil, and water to a shallow serving bowl with the raw spinach, the remaining olive oil, and a pinch of salt and pepper.

Cook the spaghetti in salted boiling water until it reaches desired doneness. I like it quite firm. Drain lightly, leaving some water with the pasta, and add to the serving bowl with the spinach. Toss well with tongs. The spinach will release a little more water and begin to wilt. There should be a little broth at the bottom of the bowl. Toss the pine nuts on top and serve the cheese and red pepper (if using) on the side.

Pea vinaigrette from Menu 18

NOTES AND VARIATIONS

I vacillate regarding my interest in and taste for whole wheat pasta. It's grainy and coarse and not really pasta to me and yet I like the idea of whole grains. To really enjoy it, I make sure it isn't overcooked and embrace the graininess rather than fighting it. For the Institute I buy classic, unbleached durum wheat pasta from Italy, usually De Cecco or Delverde. If you're flush, try one of the more expensive, traditionally made, pasta varieties, which are thicker with a rough-surface as the pasta is extruded through bronze rather than Tephlon. Brands such as Martelli or Latini are good examples, and De Cecco now has a higher-end pasta available in higher-end food stores as well.

GLAZED CARROTS

It's rare that I sweeten vegetables, but we serve glazed carrots on occasion. We often use raw sugar, but honey and maple syrup are good substitutes. **SERVES 6-8**

1 tbsp. to 2 tbsp. butter
(substitute vegetable oil,
including coconut oil, which
would work well here)

2 tbsp. raw sugar
1 tsp. lemon juice
Salt & black pepper

Bring a pot of water to boil over high heat. Add the carrots and a pinch of salt, and cook until the carrots are tender, 3 to 5 minutes. Drain the carrots and put them back into the pot. Add butter and sugar. Turn heat to low and cook until the butter is melted and the sugar coats the carrots. Turn off heat and add a bit of lemon juice to balance the sweetness. Taste and adjust the salt, and add some black pepper.

NOTES AND VARIATIONS

This glaze will be sweet and delicate. If you prefer more caramel flavor, turn the heat back up to brown the carrots. This will happen in 1 to 2 minutes. Watch the pan carefully. From the higher heat, some butter may separate out, so scoop out the carrots with a slotted spoon, transfer to a platter, and leave the excess fat in the pan.

NAPA AND ENDIVE SALAD

Napa cabbage is light, refreshing, and delicate, but is often overlooked in non-Asian recipes. In a salad it resembles endive and is much less expensive. Combined, their subtly different textures are clearly noticeable. Although both have a great crunch factor, this is a slaw that can't be left to sit too long before serving as the cabbage starts to wilt and releases water. **SERVES 6-8**

½ head Napa cabbage, cut into
¼-in. slices
Juice of 1 lemon
3 heads Belgian endive, cut into
¼ -in. slices, tossed with lemon
juice to prevent discoloring (and
for flavor)

3 tbsp. olive oil
3 tbsp. roughly chopped parsley
2 tbsp. white wine vinegar
Salt & black pepper

Toss the cabbage, endive, olive oil, parsley, vinegar, salt, and pepper together in a large bowl and serve.

GARDEN-PEA VINAIGRETTE

For information on greens and instructions on dressing a salad, see page 229. Makes 1¼ cups. **SERVES 6–8**

½ cup raw peas
½ cup olive oil
¼ cup white wine vinegar

2 tbsp. Dijon mustard
Salt & black pepper

Combine all the ingredients together in a blender and mix at high speed. Add 1 teaspoon water or a bit more as needed to achieve a creamy consistency.

HONEY-COCOA CAKE

The classic Jewish honey loaf cake is the inspiration for this recipe. Coffee is a traditional ingredient as is the cinnamon, but in place of other spices I've added lots of cocoa. I've also used butter in place of oil for richer flavor. **SERVES 8–10**

2¾ cups all-purpose, unbleached flour
1¼ cups cocoa, we use a quality brand like Valrhona
1 tbsp. baking powder
1 tsp. cinnamon
Pinch of salt
1 cup (2 sticks) unsalted, room-

temperature butter, plus more for the pan
½ cup granulated sugar
½ cup brown sugar
3 eggs
1 cup honey
1¼ tsp. vanilla
1 cup plus 2 tbsp. strong coffee

Preheat oven to 350 F. Butter a 9-inch-round cake pan.

In a bowl, mix the flour, cocoa, baking powder, cinnamon, and salt.

In the bowl of a stand mixer, beat the butter and sugars with the paddle attachment until the mixture is fluffy. Add the eggs one at a time, then the honey and vanilla. Gently mix in the flour mixture and then the coffee. Pour the batter into the greased pan and bake until the center of the cake bounces back when you press it or until a knife inserted in the center comes out clean, 17 to 18 minutes. Cool slightly before turning out onto a cooling rack. Cool completely before cutting; it's a fragile cake.

JULY MENUS

19

PASTA WITH BROWN CHERRY TOMATOES, EGGPLANT, SALT-CURED
CAPERS, MOZZARELLA, MINT, BASIL, AND GARLIC 110
RED BEAN AND GREEN PEPPER SALAD 111
RADICCHIO AND BLUEBERRIES WITH SHERRY VINEGAR AND WALNUT OIL 112
LEMON-PARSLEY VINAIGRETTE 113
BOWL OF PEACHES 114

20

HAIGA RICE, SESAME SEEDS, GREEN SHISO, AND CUCUMBER
WITH MACKEREL 114
GREEN BEANS 116
KALE WITH JAPANESE PEANUT SAUCE 116
BRONZE FENNEL VINAIGRETTE 118
CHOCOLATE BREAD PUDDING 118

21

ASIAN BEEF AND SHIITAKE SANDWICH 119
SHREDDED ZUCCHINI WITH SPEARMINT 121
CORN ON THE COB 122
PURPLE BASIL VINAIGRETTE 122
PLUMS 122

PASTA WITH BROWN CHERRY TOMATOES, EGGPLANT, SALT-CURED CAPERS, MOZZARELLA, MINT, BASIL, AND GARLIC

This recipe showcases the taste of late July when big tomatoes aren't yet ripe, but cherry tomatoes are. The varieties of cherry tomatoes just keep getting better. First we had Sweet 100s, then Sungolds. My latest favorites are the small brown heirloom varieties I find at the farmers' market and that we grow in the Institute garden. Some are more purple in color than brown, but they are all delicious, rich, and closer in taste to a full-size tomato. This recipe is already quite simple, but even if you don't have some of the ingredients it will be tasty. The combination of the capers and mint is particularly seductive. It also makes a great pizza topping. **SERVES 4–6**

1 lb. high-quality penne pasta, cooked according to package directions and drained (any shape will do)
2 cups cherry tomatoes
1 lb. fresh mozzarella, cut into 1-in. cubes (see Notes and Variations, page 111)
1 cup olive oil, divided
½ cup coarsely chopped mint

½ cup coarsely chopped basil
1 tbsp. chopped garlic (in season, the freshest garlic around is perfect)
1 tbsp. salt-cured capers, soaked for a few minutes in water
Salt & black pepper
3 cups eggplant, about one large eggplant, cut into 1-in. cubes, skin on or off

Preheat oven to 400 F. Cut the cherry tomatoes in half, or quarter them, depending on the size, and place in a serving bowl.

Add the fresh mozzarella to the tomatoes in the bowl along with ½ cup olive oil, mint, basil, garlic, drained capers, and a pinch of salt and pepper. Let the mixture stand to allow the flavors to blend while roasting the eggplant.

In another mixing bowl, toss the eggplant with the remaining ½ cup olive oil and a pinch of salt. Roast on a baking sheet until golden brown and completely tender, about 10 to 12 minutes. (Underdone eggplant is spongy and bland, yet bitter, while well-cooked eggplant is silky in texture with a more developed, sweeter taste.) Keep in a warm spot on the stovetop.

Add the just-cooked, al dente pasta and hot eggplant to the bowl with the tomato mixture. Toss together. Taste and adjust the salt and pepper. Serve warm.

NOTES AND VARIATIONS

If you can find fresh, made-that-day mozzarella that has not ever been refrigerated, it's delicious. The milk that leaks out turns to a sort of broth when mixed with the fresh tomato juice and olive oil, adding excellent flavor to the sauce. I like a spoon on the side. If your cheese isn't made fresh, take it out of the refrigerator an hour or so before using to bring it to room temperature.

RED BEAN AND GREEN PEPPER SALAD

I have come around regarding green peppers. There was a time when I carefully picked them out of take-out Chinese food, but I now find them pleasantly bitter and quite varied in flavor, depending on the variety. In this recipe, I mix green bell peppers and green chiles, mostly raw, but also roasted. I like spicy food, but for large groups I remove all the seeds and ribs from the chiles for a milder salad while offering a few sliced serranos on the side for fans of real heat. Be imaginative with this salad, it takes to the addition of scallions, celery, fennel, and parsley. **SERVES 4-6**

1 cup dried red kidney beans (or any bean you enjoy cold in a salad), rinsed, picked through for stones, and soaked overnight (substitute 3 cups canned beans, rinsed)
Assorted aromatic vegetables to cook with the beans, whatever you have on hand, including some or all of the following:
1 carrot, peeled, cut into 2-in. pieces
1 celery stalk, cleaned and cut into 2-in. pieces
A few garlic cloves, peeled and cut in half
1 quartered onion

A few sprigs parsley
A few sprigs thyme
2 poblano chiles
3 green bell peppers, cored, seeded, and cut into 2-in. strips
3 jalapeños
Up to ¼ cup olive oil
Juice of 2 lemons
½ small red onion, thinly sliced (optional)
1 garlic clove, minced
Pinch of dried, very fresh oregano (I like Turkish, optional)
Salt & black pepper
1 or 2 sliced serrano chiles, served on the side (optional)

As it's difficult to predict how long beans will take to cook, start them early in the day or the night before by simmering the soaked dried beans in a pot over medium heat with plenty of water and large pieces of aromatic vegetables. Cook for 1 to 1½ hours or until completely tender. (I like my beans fully cooked, even if that means a few might fall apart. Cook yours for less time if you like them firmer.) Drain the beans, reserving the broth if you want it for soup, and set them aside (or refrigerate them overnight if you're working ahead).

To roast the poblanos, continually turn them over on top of a gas burner until they're evenly charred. If you have an electric stovetop, place them on a baking sheet in a 450 F to 500 F oven until black. I recommend rinsing the charred skin off under a thin stream of running warm water to remove the skin. Cut the peeled poblanos into ½-inch strips and add to a mixing bowl large enough to hold all the ingredients. The poblanos may be used raw as well. Add the green bell peppers.

Cut the jalapeños, using gloves if you have sensitive skin. (If you don't use gloves, be sure to rinse your hands after cutting them and avoid rubbing your eyes.) If you want a spicy salad, slice retaining the seeds and pith and add it all to the bowl with the poblanos and green peppers.

Add the beans to the bowl with the peppers; the proportion is up to you. I like half vegetables and half beans to lighten the salad. Add the olive oil, lemon juice, sliced red onions (if using), garlic, oregano (if using), and a pinch of salt and pepper. Serve at room temperature or cold. This salad can hold, refrigerated, overnight; the peppers will absorb the lemon and garlic flavor, making them less crunchy but flavorful. Serve the serranos on the side, if you wish.

RADICCHIO AND BLUEBERRIES WITH SHERRY VINEGAR AND WALNUT OIL

At the Institute we typically buy radicchio only if we can find it locally or if we have some in the winter from a catering job. It can be quite expensive, but it's pretty with blueberries. The combination combines bitter, sweet, and tangy even before you add any dressing. For this reason I recommend you lightly dress the salad. SERVES 4-8

2 to 4 heads radicchio
1 pint blueberries
3 tbsp. to 4 tbsp. toasted walnut oil (olive oil or hazelnut oil are good substitutes)

2 tbsp. to 3 tbsp. sherry vinegar (or any vinegar you like)
1 tbsp. Dijon mustard (optional)
1 clove garlic, crushed (optional)
Salt & black pepper

One simple way to make this salad is to tear or shred the radicchio, toss with the blueberries, oil, vinegar, mustard, garlic, salt, and pepper, and serve.

NOTES AND VARIATIONS

Another tasty way to make the salad is to combine the berries, oil, vinegar, and mustard in a small bowl and microwave until warm, about 2 minutes. Toss the mixture with the radicchio to wilt the leaves slightly.

For more of a side dish, you may also sauté the radicchio in vegetable oil with the crushed garlic clove for a minute or two and toss it with cold berries, oil, and vinegar.

LEMON-PARSLEY VINAIGRETTE

For information on greens and instructions on dressing a salad, see page 229. Makes about 1½ cups. **SERVES 8-10**

3 tbsp. lemon juice
2 tbsp. mayonnaise (optional)
2 tsp. Dijon mustard
1 garlic clove, lightly smashed
Scant ¼ tsp. lemon zest

Salt & black pepper
½ cup olive oil
3 tbsp. grape seed oil
3 tbsp. chopped parsley

Whisk together the lemon juice, mayonnaise (if using), mustard, garlic, lemon zest, salt, and pepper. Whisk in the oils slowly, until emulsified, then add the parsley. Taste and adjust the salt and pepper, and remove the garlic clove. If you like a thinner dressing, add a few drops of water.

BOWL OF PEACHES

By July we usually have local peaches in the Hudson Valley. Of course, some years are good peach years and some are not. A really great peach year is rare enough that I'm happy to eat peaches plain, never even bothering to make a cobbler or pie. Though I'm not as fond of furry peach skin as I am of the smooth skin of a nectarine, I prefer a juicy, perfectly balanced sweet-and-sour, perfumed peach over any other fruit—with the possible exception of Concord grapes.

Peach growing at the Institute

MENU 20

HAIGA RICE, SESAME SEEDS, GREEN SHISO, AND CUCUMBER WITH MACKEREL

This is a room-temperature fish dish that will remind you of sushi. It can be served all mixed together as suggested below or in separate parts with the rice, the fish, and a cucumber salad in separate bowls. Add tofu instead of fish for a vegetarian version or try another fish, if you prefer. Arctic char, hake, clams, or fluke would all be good, cooked or raw. **SERVES 6-8**

8 4 oz. mackerel fillets, skin on
Salt & black pepper
½ cup vegetable oil, divided
4 cups rice (in this dish I like
to use haiga or white jasmine
best, but arborio, sushi, or even
brown rice will do nicely)
¼ cup toasted sesame oil
2 cups peeled and diced or
sliced cucumber (I like a small
dice if I have time)

½ cup rice wine vinegar
10 to 30 shiso leaves (about
1 cup total, but if the flavor is
too strong for you, use less or
substitute cilantro or basil. If you
can, use opal or Thai basil)
¾ cup sesame seeds, toasted

Sprinkle the fish with salt and pepper before cooking and then sauté it, skin-side down, over medium heat with a few teaspoons vegetable oil until the skin is crisp, 3 to 5 minutes. Turn the fish over and cook for 3 to 5 minutes more.

I typically use a rice cooker to make rice. (See page 91 for instructions for cooking rice in a pot.) When it's finished, turn the rice out onto a tray to cool. Toss the rice with sesame oil.

Toss the cucumbers in a large bowl with the vinegar. Tear the shiso leaves into pieces or cut into thin ribbons and toss them in with the cucumbers.

Mix the rice with the cucumbers, add the sesame seeds and a pinch of salt and pepper. Taste and adjust salt, pepper, vinegar, and oil, and spoon onto a serving platter. Top the rice with the fish and serve warm or at room temperature.

NOTES AND VARIATIONS

The seared pieces of mackerel may be placed skin-side up in an ovenproof dish and baked at 350 F for 6 to 7 minutes and held aside for the salad. It may also be baked just before serving if you prefer to serve the fish hot. At the Institute we sometimes sear the fish over a high flame for a very crisp skin, but I find very high-heat cooking at home too messy and smelly and generally not worth the effort.

When using Arctic char, I sear the skin because, like salmon skin, it's fatty and if it isn't rendered it can be thick and gummy. You can simply remove the skin and oven-poach or gently cook the fish in a pan on top of the stove, but I don't like searing fish flesh over high heat or on a grill as it becomes tough and dry.

GREEN BEANS

Green beans are a chore for big groups at the Institute. I am not sure why this is. I like many tedious jobs, but trimming green beans is a time-consuming task I always try to avoid. In the summer we get great beans—green, purple, yellow wax—and we cook them at least a couple of times a year. Beans are pretty easy at home, where the quantities are not so daunting. While roasted green beans are tasty, my favorite way to eat them is boiled with butter and salt. I like green beans raw or cooked all the way through, but I am not fond of medium, squeaky-to-the-bite beans. This recipe is super plain. Even though the menu is Asian, a little butter on the hot beans is a good combination, but it's optional, of course. **SERVES 6-8**

1 lb. to 2 lb. green beans, trimmed
1 tbsp. to 2 tbsp. butter or vegetable oil

2 garlic cloves, sliced (optional)
Salt & black pepper

TO BOIL

Bring a pot of water to boil over high heat. Add a pinch of salt and the beans. Cook until tender, 6 to 8 minutes. Drain the beans and then toss them in a bowl with the butter and garlic (if using). Add salt and pepper, and serve warm.

TO ROAST

Preheat oven to 450 F. Toss the beans in a bowl with the salt, vegetable oil, garlic (if using), and pepper. Spread them on a baking sheet and roast until they begin to brown, 6 to 8 minutes. Taste and adjust the salt and pepper. Serve warm or cold.

KALE WITH JAPANESE PEANUT SAUCE

This recipe is reminiscent of goma-ae, the Japanese dish of spinach with sesame sauce. Instead of kale, use blanched and squeezed-of-water spinach, chard, or watercress. **SERVES 6-8**

1 to 2 bunches kale (I like all varieties including red Russian, lacinato, and the conventional curly green-leaf variety that appears in winter when the local kale is gone)

Trim the thick stems from the kale, and cut the leaves into 1-inch ribbons.

FOR THE PEANUT SAUCE (GOMA-AE STYLE)

1 cup sesame seeds, toasted until golden brown

2 tsp. salt, plus more to taste

1 cup natural, smooth peanut butter

1 tbsp. toasted sesame oil

1 tbsp. soy sauce

1 tbsp. rice wine vinegar

1 to 2 tbsp. mirin

1 tsp. raw sugar, maple syrup, honey, or molasses (optional)

In a food processor, pulse the sesame seeds with the salt just once or twice until barely ground. (You may also use a mortar and pestle.) Set sesame seeds aside. (No need to clean the food processor if you're going to make the peanut sauce next.)

In a food processor, work together the salt, peanut butter, sesame oil, soy sauce, rice wine vinegar, mirin, and raw sugar, and slowly add cold water (up to about 2 tablespoons) until the sauce is thick but loose enough to pour. Set aside.

Bring a pot of salted water to boil over high heat. (An 8-quart pasta pot will do nicely.) Add the kale and cook until tender, 4 to 6 minutes, depending on the size and freshness of the leaves. Taste to test if it's done. Rinse the kale under cold water and squeeze it in batches to remove the excess water before placing it in a mixing bowl. Add all the peanut

Menu 20, haiga rice and mackeral with blueberries instead of chocolate bread pudding for dessert

117

sauce (or as much as you like for a dish as rich as you like) and mix thoroughly along with about half of the ground sesame seeds. Place the kale in a serving bowl or platter and garnish with the remaining sesame seeds. Serve room temperature or cold.

BRONZE FENNEL VINAIGRETTE

Bronze fennel is easy to grow in the Hudson Valley. It comes back each year and is good in all forms—the fresh fine fronds, the seeds, and the dried-out late-summer stalks. For information on greens and instructions on dressing a salad, see page 229. Makes 1 cup. **SERVES 4-6**

2 tbsp. chopped tender bronze fennel

2 tbsp. red wine vinegar or sherry vinegar

Juice of ½ lemon

1 tbsp. Dijon mustard

¼ cup olive oil

3 tbsp. grape seed oil

Salt & black pepper

Whisk together the fennel, vinegar, lemon juice, and mustard.. Whisk in the oils until emulsified. Taste and add salt and pepper. Make it thinner, if you like, by adding a few drops of water.

CHOCOLATE BREAD PUDDING

I love reused bread dishes—mique, matzo brei, chestnut stuffing, croutons, French toast, and bread pudding—savory and sweet. This recipe combines bread and chocolate in a not-too-sweet dessert, or, for me, a breakfast dish. Serve plain, with raw cherries or raspberries, or try baking some whole pitted cherries or berries right into the pudding. Plain heavy cream or coconut milk poured over the hot pudding is delicious. You can add spices and flavorings such as mint, dried chiles, mace, cardamom, ginger, cumin, cinnamon, or feel free to experiment. **SERVES 8-10**

¼ cup sugar

3 tbsp. high-quality cocoa (such as Valrhona)

2 cups heavy cream

8 cups 1½-in. toasted bread cubes (brioche or challah is a great choice, but any bread will do)

8 tbsp. (1 stick) butter, melted, plus more for the pan

1 tsp. salt, divided

3 oz. bittersweet (70%) chocolate, shaved

5 eggs, beaten

1 tbsp. vanilla extract

Preheat oven to 275 F.

Butter a 9 x 13 pan or the equivalent and set aside.

Place the sugar and cocoa in a mixing bowl. In a small saucepan, scald the cream by heating it to just boiling then turning off the heat. Slowing whisk the scalded cream into the sugar and cocoa, until dissolved. Set aside.

Place toasted croutons in another mixing bowl and toss with the melted butter and ½ teaspoon of the salt. Fold in the shaved chocolate. Set aside.

Add the eggs to the cocoa-milk mixture. along with the vanilla and remaining salt.

Add the croutons and chocolate to the greased baking pan. Pour the custard over and let the unbaked pudding sit for up to 15 minutes so that some of the custard becomes absorbed by the croutons.

Bake 20 to 25 minutes. The center of the pudding should reach 160 F on an instant-read thermometer. Serve hot or cold.

MENU 21

ASIAN BEEF AND SHIITAKE SANDWICH

This is one of many versions of Asian-inspired sandwiches popular in United States right now. Some are of Korean origin, some are riffs on Peking duck and maybe most popular, the Vietnamese sandwich known as banh mi. In this recipe I use beef and shiitake mushrooms. Sometimes we use just mushrooms or pork, shoulder or belly. And we have served duck with pickled beets in place of the carrots. All of these combinations are rich and bright and may be served on various types of bread. We often use brioche buns, but French baguettes (typical in Vietnam) or steamed buns are also good. SERVES 6-8

FOR THE BRAISED BEEF

4 lb. boneless beef chuck roast (substitute beef shanks, short ribs, pork shoulder, or pork belly)
Salt & black pepper
2 tbsp. vegetable oil
¼ cup dried shiitakes, soaked in 2 qt. hot water for at least 30 minutes, reserve liquid
2 carrots, peeled and cut into 2-in. pieces
1 Spanish onion, cut in half

6 garlic cloves, whole
2-in. piece fresh ginger, peeled and chopped
1 bouquet garni with 1 strip orange zest, cilantro stems, and bay leaf, tied together with cooking twine, or tossed in to be fished out after (optional)
2 tbsp. hoisin (optional)
2 tbsp. oyster sauce (optional)

Season the meat with salt and pepper and sear until dark brown in a saucepan over high heat in the vegetable oil. If you prefer, sear the meat in the oven at 400 F on an unlined baking sheet until brown, for 2 to 3 minutes a side.

Preheat oven to 350 F. In a hotel pan or deep baking dish large enough to hold all the ingredients, place the browned roast and the water, shiitakes, carrots, onions, garlic, ginger, bouquet garni, hoisin, and oyster sauce (if using).

Place in the oven and bake for 1½ to 1¾ hours. I like to remove the meat before it's falling-apart tender, as I think there is more flavor left in the meat when it's a little less done. Remove the roast and set aside. Reduce the broth until it's at the desired thickness, roughly by half. I like to keep the juice like a broth to moisten the bread when making the sandwich, neither too concentrated nor salty.

FOR SANDWICHES

2 cups sliced cucumbers
¼ cup rice vinegar (optional)
6 brioche buns or 1 to 2 baguettes
1 cup aioli (see recipe page 120) or 3 cloves garlic smashed and mixed into 1 cup of Hellman's full-fat mayonnaise

24 leggy cilantro sprigs
6 tbsp. sliced green chiles, jalapeño or serrano (remove seeds for less heat), or substitute premade hot sauce

Place the sliced cucumbers in a bowl with the rice vinegar (if you like a little extra tang).

To make sandwiches, cut the bread in half. If using baguette, first cut into thirds, then halve. Spread aioli or garlic mayo on both sides, using as much as you like. Place the warm meat and some juice, cucumber, a few sprigs of cilantro, and some hot sauce on top, if you like. (At the Institute we often serve the meat and topping on rice instead of a baguette.)

SHREDDED ZUCCHINI WITH SPEARMINT

I love raw zucchini in summer when it's very fresh. This is a simple slaw that would be good on top of the Asian braised meat instead of the cucumbers on the sandwich, or served with rice on a buffet. **SERVES 6-8**

3 to 6 assorted summer squash, shredded (use zucchini or ronde de Nice)

3 to 4 sprigs mint, such as spearmint

or black peppermint, or basil
Salt & black pepper
1 tbsp. lemon juice (optional)
1 tsp. sesame oil (optional)

Place the summer squash in a bowl. Pick the mint leaves from the stem and either toss them in whole or cut the leaves into ribbons. Add a pinch of salt and pepper. Serve plain or add the optional lemon juice and sesame oil (or both) and serve.

NOTES AND VARIATIONS

The same salad with lemon and olive oil is good. You can also add shredded Parmesan type cheese and/or toasted pine nuts.

Menu 21, Asian beef and shiitake sandwich with yellow summer-squash salad

CORN ON THE COB

At the Institute we boil a large pot of water and melt a little butter on top so that when we are making a lot of corn the ears are lightly buttered when we pull them out of the pot. I grew up in New Jersey, where it was a crime to boil fresh corn for more than 3 minutes. These days, I look for varieties that are not "super sweet" for a more traditional corn flavor, but any variety you like or can find is fine. Another method that's delicious but a little fussy is to slice the corn kernels from the cob and cook them with a little white wine, herbs, and garlic.

PURPLE BASIL VINAIGRETTE

For information on greens and instructions on dressing a salad, see page 229. Makes a generous ½ cup. **SERVES 2-4**

Juice of 1 lemon
3 tbsp. grape seed oil
3 tbsp. olive oil
½ cup torn or sliced purple
basil (substitute Thai basil or regular basil)
Salt & black pepper

Gently whisk together the lemon juice, oils, basil, salt, and pepper. This is a broken vinaigrette, so shake or stir before using.

PLUMS

Plums are the sturdiest and most forgiving of the stone fruits, and we often end up baking tarts, pies, and cobblers with them. In July, when we get the best sour-skinned, juicy, sweet-fleshed plums that are just past firm but not too soft, we serve them by themselves for dessert at the Institute—sometimes every other night while they're in season.

AUGUST MENUS

22

CORN CHOWDER 124
TOMATO SALAD WITH MARJORAM 125
SAUTÉED CHARD WITH MOZZARELLA AND TARRAGON 127
SORREL VINAIGRETTE 128
OVEN-POACHED PEACHES WITH ROSÉ WINE AND SPICES 128

23

HAIGA RICE AND BARLEY WITH PURPLE SHISO AND HIIJKI 129
ROASTED EGGPLANT WITH LEMON AND MISO 130
DUCK BREASTS WITH GARLIC 131
GINGER VINAIGRETTE 133
PEACHES AND CREAM 133

24

GROUND BEEF SALAD WITH PEANUTS, LEMONGRASS, ONION,
   BLACK PEPPERMINT, AND LIME 135
TIBETAN RELISH WITH TOMATO SALAD 136
RICE VINEGAR AND OLIVE OIL DRESSING 136
PANNA COTTA WITH NECTARINES 136
PANNA COTTA WITH AGAR 137
PANNA COTTA WITH GELATIN 137

CORN CHOWDER

This is a simple chowder recipe for freshly cut corn that's adaptable to include a wide range of ingredients, depending on what you have on hand. In place of the potatoes you could use root vegetables along with the corn. In winter, in place of the corn itself, use lots of carrots, extra onion, and pork shoulder for a hearty chowder stew. Of course, fish, shucked clams, or oysters are classic chowder ingredients. I was first inspired to use cobs to make chowder broth and to use fresh tomatoes in chowder by Mary J. Lincoln's corn chowder recipe in Richard J. Hooker's *The Book of Chowder*. **SERVES 8**

1½ tbsp. unsalted butter
3 cups diced onion, ½-in. dice
2 cups diced pancetta, pork belly, or bacon, cut into ½-in. or larger dice
4 cups potatoes, unpeeled, cut into ½-in. or larger dice
2 cups vegetable stock or water that has been steeped with cobs
Any or all of the following: thyme, parsley, cloves, black peppercorns, allspice, parsley, juniper, and bay leaf (it's useful to make a sachet by wrapping the spices in a piece of cheesecloth for easy removal, but I usually don't)

2 ripe tomatoes, skinned and cubed (optional; see Notes and Variations below)
Corn kernels from 8 ears of corn
1 qt. whole milk, or heavy cream for a richer chowder
Salt & black pepper

In a soup pot over medium heat, sauté the onions with the butter and pancetta until the onions are soft but not brown, stirring occasionally.

Add the potatoes, vegetable stock or cob water, and the herb sachet. Simmer until the potatoes are fork-tender.

Add the tomatoes and bring the water back to almost boiling before adding the corn and milk. Simmer gently until the corn is just done and the soup is very hot but not boiling (boiled milk will curdle), about 3 to 5 minutes. Taste and add salt and freshly ground pepper.

To remove the skin from a tomato, make a small x on the bottom with a sharp knife and dip it in boiling water for 5 seconds. The skin usually slips right off. I like to use the seeds and juice, but you may prefer to use the tomato flesh only by cutting the tomato in half along the equator and squeezing the pulp out. You can drain the seeds from the liquid and use the liquid, but I find the seeds and pulp very tasty.

You may also add 2 dozen shucked fresh clams or oysters or a few white fish fillets cut into 2 inch-cubes.

For a dairy-free version use extra tomato and vegetable stock in place of the milk.

TOMATO SALAD WITH MARJORAM

We serve tomatoes at the Institute often when they're in season. No one tires of them. Although in this menu you'll find cooked tomatoes in the chowder, I don't hesitate to serve sliced raw tomatoes on the side as well. Tomato season is short in the Hudson Valley, but we are lucky to have the amazing Jay Armour of Four Winds Farm, in Gardiner, New York, as one of our purveyors. Fresh marjoram is a great complementary herb to tomato if you want a change from basil. We switch off regularly, one leafy herb at a time, between shiso, bronze fennel, parsley, mint, and thyme, to name a few. Serve at least one whole tomato per person. **SERVES 6**

6 large ripe tomatoes, any variety   Sea salt (optional)
Leaves picked from 2 to 3 stems
of fresh marjoram (substitute
dried oregano)

Slice the tomatoes and arrange on a platter. Sprinkle with fresh marjoram leaves and sea salt (if using).

Menu 22, corn chowder

SAUTÉED CHARD
WITH MOZZARELLA AND TARRAGON

This dish is good warm or at room temperature. If you add rice or pasta and maybe some beans, it's great as a main course. **SERVES 8**

1 large bunch chard

3 to 6 cloves fresh garlic, coarsely chopped

¼ cup olive oil

Salt & black pepper

1 lb. fresh (never refrigerated, if possible) room-temperature mozzarella, cut into 1-in. cubes

1 bunch tarragon, very coarsely chopped, or the picked leaves from a whole bunch

Crushed red pepper or hot sauce (optional, to serve on the side)

I take the time to cut the stems from the leaves when preparing chard. To me, the stems taste better cooked a bit longer than the leaves. Cut the stems into ½-inch pieces and cut the leaves into larger (2-inch) pieces.

In a large (10- to 12-inch) saucepan over medium heat, lightly cook the garlic in 2 tablespoons of the olive oil until the garlic just begins to brown. Add all the chard stems and cook for 4 to 6 minutes or until the stems are tender and to your liking. Add the leaves and cook until wilted and just cooked through, another 1 to 2 minutes (see Notes and Variations below). Toss with salt and pepper and place on a platter.

Top with the mozzarella cubes and tarragon, drizzling the rest of the olive oil on top. If you like, serve crushed red pepper or hot sauce on the side.

NOTES AND VARIATIONS

I leave a little water on the chard leaves after I rinse them. It's a bit messy when you add wet leaves to a hot, oily skillet, but the leaves will end up less greasy and will wilt nicely.

SORREL VINAIGRETTE

For information on greens and instructions on dressing a salad, see page 229. Makes about 1½ cups. **SERVES 6-8**

3 tbsp. white wine vinegar
2 tbsp. mayonnaise (optional)
1 tsp. Dijon mustard (optional)
Salt & black pepper
½ cup olive oil

3 tbsp. grape seed oil
3 tbsp. chopped raw sorrel
1 garlic clove, lightly smashed
and minced

Whisk together the vinegar, mayonnaise (if using), mustard (if using), salt, and pepper. Whisk in the oils until emulsified, then add the sorrel and garlic.

OVEN-POACHED PEACHES
WITH ROSÉ WINE AND SPICES

Ripe peach halves lightly baked and basted in rosé wine and spices are delicious all by themselves. For a richer treat, spoon ice cream on top or add a crispy cookie below—or do both. Making a custard sauce or crème caramel would be delicious but more time consuming. To produce pretty peeled peach halves, it's best to use freestone peaches. **SERVES 6-8**

2 cups water
1 cup raw sugar or maple sugar
Optional flavorings, including:
1-in. or 2-in. strip lemon zest,
a split vanilla bean, 2-in.-long
cinnamon stick, bay leaf, black
peppercorns, green or black
cardamom pods, or a small
cluster of mace

4 ripe peaches
2 cups rosé wine (red or white
would work as well for a different
flavor)

Preheat oven to 350 F. In a small saucepan over medium heat, melt the sugar with the water until the sugar dissolves. Add any of the optional flavorings (if using). Turn off the heat and set aside to steep.

With a thin sharp paring knife, try to peel the ripe peaches. When peaches are in season and are perfectly ripe sometimes the skin is so thin it's easy to peel off. If it isn't so easy, bring a pot of water to boil and just like you do to peel a tomato, cut a small x in the bottom of the peach and dip the peach in the boiling water for about 3 seconds. As soon as the fruit is cool enough to handle, the skin should easily peel off. Cut the peach in half north to south and, if it's a freestone peach, when you give it a slight twist the flesh should separate easily from the stone (pit). Otherwise, cut the flesh from the stone in pieces as large as possible and poach the pieces. It will be a less fancy presentation but just as delicious.

Place the peach halves in a baking dish cut-side down and pour the sugar water and wine over the top. Be sure any spices are scattered around the pan. Bake 5 minutes, baste, and bake another 12 to 15 minutes, until the peaches are quite soft and brown on top.

You may serve the peaches as they are or with the resulting thin, light syrup. If you prefer, pour the syrup into a small saucepan and reduce until it's thicker and sweeter and then pour the syrup back over the peaches. They're good warm or cold.

MENU 23

HAIGA RICE AND BARLEY WITH PURPLE SHISO AND HIJIKI

This recipe is my take on a rice dish I had many years ago at Omen A Zen, a Japanese restaurant in New York City. When the restaurant first opened, the bowl of rice that came with most meals had a small quantity of barley and unidentifiable black specks that lent the rice an irresistible perfumed flavor. I learned later that the specks were shiso. They also served hijiki salad, which was new to me. This has become one of my favorite types of dried seaweed. Eventually, I thought to combine the two tastes. This recipe uses purple shiso, which we grow at the Institute. It's milder than the green variety, but either works. (Green shiso is easier to find in Japanese markets.) If you're thinking of growing your own, it's easily cultivated from seed. If you can't find shiso and don't garden, substitute Thai or Italian basil. SERVES 6-8

¼ cup dried hijiki	2 cups haiga rice (jasmine is a
4 to 12 purple shiso leaves	good substitute)
1 cup barley	Salt

Soak the hijiki in water until soft. Chop lightly so that the seaweed strands are bite size, and set aside.

Stack the shiso leaves and, using a sharp knife, cut into ribbons as thin as you can make them and set aside.

Bring a pot filled with 2 quarts of lightly salted water to boil. Add the barley and cook until just tender but not yet splayed, about 8 to 12 minutes (test the barley frequently as times vary depending on the variety and age of the barley). Rinse the cooked barley briefly under cool water and set aside.

I use a rice cooker to make rice. (See page 91 for instructions).

When the rice is done, add the barley and a small amount of shiso to the bowl of the rice cooker and mix thoroughly. The shiso will wilt and darken. Add salt, taste and adjust, and place rice in a serving bowl. If you love the flavor of the shiso, mix in some more or sprinkle the rest on top. Spread the chopped hijiki on top.

ROASTED EGGPLANT WITH LEMON AND MISO

Try to find long, thin Asian eggplant for this recipe. Pay attention to the roasting eggplant, as the sugar and miso in the glaze will quickly go from caramelized to burnt. **SERVES 6-8**

8 Asian eggplants, any eggplant	2-in. strip lemon zest
will work, but cut larger eggplant	2 tsp. water
into strips resembling the Asian	2 tsp. raw sugar
eggplant	½ cup miso paste (white soy
4 tbsp. vegetable oil	miso works fine for this recipe,
Juice of 2 lemons	but any miso you like will do)

Preheat oven to 350 F. Slice the eggplants lengthwise, and brush the cut surfaces with oil before placing them on a baking sheet or in a baking dish (see Notes and Variations below). Roast until the eggplant is completely tender, 10 to 12 minutes. While eggplant is roasting, make the lemon-miso mixture.

In a small saucepan, combine the lemon juice, zest (no pith), and water with the sugar and place over medium heat until the sugar is dissolved. Let the zest steep for 5 to 10 minutes before removing it and discarding. Combine the cooked lemon liquid with the miso paste. Set aside.

Remove eggplants from the oven and brush the cut side of the eggplants with the lemon-miso mixture. You won't use all of it at first; set aside the remainder.

Just before serving, bake the miso-brushed eggplant again for about 2 minutes before removing to brush with a final layer of the lemon-miso mixture. Bake until the glaze begins to color, another minute or so. Serve hot, warm, or at room temperature.

NOTES AND VARIATIONS

If you use a baking dish rather than a baking sheet, pour the whole miso mixture on top of the eggplant and baste a few times over the course of 10 to 12 minutes. You will have sauce on the side that's delicious on the rice.

If you have a broiler, you may brown the tops of the eggplant for a more caramelized, concentrated flavor, but be careful as the sugar burns quickly.

DUCK BREASTS WITH GARLIC

When I prepare duck at home or for smaller groups, I frequently buy whole birds even if I am using only the breast for a particular dish. I remove the breasts and save the rest of the bird for something else. Local garlic is available starting in the early summer, and it's a great time to prepare these breasts. Sometimes we serve them whole with a sauce on the side, or sliced ready to add to a stew, salad, or summer rolls, in which case we remove the skin altogether after cooking and use the lean meat cut into a julienne. **SERVES 4 FOR MAIN DISH, 8 FOR A SMALL-MEAT MEAL**

4 6 oz. to 7 oz. duck breasts	1 to 2 heads of garlic, preferably
Salt	fresh local garlic, but any firm
	heads will do

Using scissors or a very sharp knife, trim the extra skin and fat from around each breast so that the skin and flesh are the same size. (I use the trimmings to make cracklings for salad or finely chopped in matzo balls. See recipe for cracklings, page 58.) Score the breast skin in a crisscross pattern, not cutting all the way through the fat. Sprinkle the breasts with salt and place them skin-side down in a saucepan. They can be close together.

Fill the pan with water just up to where the skin stops so that you aren't poaching the flesh while rendering the fat.

Separate, wash, and cut the garlic cloves in half with their skin on and toss them into the water around the breasts. Start the heat high to get the water boiling and then reduce the heat so that the fat below the skin will render, but the flesh doesn't cook much, if at all. As the water evaporates, lift the breasts and move them around to keep them from sticking (though they usually stick a little anyway). The goal is a thin, crisp skin. Check to see if the skin needs more rendering. If so, add water to the pan and continue cooking until the water is gone, the skin is thin and golden brown, and the garlic cloves are cooked. Repeat this step as necessary. Depending on the heat, this takes from 7 to 10 minutes.

Turn the breasts over so that the still-raw flesh cooks briefly, 1 to 2 minutes, in the rendered fat. I like to serve duck fairly rare, but cook longer if you like your meat more well done.

Remove the breasts to a serving platter and pour off the fat and reserve for another use. There should be a bit of browned broth and lots of sticky, chewy, creamy garlic cloves to serve around the breast or on toast. (The irresistible garlic and even the cooked garlic skin often disappear in the kitchen before making it to the table.)

Flowering chives picked from our garden

GINGER VINAIGRETTE

For information on greens and instructions on dressing a salad, see page 229. Makes 1 ½ cups. **SERVES 8-10**

1 cup cup vegetable oil (I like grape seed)
¼ cup rice vinegar
¼ cup lemon juice

1 tbsp. peeled and finely minced fresh ginger
Salt & black pepper

Combine the oil, vinegar, lemon juice, ginger, salt, and pepper, and mix thoroughly.

PEACHES AND CREAM

When you have perfect peeled and sliced peaches and fresh, cold cream no other ingredient is needed. If you can find freestone peaches, use them as they are, of course, easier to pit and slice. **SERVES 4**

4 ripe peaches, peeled (see page 128 for instructions)

1 cup cold cream (not ultra-pasteurized)

Slice the peaches into a serving bowl. Serve with cold cream on the side or pour the cream right over the peaches.

NOTES AND VARIATIONS

No seasonings are necessary, but if you're inclined you might sweeten the cream with a bit of sugar, honey, or maple syrup. You can also add mace, grated nutmeg, ground cardamom, black pepper, or fragrant leaves such as hyssop, verbena, lavender, or rosemary.

Thai basil

Menu 24, ground beef salad

GROUND BEEF SALAD
WITH PEANUTS, LEMONGRASS, ONION,
BLACK PEPPERMINT, AND LIME

2 tbsp. vegetable oil
2 lb. ground beef
1 stalk lemongrass
1 cup unsalted peanuts
½ cup loosely packed cilantro
leaves with some stem attached
¼ cup mint leaves (we grow
black peppermint, but any mint
is fine) or Thai basil
3 tbsp. Asian fish sauce (nam pla)
Juice of 2 limes

1 red onion, very thinly sliced
4 scallions, sliced (optional)
1 to 2 hot fresh chiles, such as
Thai red, or hari mirchi chiles,
the small slightly wrinkled green
chiles used in Indian cooking, or
serrano, thinly sliced (optional)
1 clove garlic, minced
Salt
1 to 2 heads Bibb or romaine
lettuce, washed and dried

Heat the vegetable oil in a saucepan over medium heat until warm. Add the ground beef, crumbling with a wooden spoon as it cooks. Cook through, about 5 to 6 minutes. Drain the fat from the meat and transfer to a mixing bowl.

Peel the outer leaves from the lemongrass stalk; cut about a ¼ of the stalk off the bottom. What you're left with should be the most tender part, though the whole lemongrass stalk is fairly tough. Cut the stalk into very thin slices starting from the bottom root end until it's too tough to use (might be 1 inch or up to 3 inches) and then chop the thin rounds. Add the lemongrass, peanuts, cilantro, mint, fish sauce, lime juice, red onion, scallions, chiles (if using), and garlic to the bowl with the meat. Taste and add salt.

Spread lettuce leaves on a platter and serve the ground meat salad over the top or on the side along with the jasmine rice (see recipe, page 91).

TIBETAN RELISH WITH TOMATO SALAD

The Dalai Lama has visited the Institute on a few occasions. On one trip he came to meet with Tibetan students studying in the United States. That time there were a few young chefs from Tibet who came along to help cook for the monks, who require a strictly traditional diet. One of the condiments they served was this simple, very spicy, really good relish, which they ate with steamed meatballs. What's interesting about the recipe is not so much what's in it, but what isn't. It contains no acid, no oil, and no salt. **SERVES 8 TO 12 PEOPLE WHO LOVE VERY SPICY FOOD AND AN ARMY OF THOSE WHO DON'T**

1 cup finely chopped cilantro
1 onion, finely diced about 1/8 inch
1 ripe raw tomato, finely chopped

2 to 4 very hot chiles, such as habaneros, very finely chopped
2 garlic cloves minced
1-in. piece fresh ginger, peeled and finely chopped

Mix all ingredients together in a bowl and serve.

RICE VINEGAR AND OLIVE OIL DRESSING

For information on greens and instructions on dressing a salad, see page 229. Makes ¾ cup. **SERVES 4-6**

½ cup olive oil
¼ cup rice vinegar

Salt & black pepper

Combine the oil, vinegar, salt, and pepper, and mix thoroughly. This is a broken vinaigrette.

PANNA COTTA WITH NECTARINES

Panna cotta is a simple-to-make custard—cream thickened with gelatin or agar, rather than French custards, which use egg. I am including two recipes, one that uses gelatin and equal parts milk and cream, and one made with agar and extra cream. Both recipes are delicious with vanilla, but if you have really good fresh cream you might try it with nothing other than the sugar. Gelatin such as rennet in cheese is not strictly vegetarian. Agar is made from algae. The difference in flavor in these recipes is subtle but worth exploring. **SERVES 8-10**

PANNA COTTA WITH AGAR

3⅓ cups cream
1 cup milk
⅓ cup sugar

2 vanilla beans, split
½ tsp. agar

Combine cream, milk, sugar, and vanilla in a saucepan over low heat. Heat slowly, whisking frequently. As soon as the mixture begins to bubble on the edges or shows signs of boiling, turn off the heat and set pan aside to steep for at least 30 minutes or for up to 2 hours. Return the pan to stove and set over low heat. Once again, bring the mixture to almost to a simmer but this time add the agar when it's nearly boiling. Continue to heat, whisking all the while. The agar must reach a full boil (or 90 F) for it to set the custard properly. Remove from the heat, whisk in the milk mixture and pour into small glass bowl or small custard cups (about 10 4-ounce cups). Chill until thoroughly cool to set. Remove the custard from the refrigerator 30 minutes before serving (unless the weather is very hot) to take the chill off. Top with sliced, ripe nectarines.

PANNA COTTA WITH GELATIN

SERVES 8–10

2 cups heavy cream, not ultra-pasteurized, divided
½ oz. gelatin (if you're using a typical paper sleeve from the supermarket that means roughly 1½ packages)

½ cup sugar
½ vanilla bean, split lengthwise, or 1 tsp. vanilla extract
2 cups whole milk, not ultra-pasteurized

Heat 1 cup of cream with the gelatin in a saucepan over very low heat until the gelatin is completely dissolved, 2 to 3 minutes. Whisk in the rest of the cream and the sugar. Scrape the split vanilla bean and add the moist seeds and the pods to the cream mixture. Cook over medium heat until the mixture is very hot, not boiling, about 5 to 7 minutes. Pour into 10 4-ounce custard cups or into a single baking dish and refrigerate until the custard is set, about 1 hour. Cover with plastic wrap so it doesn't absorb other smells. You may slide a knife around the side and invert the custard onto a plate or serve right from the dish topped with peeled, sliced nectarines. Nectarines may be raw or baked as in the oven-poached peach recipe (page 128). You may, of course, substitute any fruit for the nectarines or serve the custard plain. For a richer custard use more heavy cream in place of the milk.

Pond in autumn at the Institute

SEPTEMBER MENUS

25

BRAISED BEEF SHANKS WITH TZATZIKI 140, 141
BAKED PLUM TOMATOES WITH BREADCRUMBS 142
EGG NOODLES WITH CHIVES 143
OLIVE VINAIGRETTE 144
CONCORD GRAPES 144

26

THAI-STYLE EGGPLANT CURRY WITH COCONUT MILK, LEMONGRASS,
    SHIITAKES, TURNIPS, AND LIME 145
JASMINE RICE WITH PEANUTS AND BROWN SHALLOTS 149
PICKLED CARROTS 149
CUMIN VINAIGRETTE 150
SLICED WATERMELON 150

27

FISH SOUP 150
MIXED RADISH AND RAW-CORN SALAD 154
TARRAGON VINAIGRETTE 155
PEARS 155

BRAISED BEEF SHANKS WITH TZATZIKI

Beef shanks are naturally rich and flavorful. In this recipe they are cooked in the oven uncovered, not fully submerged in liquid—a combination of roasting and braising. This recipe has lots of different vegetables listed as ingredients for a very flavorful broth or sauce. Feel free to make simpler variations with just one or two vegetables. In summer, beef shanks are enhanced by a cold tangy condiment like tzatziki served on the side. In spring, rhubarb sauce is a refreshing condiment. If you're interested in a less meaty meal, braise the meat with extra vegetables, take the meat off the bones, cut it up, and toss it with the vegetables to serve. Don't forget to eat the marrow! **SERVES 4-8**

FOR THE BEEF

4 pieces beef shank (approximately 5 lb. to 8 lb.)

Salt & black pepper

¼ cup vegetable oil

1 Spanish onion, cut into ½-in. dice

4 garlic cloves, sliced

2 fresh tomatoes, peeled and rough chopped (or 1 cup canned)

1 tbsp. tomato paste (optional)

1 cup red wine (or white wine is fine)

2 cups water, vegetable or beef stock

¼ cup finely chopped dried mushrooms (porcini, Polish mushrooms, shiitakes, or any combination will do), soaked in 1 cup hot water for at least 30 minutes, broth reserved

3 celery ribs, cut into 2-in. pieces (optional)

2 turnips, peeled and cut into bite-size pieces (optional)

2 parsnips, peeled and cut into 2-in. pieces (optional)

2 carrots, peeled and cut into 2-in. pieces (optional)

1 leek, split in half, washed, and cut into 2-in. pieces (optional)

2-in. slice pancetta, pork belly, or bacon (optional)

Aromatics such as: 4 sprigs dill, 3 sprigs thyme, 1 bunch parsley (I like a lot of parsley, but a few sprigs are fine), 1 bay leaf, a few juniper berries or cloves

Preheat oven to 350 F. Sprinkle the beef with salt and black pepper. Heat the oil in a saucepan over medium heat. When the oil is hot, add the meat and brown for 10 to 12 minutes. Place the seared shanks in an ovenproof baking dish. If the pan becomes dry, add a little more oil to the saucepan and sauté the onions and garlic until they're soft and beginning to brown. Add the tomato and cook with the onions and garlic until slightly thickened, 5 to 10 minutes. Add the tomato-onion mixture to the baking dish with the meat. Add wine (or water) to deglaze the pan (this will remove any tasty leftover, stuck bits), and pour over the beef. Add the water and mushroom-soaking liquid. Scatter around the meat any or all vegetables, pancetta, and any aromatics you choose to use. Bake uncovered for 1½ to 2 hours, turning the shanks every 20 minutes or so. Be sure that the browned side of the meat gets turned into the sauce for extra flavor. If your oven runs hot and the liquid gets too low, just add extra water. I like to remove the meat before it is so tender that it falls off the bone. To my mind, much of the flavor is lost to the sauce. I want a gelatinous, even slightly chewy texture left in the meat. But cook the way you like it (see Notes and Variations below).

Transfer the shanks to a serving platter, drain the broth from the vegetables, and pour the broth into a saucepan. Skim the excess fat from the top. (You may serve the soft cooked vegetables on the side or keep them for lunch the next day and serve freshly roasted vegetables with the shanks.) I like the sauce the consistency of broth, but reducing it by half or more will concentrate the flavors. Taste and adjust the salt and pepper, and serve with tzatziki on the side (see page 141).

NOTES AND VARIATIONS

This recipe lists lots of ingredients, but braising meat may be as simple or as time consuming as your mood, schedule, or on-hand ingredients permit. If need be, you may put the beef shanks in an ovenproof baking dish, fill about halfway up with liquid, add a few herb sprigs along with an onion cut in half and roast for a few hours until the meat is so tender it comes easily off the bone. I used to cook these fattier, bony cuts until they were fork-tender, but recently I have realized how overcooked that meat is. It makes good sauce, but if you want the meat to taste good, to my mind it's better to stop your braise when the meat is quite firm and there is still juice, fat, collagen, and flavor left It might require a knife to eat, but it's worth the effort. Especially if you're cutting back on how much meat you eat, you want the little you eat to taste as good as possible.

TZATZIKI

This sauce is refreshing and light with traditional whole milk yogurt. For a richer dish, drain the yogurt in cheesecloth or a strainer for at least 10 minutes to thicken, or use a thick,

Greek-style whole milk yogurt. I like the very creamy Old Chatham sheep's-milk yogurt, which I don't drain. **SERVES 6-8**

2 full-size cucumbers or 4
Kirby cucumbers, peeled, cut
lengthwise, and seeded
2 cups yogurt
4 garlic cloves, mashed to paste

2 tbsp. lemon juice
2 tbsp. olive oil
4 tsp. chopped mint
Salt & black pepper

After scraping out the cucumber seeds with a teaspoon, either dice into ¼-inch cubes or shred using a box grater or food processor. Place in a mixing bowl large enough to hold all the ingredients. Sprinkle the cucumber with salt, toss, and let it sit for at least 10 minutes. Rinse the salt and drain the excess water. For a rich sauce, squeeze the cucumber dry and blot on a towel. Put the cucumber back in the dried mixing bowl and add the yogurt, garlic, lemon juice, oil, and mint. Mix well and season with salt and pepper.

BAKED PLUM TOMATOES
WITH BREADCRUMBS

This recipe uses some of the last tomatoes at the market in September and even October—if we're lucky and there's a late frost. I've recently been surprised at how delicious some of the heirloom paste tomatoes are eaten raw or very simply cooked, as in this easy recipe. Try making your own rustic breadcrumbs; the larger crumbs catch the tomato juice like warm panzanella.
SERVES 6-8

2 large slices sourdough bread,
the equivalent, or any type you
like (brioche also works well but
watch because it burns quickly)
3 tbsp. olive oil
1 tsp. lemon juice

2 garlic cloves, minced
2 sprigs fresh marjoram, leaves
only, chopped
Salt & black pepper
8 ripe plum tomatoes, cut in half
lengthwise

Preheat oven to 450 F. Toast the bread to dry it out. Break the bread into pieces and process in the food processor, pulsing 3 or 4 times to end up with uneven, fairly large crumbs. In a bowl, mix the breadcrumbs, oil, lemon juice, garlic, marjoram, salt, and pepper.

Place the cut tomatoes on a baking sheet. Top each one with an equal portion of the breadcrumb mix. Bake just 5 minutes before checking the crumbs. If they're starting to burn, lower the temperature to 350 F, and cook for 5 or 10 minutes more. Serve as a side dish.

EGG NOODLES WITH CHIVES

At the Institute I often serve something easy like egg noodles on the side of braised beef shanks that have been prepared with more vegetables than beef. Mashed potatoes, or spaetzle if you have the time, are also good complements. **SERVES 6-8**

1 lb. dried egg noodles	Salt & black pepper
3 tbsp. unsalted butter, or substitute olive oil	3 tbsp. snipped chives or parsley

In a large pot over high heat, bring salted water to boil. Add noodles and cook until al dente, according to the package directions. Drain, toss with butter, salt, and pepper, and place on a serving platter topped with snipped herbs.

NOTES AND VARIATIONS

Spaetzle isn't that time consuming and is delicious. This recipe makes 3½ quarts and serves 12 to 14 generously, but you can freeze extra spaetzle and bake to reheat another time.

1⅓ cups milk	unbleached flour
8 eggs	2 tbsp. chopped parsley
4 egg yolks	2 tbsp. snipped chives
2 tsp. salt	4 tbsp. butter (optional)
½ tsp. black pepper	½ cup homemade breadcrumbs (optional)
½ tsp. freshly grated nutmeg	
4¼ cups all-purpose,	

Whisk together the milk, eggs, egg yolks, salt, pepper, and nutmeg. Sift in the flour and stir in the herbs before covering and setting the dough rest for 1 hour or so.

Bring a large pot of salted water to boil over high heat. To cook, press the batter through a perforated hotel pan, colander, or spaetzle maker. You may also place the dough into the boiling water a few small pieces at a time for more of a dumpling. Spaetzle are done 1 minute after they've risen to the surface. Prepare a bowl of ice water and put the spaetzle in as soon as they come out of the cooking water. Drain well.

For added flavor, warm the spaetzle in a saucepan with butter and homemade breadcrumbs. (If you use breadcrumbs in the spaetzle you might leave them off the tomatoes.)

OLIVE VINAIGRETTE

For information on greens and instructions on dressing a salad, see page 229. Makes about 1 ¼ cups. **SERVES 6-8**

3 tbsp. mixed citrus juice (or a combination of any two or three including lemon, lime, orange, tangerine, and grapefruit)
2 tbsp. mayonnaise (optional)
1 tsp. Dijon mustard
Scant ¼ tsp. lemon zest (optional)

Salt & black pepper
½ cup olive oil
3 tbsp. grape seed oil
3 tbsp. chopped, pitted olives of your choice
1 garlic clove, lightly smashed and finely chopped

Whisk together the citrus juice, mayonnaise (if using), mustard, lemon zest (if using), salt, and pepper. Slowly whisk in the oils until emulsified before adding the olives and garlic.

CONCORD GRAPES

Concord grapes are one of my absolute favorite fruits. They're very typical of New York State and are at their peak in September, although, depending on the year, you can find them from late August through early October. Concord are the small, round, slightly bloomy, very dark purple, deeply fragrant "wine" grapes that make better eating out of hand than they make wine. Close relatives, the Niagara (white or otherwise known as green) and red Delaware grapes are also usually at the market at the same time. They're fragrant and wonderful, but to my mind no grape beats the Concord for eating plain or making jam and jelly. Growing up, I was taught to eat only the firm grapes, one at a time, by squeezing and then sucking the skins to release only the inner grape into my mouth. I then worked the grape around my mouth to remove the seeds so I could spit them out. An arduous process to be sure, but I am fast and can easily eat a quart of grapes in one sitting. My boys are even more efficient; they eat the whole grape, seeds, skins, and all.

THAI-STYLE EGGPLANT CURRY
WITH COCONUT MILK, LEMONGRASS,
SHIITAKES, TURNIPS, AND LIME

My first cooking experiments with curry were Southeast Asian, which seemed more accessible to me than Indian curries. Maybe that's because it's so easy to love the flavors of coconut milk, lime, Thai basil, kaffir or makrut lime leaves, lemongrass, chiles, and cilantro. This is a summer recipe with eggplant, summer squash, turnips, and green beans. In fall, I use root vegetables; in winter, leeks, canned tomatoes, and potatoes are good. This curry is also delicious with meat or fish. For variation, if you leave the curry spices out, this dish would resemble the Thai soup, tom kha gai without the galangal. This recipe is a mainstay at the Institute. **SERVES 6–8**

3 cilantro roots, peeled as necessary and chopped (optional)

2 stalks lemongrass, crushed

2 cups unsweetened coconut milk

1 medium eggplant, cut into 1-in. dice (with or without skin)

3 tbsp. vegetable oil, divided

4 medium turnips, cut into 1-in. dice

6 to 8 dried shiitakes, reconstituted in hot water, 2 cups soaking liquid reserved (see Notes and Variations below)

2 tsp. chopped cilantro (with stem is fine)

5 scallions, coarsely chopped

2 cloves garlic, chopped

1-in. piece fresh ginger, peeled and chopped

1 serrano chile, thinly sliced

2 tsp. sweet curry powder blend (see Notes and Variations below)

1 lb. fresh green beans, trimmed and cut into 1-in. pieces

1 tbsp. Asian fish sauce (*nam pla*), vegetarians may substitute soy sauce

1 tbsp. lime juice

½ tsp. crushed dried arbol chile (optional)

Salt & black pepper

5 serrano chiles, thinly sliced for extra heat (for garnish)

1 bunch Thai basil leaves (for garnish)

Lime wedges (for garnish)

Steep cilantro root and lemongrass stalks in the coconut milk for 15 minutes over low heat. Remove lemongrass.

Preheat oven to 400 F. Toss the eggplant with 1 tablespoon of the oil, and roast on a baking sheet until slightly brown, but

Menu 26, Thai-style eggplant currry, plus cucumbers and Thai basil

still firm, 5 to 10 minutes. Set aside. Do the same with the turnips (see Notes and Variations below). These vegetables will be slightly underdone as they will finish cooking in the stew.

Cut the reconstituted shiitake mushrooms into ⅛-in. slices.

Heat the remaining tablespoon of oil in a saucepan over medium heat. Add the shiitake slices, chopped cilantro, scallions, garlic, ginger, and serrano chile, and sauté for 1 minute, then add the curry powder. Stir and heat for another minute, then add the mushroom-soaking liquid and lemongrass-steeped coconut milk. Heat the mixture until warmed through before adding the partially cooked eggplant, turnips, and raw green beans, and cook until the vegetables are tender, 6 to 8 minutes. Add the Asian fish sauce (nam pla), lime juice, arbol chile. Taste and add salt and pepper. Garnish with sliced green chiles, Thai basil, and lime wedges.

NOTES AND VARIATIONS

If I'm rushed and don't want to make my own curry-powder blend, I use sweet curry powder from Penzey's. Their blend includes: turmeric, coriander, cumin, fenugreek, ginger, nutmeg, fennel, cinnamon, white pepper, cardamom, cloves, black pepper, and cayenne pepper. Sometimes, for Thai curry, I use a simpler version with these toasted and ground spices: turmeric, coriander, cumin, fennel, black pepper, and spicy dried red chiles. We also buy or make a Thai-style curry paste (see recipe on following page).

CURRY PASTE

If you make this recipe you can freeze small containers for later use. It won't be quite as bright, but it is a bit time consuming to make and it is satisfying to have around. Use this paste in place of the curry powder. **MAKES ABOUT 2 CUPS**

½ cup scallions, minced
8 fresh green chiles
2-in. piece fresh ginger, minced
2 stalks lemongrass, very finely minced
4 cloves garlic, minced
1½ tbsp. sweet paprika
2 tsp. caraway seeds, toasted and ground

2 tsp. coriander seeds, toasted and ground
2 tsp. sea salt
2 tsp. turmeric
1 tsp. fenugreek, toasted and ground
1 large pinch saffron
1 cup vegetable stock or water

Purée all ingredients in food processor with just enough vegetable stock to form a thick paste. Purée well, scraping down sides of the processor with rubber spatula.

Roasting the vegetables first is an extra step and may be skipped, but partially roasting the vegetables helps control the timing and doneness of the vegetables, and the caramelization adds flavor and texture to the finished curry.

NOTES AND VARIATIONS

A few suggestions for adding meat, poultry or seafood:

Sauté duck breasts with sea salt until rare, 3 to 4 minutes on each side. Slice before serving and top the curry. The same method works for rare, sliced lamb or duck (see recipe, page 131).

Poach a whole chicken in water or vegetable stock until just done, about 1 hour. Remove the meat from the carcass, cut into bite-size pieces, and add to the curry when you add the roasted vegetables. Do the same with a whole fish. Raw boneless fish may be also be added at the very end.

Roast a duck, chicken, or lamb shoulder until medium. Remove the meat from the bones, cut into bite-size pieces, and add to the curry when you add the vegetables. Remove the fat from roasting pan, but add any pan juice and brown bits to the curry.

JASMINE RICE
WITH PEANUTS AND BROWN SHALLOTS

The chewy, slightly crisp brown shallots that normally top the curry are, for a change, mixed with the rice. They take awhile to cook and lose lots of volume, so we use them for flavor. **SERVES 4-6**

6 shallots, very thinly sliced into rings or half rings
¼ cup vegetable oil

Salt & black pepper
2 cups jasmine rice

Combine the oil and shallots in a saucepan over medium heat and cook slowly until the shallots are completely brown, 10 to 12 minutes or more, stirring occasionally for even cooking. Drain on a towel and sprinkle with salt and black pepper. They will be crisp when they're cool.

I use a rice cooker to make rice. (See page 91 for detailed instructions on cooking rice.) Toss the cooked rice with the brown shallots or sprinkle the shallots on top of the rice in the pot or serving bowl.

PICKLED CARROTS

These may be served as a condiment, or you may make enough for a side dish. They're a bright complement to the rich, spicy curry. Sliced, small round, lemon cucumbers in season from the market or your garden would be a good substitute. **SERVES 6-8**

4 large carrots, peeled and thinly sliced
⅓ cup water
⅓ cup rice vinegar

1 tbsp. salt
1 tbsp. raw sugar (substitute any sweetener or leave it out)

The carrots can be sliced using a mandoline or shredded using a box grater or food processor. In a small pot over medium heat combine the water, vinegar, salt, and sugar and cook until the sugar is dissolved. Pour the liquid over the carrots and let them sit in the refrigerator for at least 10 minutes. (You may make the carrots a day or two in advance and store them in the refrigerator.)

CUMIN VINAIGRETTE

For information on greens and instructions on dressing a salad, see page 229. Makes scant cup. **SERVES 4-6**

¼ cup rice vinegar
2 tbsp. Dijon mustard
1 tsp. toasted, ground
cumin seeds

¼ cup grape seed oil
¼ cup olive oil
Salt & black pepper

Whisk together the vinegar, mustard, and cumin. Slowly whisk in the oils until emulsified. Taste and add salt and pepper.

SLICED WATERMELON

Watermelon is a super-popular and refreshing dessert fruit at the Institute. In season, we buy small seedless melons for large groups, always hoping when we cut them open they will reveal crisp, juicy, dark-pink flesh. I have yet to figure out a way to consistently avoid the dreaded mealy, tasteless melon. We keep oranges in the refrigerator as backup for those not-so-special occasions.

MENU 27

FISH SOUP

This recipe is a relatively simple version of the classic soupe de poisson, which itself is a simplified version of bouillabaisse. This is one of those recipes in which it's particularly wise to read through before you start. (It looks more complicated than it is.) It has many parts, but isn't hard to make and is well worth the effort. Keep in mind that a little fish will go a long way. Like all the recipes in the book, I include many ingredients for the most exhaustive version, but if you have a can of clams, a loaf of bread, a can of tomatoes, a few garlic cloves, some oil, and an onion, you can read through this recipe and cook creatively with what you have and you will have a great soup—although a little saffron is an asset. **SERVES 6-8**

FOR THE FISH STOCK

¼ cup vegetable oil
4 sprigs flat-leaf parsley
2 garlic cloves, sliced
2-in. piece of orange zest
(optional)
1 onion, cut into ½-in. dice
1 fresh fennel bulb or a few
stalks bronze fennel, cut into
1-in. pieces
1 carrot, peeled and cut into
1-in. pieces

1 leek, halved, rinsed well, and
cut into 1-in. pieces
Fish bones from the non-oily
white fish you're using in the
soup (see page 153)
1 qt. cold water
1 lb. to 3 lb. mussels for broth
(substitute 6 live blue crabs,
which make a great broth, if you
can find them)
Salt & black pepper

In a soup pot, heat oil over medium heat until it's warm. Add the parsley, garlic, orange zest (if using), onions, fennel, carrot, and leek, and cook until the carrots are almost tender and the onions are soft, 5 to 6 minutes. Add the fish bones and water, and simmer for 20 minutes. Add the mussels (or live crabs, if using), and cook for another 5 minutes. Drain and set aside (see Notes and Variations below). Taste and add salt and pepper.

FOR THE ROUILLE

1 slice toasted sourdough bread
(any bread you like is fine)
¼ cup fish stock (mostly broth
but a stray piece of vegetable
is fine)
2 tbsp. lemon juice

3 garlic cloves
2 egg yolks
1 to 2 dried red chiles, as hot a
variety as you like
Salt & black pepper
1 cup olive oil

Soak the toasted slice of bread in lukewarm or cold fish stock until soft. In the bowl of a food processor combine the bread, lemon juice, garlic, egg yolks, chiles, salt, and pepper, and process until slightly thickened. Add olive oil in a thin stream until the mixture emulsifies. Put the sauce in a bowl and set aside. (If you prefer you can substitute store-bought mayonnaise for the egg and oil or just eliminate the egg and use the bread only; the sauce should still emulsify.)

Menu 27, fish soup

FOR THE SOUP

1 lb. fedelini (substitute spaghettini or spaghetti)

½ cup plus 1 tbsp. olive oil

3 ripe tomatoes (local plum tomatoes or beefsteak are fine; the sweeter and riper the better)

1 large onion, cut into ½-in. dice

3 leeks, halved, rinsed well, and sliced into ¼-in. rings

6 garlic cloves, sliced

4 sprigs thyme

1 tsp. ground fennel seed (optional)

1 generous pinch Spanish saffron

1 bay leaf

1 pinch dried savory (optional)

Salt & black pepper

3 lb. seasonal nonoily white fish, filleted as you would blackfish or halibut

1 cup grated cheese (classically Gruyère, but any local, firm cow's-milk cheese you like is fine), for garnish

4 slices sourdough bread, or any bread you like, for garnish

To make the soup: Preheat oven to 375 F. To prepare the pasta for the soup, break the fedelini into ½-inch or 1-inch pieces and toss in a mixing bowl with 1 tablespoon of the olive oil. Spread the broken pasta onto a baking sheet and toast in the oven until light brown, 5 to 6 minutes, and set aside.

Remove the skin from the tomatoes by cutting a small x on the bottom of each one and dipping them in boiling water for 3 seconds (literally). The skin should slip right off.

Chop the tomatoes into a 1-inch dice and set aside. (I use the seeds and pulp.) In a soup pot over medium heat, warm the remaining olive oil before adding the onions, leeks, and garlic. Cook until soft, 5 to 6 minutes. Add the tomatoes, strained fish stock, thyme, fennel seed, saffron, bay leaf, savory, salt, and pepper. Bring to a boil, reduce heat, and simmer for 10 minutes. Remove bay leaf. Add the noodles and simmer until the noodles are just done, about 10 minutes more. Add the raw fish in big pieces and stir so it falls apart after it's cooked. Taste and adjust salt and pepper.

Serve the soup with a platter of croutons, grated cheese, and a dollop of rouille. Suggest everyone spread a generous amount of rouille on a piece of toast and float it in the soup.

NOTES AND VARIATIONS

For a long time mussels and crabs were cheap and it wasn't odd to buy them just to make stock. They're expensive now; when I make stock, I nibble the crabs the next day cold. The mussels will be a little over cooked but with mayonnaise and celery root or celery and mustard they make a good salad.

I use various websites such as Seafood Watch to keep track of fish recommendations. We have a good local purveyor who goes to the fish market. When we can, we buy fish at the farmers' market that comes from Long Island. If I'm feeling flush I buy directly through a website that enables fisherman to ship direct from the dock. Check out sea2table.com. We use a fair amount of arctic char for large groups. It's a farmed fish with an excellent rating that's very popular. Char is a lake trout that tastes like a cross between trout and salmon, whereas many successful (from an environmental perspective) farmed fish are muddy tasting (farmed striped bass, for example). Tilapia is growing in popularity. It's a fish I found quite boring, but it can be good in fish tacos. Although they're not local, I occasionally buy Florida Gulf shrimp that have been flash frozen. (They contain none of the additives that contaminate shrimp from Southeast Asia.) I use hake, mackerel, clams, fluke, and bluefish, depending on which are running. I buy wild striped bass when it is available and occasionally halibut. I love fish and would buy it more often, but I think we need to go easy on our oceans, if possible allowing overfished stocks to replenish themselves.

MIXED RADISH AND RAW-CORN SALAD

Corn is a vegetable I only recently started to like raw. The nibs buried in the cob are good, so be sure to scrape the cob. In this salad, the sweet kernels of corn combined with spicy, crunchy radishes make a tasty and very pretty combination that has the added advantage of the late-summer and early fall, second radish season. **SERVES 4-6**

4 ears fresh sweet corn
2 bunches small radishes, cleaned and cut into bite-size pieces (French breakfast, Easter egg, or any variety or assortment is fine)
3 tbsp. good olive oil
2 tbsp. lemon or lime juice (white wine vinegar is a fine substitute)

Salt & black pepper
1 tsp. fresh thyme leaves (optional)

To remove the kernels from the cobs, use a sharp knife and hold the cob inside a mixing bowl as you shave. Avoid cutting too deeply into the cob as the pieces will be tough and sharp (see Notes and Variations below). Combine the radishes with the corn kernels in a bowl and season to taste with oil, citrus juice, salt, pepper, and thyme (if using), and serve.

NOTES AND VARIATIONS

The cut cobs are good to nibble or to boil to make stock for chowder or any soup. Corn stock is even good to add to the fish broth, instead of water, for the Fish Soup on page 153.

TARRAGON VINAIGRETTE

For information on greens and instructions on dressing a salad, see page 229. Makes a generous cup. **SERVES 6–8**

3 tbsp. white wine vinegar	1 garlic clove, lightly smashed
2 tbsp. mayonnaise (optional)	(optional)
1 tsp. whole-grain mustard	½ cup olive oil
½ tsp. salt	3 tbsp. grape seed oil
½ tsp. black pepper	3 tbsp. chopped fresh tarragon

Whisk together the vinegar, mayonnaise (if using), mustard, salt, pepper, and garlic clove in mixing bowl. Slowly whisk in the oils until emulsified, and add tarragon.

PEARS

Pears take a little advance planning, as they're picked unripe on purpose. Sometimes it takes days before they're ready to eat. Elusive, at times they rot before they ripen. A fragrant, juicy pear (I like them peeled) is heaven. A hard, dry or mealy one, not so much. Usually the imperfect-to-eat-as-dessert pears are quite tasty in a scone or a pound cake. Pear season in the Hudson Valley is from late August until they last, sometimes until Thanksgiving, depending on the farm. Because they do travel well, pears are a fruit we will buy all winter long from faraway parts.

Woods on the property

OCTOBER MENUS

28

29

30

BUTTERNUT SQUASH LASAGNA

Lasagna is a project at the Garrison Institute, but it's also something that can be easily done a day or two in advance and be ready to heat and serve when needed. In addition to the two recipes here, I encourage you to experiment. We make many varieties of lasagna, including spinach or chard, with and without béchamel or ricotta, and tomato, eggplant, sausage, and mushroom. **SERVES 12**

1 recipe béchamel (for recipe, see page 63)
¼ oz. dried porcinis (optional)
¼ cup olive oil, divided, plus more for oiling the pan
4 oz. pancetta, cut into ¼-in. dice (optional)
1 large Spanish onion, cut into ¼-in. dice
4 celery ribs, cut into ¼-in. dice
2 garlic cloves, finely chopped
1 medium butternut squash, cut into 1-in. cubes, about 2 cups (see Notes and Variations below)

Pinch freshly grated nutmeg
Salt & black pepper
1½ lb. to 2 lb. pasta sheets for lasagna (see recipe, page 153; or use dry, frozen, or no-boil noodles. You'll need enough to make 4 layers in an approximately 13 x 9 baking dish)
8 to 10 fresh sage leaves, thinly sliced
2 cups grated Parmesan
¼ cup flat-leaf parsley leaves, chopped

Preheat oven to 350 F.

If you're using the dried porcinis: Cover dried mushrooms with boiling water and let them sit for 15 minutes. Remove them from the water (reserve liquid for future use), rinse to remove any grit, and chop finely.

In a large saucepan, heat 2 tablespoons of the olive oil and the pancetta (if using) over medium heat. After the pancetta has released some fat, add the onions and celery. When the vegetables have softened, 2 to 3 minutes, add the garlic and porcinis. Cook until the vegetables are soft, about 5 minutes more, and set aside.

In a mixing bowl, toss the squash cubes with the remaining 2 tablespoons olive oil, nutmeg, salt, and pepper. Roast the squash on a baking sheet until completely tender, 20 to 25 minutes.

To assemble the lasagna, lightly oil a baking pan, about 13 x 9. Spread a thin, even layer of béchamel on the bottom of the baking dish. Place one layer of pasta sheets, then a layer of squash and vegetables or the squash puree, ½ cup cheese, ⅓ of the parsley and ⅓ of the sage. Add salt and pepper and ½ to 1 cup béchamel. Lay down another layer of pasta and repeat the previous steps twice. On the fourth, final, layer of pasta, spread a generous layer of béchamel so that all the pasta is covered thoroughly. Sprinkle with the remaining ½ cup cheese, salt, and pepper.

Bake the lasagna until the top is golden and the sides are bubbling, 45 to 50 minutes. Let sit for a few minutes before cutting and serving (see Notes and Variations below).

NOTES AND VARIATIONS

Any winter squash is fine. Butternut has the best yield, is easiest to cut, and I love the texture and flavor. If you want a smoother filling, puree the squash with the vegetables and a bit of the mushroom-soaking liquid, as needed.

Lasagna may be made a day in advance. Bring the pan to room temperature before you bake or bake cold at 325 F for 1 to 2 hours. You may also freeze the lasagna before or after it is cooked.

Substitute spinach, mushrooms, roasted onions, kale, broccoli, or other vegetables for the winter squash. Substitute marinara sauce for the béchamel for a lighter recipe or use Bolognese sauce for a classic meat meal. At the Institute, when we make lasagna Bolognese, we add a lot more carrot and celery than a traditional recipe would call for (see recipe, page 161).

PASTA DOUGH—ALL PURPOSE

At the Institute we don't have time to make our own pasta. We use frozen fresh egg-pasta sheets. If you want to experiment with a scratch recipe, here is my basic recipe for pasta dough. It will make a difference, particularly if you use really good, fresh eggs. **MAKES 2 POUNDS**

7 cups all-purpose, unbleached flour	1 tbsp. salt
8 whole eggs plus 6 egg yolks	Cornmeal (for sprinkling)

Place flour, eggs, egg yolks, and salt in a food processor, and pulse until meal resembles couscous. (It should be pretty dry, although it should hold together if you press it together in your fist.) If the dough is wet, add a little more flour. If

Menu 28, lasagna two ways

it's too dry, add another yolk, then adjust with a bit more flour if necessary.

Wrap the dough in plastic wrap and set it to rest at room temperature for about 1 hour.

To roll lasagna sheets, begin with pasta machine set at the thickest setting, #1, and work down to the thinner #6.

As you produce a sheet of pasta, place it on a baking sheet and sprinkle lightly with cornmeal to prevent sticking. For this recipe, the pasta does not have to be cooked before building the lasagna. If you want to make the pasta in advance, I would use sheets of parchment between the layers along with the cornmeal. Wrap the sheets in plastic wrap and lay them flat in the freezer to store. If you want to cook these sheets to make a fancy free-form plated lasagna, cook the sheets in salted boiling water for 2 minutes, drain, and serve.

LASAGNA BOLOGNESE

This is a classic recipe from Bologna, using meat sauce and béchamel. At the Institute we use more vegetables in the ragù (meat sauce) than is typical in Italy. **SERVES 12**

3 to 4 cups béchamel (see recipe, page 63)
1½ lb. to 2 lb. pasta sheets for lasagna (see recipe, page 159; or use dry, frozen, or no-boil noodles. You'll need enough to make 4 layers in an approximately 13 x 9 baking dish)

3 cups grated Parmesan, best quality you can afford

FOR THE RAGÙ

3 tbsp. olive oil
4 oz. pancetta, cut into a fine dice (optional)
6 celery ribs, cut into a fine dice
3 small carrots, peeled and finely diced or shredded
1 yellow onion, cut into a fine dice
Salt & black pepper
2 cloves garlic, finely chopped

2 lb. ground beef
Pinch freshly grated nutmeg
1 cup dry white wine
2 bay leaves
2 sprigs thyme
1 cup milk
3 cups canned whole plum tomatoes, pureed for a classic sauce, rough-chopped for texture

Preheat oven to 350 F. Heat the oil and pancetta (if using) in a 6-quart saucepan over medium heat. After the pancetta has released some fat, add the celery, carrots, onions, and a pinch of salt and pepper and cook for 5 minutes. When the vegetables have softened a little, add the garlic and cook until the vegetables are completely soft, 6 to 8 minutes more.

In same pan add the meat, nutmeg, and another pinch of salt and pepper. Cook over medium-high heat until the meat appears to be cooked, 5 to 7 minutes. Turn the heat to medium, and add the wine, bay leaves, and thyme. Cook at a slow simmer until the liquid evaporates. Add the milk, and when it evaporates, add the tomatoes. Reduce the heat and simmer for 2 to 3 hours. Skim the fat off the top as the sauce cooks. When it's finished, the sauce should be velvety and the meat tender.

To assemble the lasagna, place a little ragù on the bottom of a 13 x 9 baking dish. Cover with sheets of pasta one layer thick. Add ⅓ of the remaining ragù, 1 cup béchamel, ⅓ cup grated Parmesan, and repeat twice. After adding the final layer of pasta (the 4th), cover the top with a generous layer of béchamel and grated cheese, and bake 45 to 50 minutes. (You can make this the night before and refrigerate, but a cold lasagna will take longer to cook.) When it's done, the surface should be golden and bubbling. Let the lasagna rest for a few minutes before cutting.

NOTES AND VARIATIONS

When I have lots of time, I let the Bolognese cook for up to 4 hours for a classic, rich, very tender, sweet sauce. When I'm in a hurry I serve the sauce after it has cooked for only 1 hour. I might add extra tomatoes, but the resulting very homey, meaty sauce has a pleasant chewy texture when the tomatoes are less incorporated. It is also popular at home over penne with lots of cheese and a touch of butter.

BRUSSELS SPROUTS WITH GARLIC

Brussels sprouts are bitter for some folks, but they are more popular as time goes on. Sometimes we roast them. In this recipe they are sautéed and steamed. **SERVES 4-6**

½ cup olive or vegetable oil
2 to 8 garlic cloves, smashed or
roughly chopped
1 lb. Brussels sprouts, base
trimmed and cut in half

½ cup water
Salt

Heat the oil in a saucepan over medium heat until it's hot. Add the garlic, and when it begins to color add the Brussels sprouts and water to create steam. Cover and cook for 2 to 3 minutes. (Be careful, the oil may spatter when you add the water.) Uncover, letting the water evaporate while cooking until the Brussels sprouts are tender, 10 to 12 minutes. Toss occasionally to help them cook evenly, and serve with a pinch of salt.

APPLE WITH SAGE, MAPLE, AND LEMON

Fresh green apples such as Crispins, Mutsus, or Granny Smiths are just tart enough to be a used in this simple savory salad. **SERVES 6-8**

15 to 18 fresh sage leaves,
thinly sliced
3 tbsp. vegetable oil
4 to 6 fresh, crisp green apples

Juice of 2 lemons
2 tbsp. olive oil
2 tsp. maple syrup
Sea salt & black pepper

In a small saucepan over medium-low heat, combine the sage and vegetable oil, and cook until the sage curls up and darkens. When the leaves are done, you'll be able to see, after 2 to 3 minutes, that all the moisture in the leaves has been cooked away. Transfer the leaves to a paper towel using a slotted spoon. They should quickly stiffen and crumble when you crush one. Sprinkle with sea salt and set aside.

Slice the apples, skin on, or julienne and place in mixing bowl. Toss the apple with the lemon juice to season and prevent the apple from turning brown. Add the olive oil, maple syrup, and a pinch of salt and pepper. Place in the serving bowl, gently toss, top with the fried sage, and serve.

GRAIN MUSTARD VINAIGRETTE

For information on greens and instructions on dressing a salad, see page 229. Makes about ¾ cup. **SERVES 4-6**

¼ cup red wine vinegar, or substitute whichever vinegar you prefer
2 tbsp. whole-grain mustard

¼ cup olive oil
¼ cup grape seed oil
Salt & black pepper

Whisk together the vinegar and mustard. Slowly whisk in the oils until emulsified. You may use all olive oil; taste and see if that's your preference. Add a few drops of cold water at the end if you want to thin the vinaigrette slightly. Add salt and pepper, taste, and adjust.

POACHED PEARS

This is a fancy-sounding but uncomplicated and popular dessert. At the Institute a poached pear is a simple dessert to make and serve plain. At home, my family will look for a cookie or pound cake accompaniment. **SERVES 6-8**

4 ripe pears, peeled, halved, and cored
2 qt. liquid, all water or half white or red wine (see Notes and Variations below)

½ cup raw sugar or maple sugar
2-in. piece cinnamon stick (see Notes and Variations below)

Put pears, water (or water and wine), sugar, and cinnamon stick in a saucepan over medium heat. Simmer until the pears are tender, 5 to 15 minutes. The cooking time will vary depending on the ripeness of the fruit. Serve the pears plain with their own syrup or accompanied by cake or a cookie. You may also top with cream or ice cream.

NOTES AND VARIATIONS

If you use a sweet wine, adjust the amount of sugar to your taste. The more you reduce the volume of the syrup, the sweeter it will be. You can always adjust the tanginess by adding a squeeze of fresh lemon juice.

You may add to or replace the cinnamon stick with one or all of the following spices: bay leaves, cloves, juniper or allspice berries, black peppercorns, cardamom pods, coriander, fennel seed, or citrus zest.

Local apples and pears in season

MENU 29

HUMMUS WITH PARSLEY SALAD, ROASTED RED ONIONS, TOMATOES, AND ARUGULA (WRAP OPTION)

Hummus is so widely available in supermarkets today it may not seem worth the effort to make your own. I still make my own so that I can adjust the ingredients just the way I like—a little more lemon or garlic or extra tahini, depending on my mood. Tomatoes are a good addition to this wrap if the tomato season lasts through October, which it does in good years. **SERVES 4**

1 batch hummus (see recipe, page 166)
1 red onion, thinly sliced
2 tbsp. olive oil, divided
Salt & black pepper
2 cups flat-leaf parsley leaves, loosely packed
1 tbsp. of your favorite vinegar (I like sherry in this recipe)

4 12-in. flour tortillas for wraps, (we like the whole wheat variety from Harbar, but any will do)
2 bunches arugula, rinsed and dried
2 ripe tomatoes, sliced or chopped
Hot sauce (optional)
Lemon wedges (optional)

Toss the sliced onions with 1 tablespoon olive oil, salt, and pepper. Set aside.

Dress the parsley leaves with vinegar, remaining 1 tablespoon olive oil, salt, and pepper. Set aside.

To make a hummus plate, arrange a spoonful of hummus, a pile of onions, parsley salad, arugula leaves, and tomatoes on individual plates or place items on one big platter. Serve with optional hot sauce and lemon wedges on the side.

To make wraps, char the tortillas over a medium flame on your stovetop or in your broiler, or toast them in a dry skillet. Move them around often, taking care that the tortillas don't burn or get brittle. Place a tortilla on a cutting board. Spread a generous amount of hummus in a wide band in the middle of the tortilla, leaving a 2-inch border on each side with no spread.

Add ¼ of the arugula, ¼ of the onions, and ¼ of the parsley salad to each wrap. It takes a little practice not to overstuff the wrap; then again, understuff it and you'll have too much bread. Fold both sides of the tortilla in toward the middle and, starting at the end nearest you, roll away from yourself. Try to roll tight enough that you can cut the wrap in half (see Notes and Variations below).

HUMMUS

My hummus recipe is dense with flavor and richness. To lighten it, add a little extra water or chickpea broth. I like to squeeze in lots of lemon, hot sauce, and extra olive oil. I prefer the flavor and texture of dried chickpeas and the resulting broth, both of which we use to make hummus. Chickpeas cook faster if they're soaked overnight, but it isn't essential. They tend to cook faster than most other dried beans, more like lentils.

MAKES ABOUT 3 GENEROUS CUPS

1 cup dried chickpeas, soaked overnight in water (substitute 1 cup of rinsed canned chickpeas)
Aromatic vegetables for cooking beans—any or all of the following:
1 bay leaf
1 carrot, peeled and cut into 2-in. pieces
1 bunch of cilantro stems, rough chopped
3 garlic cloves, peeled and sliced in half
A few celery stalks, cut into 2-in. pieces

½ onion
A few parsley sprigs
⅓ cup tahini
¼ cup freshly squeezed lemon juice
3 garlic cloves
¼ to ½ cup reserved chickpea broth (substitute water or vegetable stock if you're using canned chickpeas rather than the liquid in the can)
½ cup olive oil
1 tsp. salt
½ tsp. black pepper

Chickpeas will cook without soaking them, just allow extra time. Cook the chickpeas over medium heat in a large pot covered with water along with the aromatics until tender, 1 to 1¼ hours, less for soaked chickpeas. The time will vary depending on the age of the beans. (The soaking and cooking can be done a few days in advance.) Drain the chickpeas and reserve the cooking liquid.

In the bowl of a food processor combine the chickpeas, tahini, lemon juice, and garlic. Process until smooth. Add ¼ cup of the cooking liquid or water. If the mixture is too stiff, add more of the cooking liquid (hummus will thicken when it's cold; see Notes and Variations below). Drizzle in the olive oil and add salt and pepper.

NOTES AND VARIATIONS

This is just one of the many wraps we make at the Institute. Other ingredients we use in various combinations include: baba ghanoush, roasted peppers, roasted summer squash, red wine vinegar, olive oil, basil, lettuce, feta, olives, romaine, lemon, cherry tomatoes, olive oil, and mint.

BUTTERNUT SQUASH (OR SWEET POTATO) SALAD WITH JALAPEÑO, CILANTRO, AND LIME

Naturally sweet vegetables pair well with spicy, tangy flavorings in this dish. No need to add extra oil to the salad, as the squash is tossed in oil before it's roasted. **SERVES 4-8**

1 medium butternut squash, peeled and cut into 1-in. to 2-in. pieces, about 4 cups (substitute 4 medium sweet potatoes, peel on)
¼ cup vegetable oil
Salt & black pepper
3 jalapeños, sliced (remove all seeds and membranes for a mild salad, use the whole pepper for more heat)

Juice of 3 limes
1 bunch cilantro, rough chopped
3 scallions, cut into ¼-in. slices (use the whole trimmed scallion, green and white parts)
2 tsp. fresh red chiles, sliced (optional)
½ cup toasted pumpkin seeds (optional)
1 roasted red onion (optional)

Preheat oven to 400 F. Toss the squash in a bowl with the oil, salt, and pepper, and spread on a baking sheet. Roast until tender and as golden brown as you like, about 17 to 20 minutes. Set aside to cool.

In a mixing bowl, toss the squash together with the jalapeños, half the lime juice, cilantro, scallions, red chiles (if using), and pumpkin seeds (if using). Taste and adjust the flavor with the remaining lime juice, salt, and pepper.

NOTES AND VARIATIONS

For a quick version, toss the roasted squash or sweet potatoes with salt, lemon, and ancho chile powder. Or serve a premade sauce like Sambal Oelek plain or mixed with mayonnaise on the side.

CUCUMBER WITH YOGURT, GARLIC, AND DILL

This cucumber recipe has similar ingredients to tzatziki but with more cucumber, making it a salad rather than a sauce or condiment. When tomatoes are in season, add a few wedges, likewise radishes or red peppers. **SERVES 6–8**

4 to 6 full-size cucumbers, or twice as many Kirby cucumbers, peeled	3 tbsp. olive oil
	4 tsp. fresh dill, snipped (optional)
½ cup plain yogurt, your favorite brand	4 tsp. fresh chives, snipped (optional)
1 tbsp. white wine vinegar	Salt & black pepper

If the cucumber seeds are large or you simply prefer to remove them as I do, split the cucumbers lengthwise and use a spoon to scrape out the seeds. Slice the cucumbers into half moons, place them in a mixing bowl, and toss together with the yogurt, vinegar, oil, and if using, the mint, dill, and chives. Add salt and pepper, taste, and adjust.

NOTES AND VARIATIONS

To be more frugal, or if you like the cucumber seeds, leave the cucumbers whole and cut them into quarters lengthwise and then into 1-inch chunks. This is good for big groups, but if you leave the seeds in, dress the cucumbers just before serving, as they will release more liquid with the seeds remaining.

There are many appealing variations you may want to try using this recipe as a base. Consider using lemon juice or red wine vinegar in place of the white wine vinegar, and adding minced garlic, sliced green peppers, radishes, or chopped raw asparagus.

RED WINE VINEGAR AND OLIVE OIL DRESSING

For information on greens and instructions on dressing a salad, see page 229. Makes ¾ cup. **SERVES 4–6**

½ cup olive oil	Salt & black pepper
¼ cup red wine vinegar	

Combine oil, vinegar, salt, and pepper, and shake before using. This is not an emulsified dressing.

BAKED APPLES

Baked apples are good plain, which is how we serve them at the Institute. For a fancier dessert, serve with whipped cream, custard sauce, ice cream, heavy cream, yogurt, sour cream, cheddar cheese, pudding, or cookies. **SERVES 4**

4 apples, any variety (see Notes and Variations below)

4 tsp. to 8 tsp. raw sugar, maple syrup, honey, or brown sugar (see Notes and Variations below)

2 tsp. ground cinnamon (see Notes and Variations below)

Juice of 1 lemon

4 tsp. unsalted butter (optional)

2 cups to 3 cups water and/or wine, any type will do (f you use a sweet wine, adjust the sugar by cutting it in half or to your taste)

Preheat oven to 350 F. Leaving the apples whole, peel each one at least halfway or more down, leaving an inch or so of peel around the bottom of the apple. I like to peel most of the apple so that the outside is exposed to the heat and will caramelize. Cut out most of the core, leaving a bit at the bottom so that the hole is a deep bowl that gathers sweet syrup. If the apples are soft, they may fall apart, but they will still taste good.

Place the peeled and cored apples in a baking dish that just holds them. Place a teaspoon of butter (if using) in each core hole. Mix the sugar and cinnamon in a bowl, and sprinkle ¼ of the amount on top of each apple. Add enough water or wine to the pan so that it's about ½-inch deep.

Bake the apples for a total time of 40 to 45 minutes. After the first 15 minutes, baste the apples with the water in the pan so that it mixes with the butter, sugar, and cinnamon . If the pan is dry add a little more water. Repeat this step in 10 minutes and again in 10 more. After 40 to 45 minutes total, the apples should be done, depending on how large they are. A paring knife should go through the center easily, like a well-done baked potato. Some varieties, such as McIntosh, will be softer than others, some will stay firm, like Crispins. Serve hot, room temperature, or cold with the sweet syrup from the pan.

A typical baking apple is a Rome. Big and meaty, when it bakes it gets soft and juicy. A sweeter apple such as a McIntosh or Golden Delicious is also good. A tangy, green Crispin will remain tart and firm.

I love maple syrup and maple sugar as sweeteners. In this simple recipe you're free to use whatever you like. The amount you use is also flexible depending on your taste and the variety of apple you choose. It's possible to use no sugar at all and enjoy only the natural sweetness of the apple. If you use honey, be aware that it burns easily, so watch the apples carefully.

When I buy cinnamon from Penzey's, I tend to use the Chinese for savory applications and the Vietnamese for desserts. For baked apples, the mellow Chinese cinnamon is quite nice. You may use any variety or put a small piece of cinnamon stick in each apple instead. You may also substitute nutmeg or mace for the cinnamon.

MENU 30

MOROCCAN VEGETABLE STEW

Years ago I spent a summer in Morocco, and I had the good fortune to return to an apartment in Rabat every two weeks where I could cook with the ingredients I had bought at the local markets. I bought cookbooks in Morocco although I already owned Paula Wolfert's *Mediterranean Cooking* and *Couscous and Other Good Food from Morocco*. When I returned to New York, I made the same recipes over and over using the ingredients I had become so familiar with while traveling, until the food almost felt like it was part of my own heritage. In the Hudson Valley we usually don't get a frost until late October and just before the frost we have the most amazing selection of late summer and early autumn vegetables, perfect for preparing this recipe fully vegetarian. If I want meat, I braise it on the side and folks add as desired. In winter, with canned tomatoes, if no one is vegetarian I might braise chicken or lamb right in the stew from the start. (If you'd like to add meat, see Notes and Variations below.) In winter, I use yams, winter squash, parsnips, or celery root instead of green beans and summer squash for a heartier stew. In spring, if you have the patience, try fava beans. **SERVES 6–8**

A plate from Menu 30

1½ cups cooked chickpeas (see recipe, page 84)
4 tbsp. unsalted butter (olive oil may be substituted or a combination of both)
1 cup chopped cilantro
1 large onion, cut into ¼-in. dice
1 3-in.-long cinnamon stick or 1 tsp. ground cinnamon
1 tsp. salt
½ tsp. black pepper
3 long dried red chiles, such as arbol or pequin (optional)
6 to 8 ripe tomatoes, peeled and roughly chopped (plum tomatoes are best, but beefsteak tomatoes work fine; see Notes and Variations below)
2 cups liquid reserved from cooking chickpeas, or water if you're using canned chickpeas

½ cup raisins
Generous pinch of saffron (or substitute turmeric)
2 carrots, peeled and cut into ½-in. dice
2 turnips, peeled and cut into ½-in. dice
1 cup green beans, cut into 1-in. pieces
2 summer squash, cut into ½-in dice
1 to 2 cups harissa (see recipe, page 175)
2 cups rough chopped cilantro (for garnish)
1 cup almonds, toasted and chopped (for garnish)

Cook chickpeas according to recipe on page 84. Set aside along with 2 cups of the cooking liquid.

In an 6-quart pot, heat the butter or olive oil and add cilantro, onions, cinnamon stick, salt, pepper, and dried red chiles (if using), and cook over medium heat until the onions are soft but not brown, about 8 to 10 minutes.

Add the tomatoes, chickpea cooking liquid or water, raisins, and saffron. Let the stew simmer for 8 to 10 minutes. Add the carrots and turnips and simmer for another 15 minutes. Add the green beans and cook for 5 minutes before adding the summer squash and simmering for another 2 minutes. Remove from the heat and garnish with harissa (see page 175), cilantro, and almonds (if using).

NOTES AND VARIATIONS

To prepare with braised meat, make a marinade of 3 cloves garlic, 1 medium onion, 6 sprigs cilantro, ¼ cup olive oil, and juice from one lemon juice in a blender, and marinate a whole lamb shoulder or whole chicken, from 1 hour to overnight. You can braise it alone in a baking dish with 2 inches water at 350 F until cooked but not falling off the bone, 1 to 1½ hours for the lamb, 50 to 60 minutes for the chicken, until it reaches 160 F on an instant-read thermometer. Take the meat off the bone and set aside. Heat the braising liquid again for another 8 to 10 minutes (reduce the sauce as much as you like, to concentrate the flavor) and right before serving, add the boneless cut-up meat back to the reduced sauce and serve on the side of the vegetarian stew. You can also braise the marinated meat right in the stew by adding it when you add the tomatoes.

For a quicker version, use boneless meat, chicken thighs, or lamb shoulder. Marinate the meat the same way, if you have time, but marinating isn't necessary. Braise the meat in 2 inches of water in a baking dish at 350 F until the juice from the chicken is clear when you insert the point of a knife, 20 to 25 minutes. The lamb will need 35 to 40 minutes. Cut up the meat and either add to the stew at the last minute or serve separately for people to add as they wish.

For instructions on peeling fresh tomatoes, see page 125.

Menu 30, Moroccan stew, prepared right after the frost with lots of root vegetables

HARISSA

Harissa is the spicy paste of chiles, garlic, and caraway seeds used to season and spice the finished Moroccan stew.

MAKES ABOUT 1¾ CUPS

1 ripe tomato, roasted
(substitute a roasted red
pepper)
3 cloves garlic
Juice of 1 lemon
1 tsp. caraway seeds, toasted
and ground

1 tsp. cayenne pepper
(substitute the equivalent of
dried or fresh red hot chile or 1
tbsp. hot sauce)
Salt & black pepper
1 cup olive oil

Combine tomato, garlic, lemon juice, caraway seeds, cayenne, salt, and pepper in a food processor and work until smooth, about 1 minute. Slowly add the olive oil to emulsify.

COUSCOUS

I use the regular (not instant) variety of couscous. I like whole wheat couscous as well as white, and I use the quick-cook method as opposed to steaming the pasta over the stew. **MAKES 4 CUPS**

2 cups couscous (I like whole
wheat or white)
2 tbsp. olive oil
2 cups boiling water
Salt & black pepper

1 cup amount harissa
1 cup amount chopped and
toasted almonds
1 cup amount chopped cilantro

While the stew is cooking, toss the couscous in a bowl with the olive oil and salt. Add 2 cups boiling water to the pasta. Toss with a fork. Cover with plastic wrap or a lid for 2 to 3 minutes. Uncover and loosen the couscous with a fork to fluff. Serve with the stew and garnish with harissa, chopped almonds, and cilantro.

BEETS WITH BUTTER AND ANISE SEED

Often we serve beets cold in slaw or pickled. In this dish we serve the beets warm with fragrant spice. **SERVES 6-8**

3 beets skin on, tops cut off	Salt
1 tsp. unsalted butter or olive oil	2 tsp. lemon juice (optional)
1 tsp. anise seeds	1 tsp. vinegar (optional)

Preheat oven to 400 F.

Wrap the beets in foil and roast on a baking sheet until knife-tender, about 1 hour. They're done when the jackets slip off easily. Peel the beets under thin stream of water to speed the process and keep your hands from staining quite so much. (If the beets have been in storage and have no tops you may have to peel the skin off with a knife.)

Slice or dice the beets and toss warm in a bowl with butter or olive oil, anise seeds, and salt.

You may add a little lemon or vinegar to this dish.

WATERCRESS VINAIGRETTE

For information on greens and instructions on dressing a salad, see page 229. Makes about ¾ cup. **SERVES 4-6**

1 bunch of watercress, cut into	2 tbsp. vinegar white wine
1-in. pieces, stems and all	vinegar
4 tbsp. olive oil	Salt & black pepper

Mix the watercress, oil, vinegar, salt, and pepper in a blender. This may break if you don't use it right away, which is fine, just shake before using.

POUND CAKE
WITH QUINCE AND ORANGE FLOWER WATER

I use Edna Lewis's pound cake recipe as a guide for all the pound cakes I make. In this recipe I add baked quince and orange flower water to the batter, and I sprinkle raw sugar on top. Orange flower water doesn't last long. Smell it before you use it, and make sure it's beautifully perfumed. Buy a small bottle and replace as needed. **SERVES 8**

1 quince, peeled and cut into ½-in. chunks (substitute pears or apples)

1 cup water

2 tbsp. sugar plus ⅔ cups sugar

1 cup (2 sticks) unsalted, room-temperature butter

2 cups unbleached all-purpose flour (Edna recommends sifting, which is no doubt worth the trouble, but I never do)

¼ tsp. salt

5 eggs, beaten

1 tbsp. vanilla extract

1 tsp. orange flower water (substitute fresh lemon juice, cognac, or rum)

Pound cake with quince and orange flower water

Preheat oven to 300 F.

Combine the quince, water, and 2 tablespoons sugar in a saucepan over high heat. Boil until the quince is tender, 5 to 6 minutes. Quince is spongy and bitter when raw, but silky and tangy like a fragrant, creamy apple when cooked. It needs sweetening.

Prepare a 9 x 5 loaf pan by greasing generously with butter.

Cream the ⅔ cup sugar and butter with a wooden spoon in a mixing bowl or use the paddle attachment of a stand mixer until the butter is soft, pale yellow, and fluffy.

In a mixing bowl, combine the flour and salt.

Still using either a wooden spoon or paddle attachment, alternate adding ⅓ flour mixture and ⅓ beaten eggs until each is incorporated into the batter. Add the vanilla and orange flower water.

Fill the loaf pan with the batter and bake until a knife comes out clean when inserted into the middle of the cake. Depending on your oven, it will take just over 1 hour to bake. Cool for 10 minutes before removing from pan and transferring to a cooling rack. Cool completely before cutting and serving.

The Institute in early November

NOVEMBER MENUS

31

FLAT BREAD THREE WAYS: 180
    CURRIED POTATOES AND MUSTARD SEEDS WITH GREEN YOGURT SAUCE 182
    FETA, MOZZARELLA, WALNUTS, OLIVES, AND MINT 183
    TURNIPS, GREENS, CHEESE, BACON, AND ONIONS 184
BROCCOLI WITH GARLIC 184
GIANT WHITE BEANS WITH PARSLEY AND DILL 185
SHALLOT VINAIGRETTE 186
CHOCOLATE PUDDING 186

32

SPICY CABBAGE WITH BROWN MUSTARD SEEDS 188
WILD RICE 188
CURRIED LENTILS 190
LIME AND TOASTED SESAME SEED VINAIGRETTE 191
WALNUT BAR 191

33

NOODLE SOUP WITH SHIITAKES AND SCALLIONS 192
PORK BELLY 195
NAPA CABBAGE SLAW 196
CIDER-CARDAMOM VINAIGRETTE 198
PEAR TART 198

FLAT BREAD THREE WAYS

When serving flat bread to large groups, it is best to make a crust that is good to eat as the bread comes to room temperature. One way to achieve this is to brush the dough generously with oil. I have included a traditional pizza dough recipe if you're up to making your own. You may, of course, buy a basic dough from your local pizza place to save time. If you make these in advance at home, heating them over a low wood-burning fire is great.

MAKES APPROXIMATELY 6 SMALL OR 1 LARGE PIZZA

1 recipe Pizza Dough (see page 180) or 1 large restaurant-bought
    pizza dough **AND**
1 recipe Curried Potatoes and Mustard Seeds
    with Green Yogurt Sauce (see page 182) **OR**
1 recipe Feta, Mozzarella, Walnuts, Olives, and Mint (see page 183) **OR**
1 recipe Turnips, Greens, Cheese, Bacon, and Onions (see page 184)

FOR THE PIZZA DOUGH

Allow 1½ hours to make the dough, including the rise. You may also make it the night before and allow 30 minutes for it to come back to room temperature. One dough recipe serves 3 to 4, but you can increase the recipe to make a larger batch.

1½ cups water, approximately 100 F (warm tap water is fine)	½ tsp. raw sugar
½ oz. fresh yeast or 1 tsp. dry active yeast	1 tsp. salt
3½ cups unbleached, all-purpose flour (use bread flour if you prefer)	2 tbsp. olive oil plus more for coating the dough and oiling the pan
	Black pepper

Preheat oven to 550 F (or as high as it goes).

Dissolve the water and yeast in a mixing bowl. When a bit of foam starts to float to the surface, you have proofed the yeast and know it's active and okay to use. (In the rare case that your yeast is inactive you will have to try a new batch.) Add the flour and stir with a wooden spoon or use the dough hook of a stand mixer. Add the sugar, salt, and olive oil. Knead with the hook attachment or by hand until the dough is smooth and elastic, 3 to 4 minutes by machine, about 6 to 8 minutes by hand. Form the dough into a ball, coat with oil, and place in a large bowl covered with plastic wrap. Set aside to rise in a warm spot where it should double in size, depending on the temperature of your room, in a little more than an hour. You may also portion the dough into a few small balls for individual flat breads. Refrigerate or freeze the dough at this point for future use if you're working ahead.

Stretch the dough gently until it is as thin as you like. This takes a bit of practice. If you aren't familiar with making pizza, you may use a little flour and a rolling pin to flatten the dough. An irregular shape or thickness is fine. The thinner parts will be more crispy and the thicker parts will be more chewy. I like to hold the ball and slowly let the weight of the dough stretch the ball as I turn it gently, letting it get bigger and bigger until it's quite thin. Use a baking sheet brushed with olive oil to cook this pizza. You may also use a pizza stone. Lay the dough on the oiled pan and stretch the edges a bit more so that the edge is thin (if you prefer a thicker edge that's fine, too). Brush the dough with a little more oil on its surface, and sprinkle with salt and pepper.

Bake the flat bread for 5 to 6 minutes.

Spread whichever topping you've chosen over the surface of the pizza. There should be a generous layer, but I leave spots of dough showing randomly throughout so that there are crispy spots when it's finished.

Rotate the pan and bake for another 5 to 10 minutes until the crust is quite brown. Reduce the oven temperature slightly if you think the topping is cooking too fast. You may like your crust paler, so feel free to experiment with time and temperature.

Remove the flat bread from the oven and slide it on to a cutting board. Cut into pieces with a large knife or a pizza cutter. (If you've made the Curried Potatoes and Mustard Seeds option, top the pieces with Green Yogurt Sauce, or serve it on the side at the table.)

CURRIED POTATOES AND MUSTARD SEEDS WITH GREEN YOGURT SAUCE

The curried potato recipe produces a cross between a samosa and a pizza. The yogurt sauce can be drizzled on top or served on the side. **SERVES 3-4**

2 tbsp. vegetable oil
1 tbsp. sweet curry or Madras curry powder (substitute any curry spice blend; see Notes and Variations, below)
2 lb. potatoes, peeled and cut into a ¼-in. or ½-in. dice (any variety is fine)

2 large Spanish onions, cut into a ¼-in. dice
2 tbsp. brown mustard seeds (yellow are fine)
Salt & black pepper

In a large saucepan over medium heat, pour in the vegetable oil and heat until hot, not smoking. Add the curry powder, then the potatoes and onions, and cook until the potatoes are completely tender and golden and the onions are soft and brown, about 15 to 20 minutes. If the mixture starts to stick, scrape it with a wooden spatula or a spoon. Don't worry if the potatoes and onions start to blend. If the mixture sticks too much, turn off the heat and cover the pan for a few minutes. The steam will release the mixture, and you may continue cooking. Add the mustard seeds, salt, and pepper, and cook 1 minute more. Add to flat bread and bake (see recipe, page 180).

FOR THE GREEN YOGURT SAUCE

1 pint plain yogurt (I like whole milk yogurt, but any yogurt will do), divided
½ cup fresh cilantro, roughly chopped
3 tbsp. lemon juice
2 tbsp. olive oil
3 garlic cloves

2 scallions, roughly chopped
1 to 2 jalapeños, sliced (substitute any chile, depending on the spice level you want, including serrano, or a single scotch bonnet for lots more heat)
Salt & black pepper

Drain the yogurt in a fine mesh strainer over a bowl for 5 to 10 minutes to thicken it (see Notes and Variations below). You may also use thick Greek-style yogurt, which does not need to be drained. Place ½ cup of the drained yogurt, cilantro, lemon juice, oil, garlic, scallions, jalapeño, salt, and pepper in a blender or food processor, and work until smooth. Fold the mixture into the rest of the thickened yogurt, taste, and adjust the salt and heat. If you want a thinner sauce you can pour, stir some of the drained yogurt water back into the sauce.

NOTES AND VARIATIONS

A fresh commercial curry powder blend such as Penzey's sweet curry powder is good, but you may also toast and grind your own blend. For potatoes I might use: 1 tsp. cumin seed, 2 dried red chiles, 2 tsp. fennel seed, ½ tsp. anise seed, 4 cloves, and 1 brown cardamom pod. These amounts will yield more curry powder than you will use in this recipe.

The water that drains from the yogurt may be used in baking recipes in place of buttermilk—to make cornbread, for example. It will last in the refrigerator for a few days.

The potato mixture makes a great roti filling for a meal easier than making pizza. At home I serve a bowl of the warm topping/filling with sides like sliced red onion, yogurt, tomatoes, chiles, mint, and lemon wedges with warm wheat wraps for folks to fill their own way. Sliced lamb is a good small-meat addition.

FETA, MOZZARELLA, WALNUTS, OLIVES, AND MINT

This recipe is tasty hot from the oven or at room temperature like a fancy cracker with topping. It's great with a glass of rough—say, Greek or Algerian—red wine. **SERVES 3-4**

1 lb. feta, crumbled (substitute ricotta salata or any cheese you like)	chopped (I like picholine, arbequina, or niçoise, but any variety will do)
1 lb. fresh mozzarella, cut into ½-in. cubes or sliced	¼ cup olive oil, divided
	Salt & black pepper
4 oz. walnuts, roughly chopped	2 tbsp. roughly chopped mint leaves
4 oz. olives, pitted and roughly	

In a bowl, mix the feta, mozzarella, nuts, olives, and 2 tablespoons of the olive oil, salt, and pepper. Add this topping to the prebaked flat bread. Drizzle with the remaining 2 tablespoons olive oil, and sprinkle with mint leaves.

TURNIPS, GREENS, CHEESE, BACON, AND ONIONS

Bacon is a great way to add a satisfying meat flavor to a meal without adding much meat. Topping varieties are endless, but here is one that's great for the winter. I like the classic condiments of dried oregano and crushed red pepper on the side. **SERVES 3–4**

½ lb. sliced, good-quality bacon, cut into ½-in. pieces and lightly cooked

2 cups boiled white turnips, cut into ¼-in.-thick slices

2 cups sautéed greens such as dandelion, kale, spinach, with or without garlic

1 large Spanish onion, diced and sautéed lightly in 2 tbsp. grape seed oil or bacon fat

8 oz. medium soft cheese (I like Sprout Creek's Pawlett, which has the texture of a young Gouda, but any cheese you like will work)

Salt & black pepper

Crushed red pepper (optional condiment)

Dried oregano (optional condiment)

Combine the bacon, turnips, greens, and onions, and cover the prebaked flatbread. Cook for another 8 to 10 minutes or until medium brown. Add the cheese and bake until melted, about 1 minute more. Add pinch of salt and pepper and crushed red pepper and oregano, if using.

BROCCOLI WITH GARLIC

Broccoli is a great vehicle for garlic, raw or cooked. At home I take the time to peel the stems. At the Institute we slice the head into long strips so that the stems are split and cook through. **SERVES 6–8**

1 to 2 heads broccoli

¼ cup olive oil

12 cloves garlic, more or less according to your taste (see Notes and Variations below), sliced

1 to 2 dried red chiles (optional)

Salt & black pepper

Use the broccoli stems, but peel away the toughest skin. Cut the broccoli into manageable pieces, either thin, full-length florets, or chopped into 2-inch pieces, stem and all.

Heat the oil in a small saucepan over medium heat. Add the garlic slices and red chiles (if using), and sauté until the garlic begins to turn golden brown. Remove the pan from the heat and stir occasionally, as the garlic will keep cooking.

Boil or steam the broccoli until it reaches the desired doneness. I like broccoli tender, but still bright green. Drain and toss with garlic, salt, and pepper.

NOTES AND VARIATIONS

How you prepare the garlic depends on your time and inclination. For large groups, we purée the cloves with vegetable oil and salt and then toss or drizzle the garlic oil over the cooked broccoli before serving. Finely chopping the garlic and adding it raw or sautéing lightly cooked broccoli with the garlic are also good.

GIANT WHITE BEANS WITH PARSLEY AND DILL

These large white beans are in the lima bean family. We buy dried varieties, and Divina makes a good-quality canned version.

SERVES 8

½ lb. dried large white beans, debris removed and soaked overnight and drained
1 head garlic, peeled
2 celery ribs, peeled and cut into 2-in. pieces
1 carrot, peeled and cut into 2-in. pieces
Stems from a bunch each, dill and parsley (tie with string if you want to remove the stems easily from the pot)

1 cup roughly chopped flat-leaf parsley
¼ cup chopped dill
2 tbsp. olive oil
Juice of 3 lemons
Salt & black pepper

Place the soaked beans, garlic, celery, carrot, and herb stems in a soup pot with enough water to cover the contents by 2 inches. Bring to a boil, skim the foam, and simmer over low heat until the beans are tender. This may take from 1 to 3 hours depending on the beans. They should be fully tender and creamy inside. Drain the beans, reserving the cooking liquid, but discarding the vegetables and herb stems.

Toss the beans in a salad bowl with parsley, dill, ¼ cup of the cooking liquid, olive oil, lemon juice, salt, and pepper. Serve warm, cold, or at room temperature.

NOTES AND VARIATIONS

Sometimes we add thinly sliced red onions, roasted red peppers, celery, fennel, fresh herbs, sliced raw chiles, or dried oregano to these beans. For beans and greens, mix equal amounts sautéed greens (see recipe, page 29) and these beans.

SHALLOT VINAIGRETTE

For information on greens and instructions on dressing a salad, see page 229. Makes ¾ cup. **SERVES 4-6**

3 tbsp. sherry vinegar
2 tsp. Dijon mustard
½ cup olive oil, or use half grape seed oil

2 tbsp. finely chopped shallot
Salt & black pepper

In a bowl, whisk together the vinegar and mustard. Slowly whisk in the oil until emulsified. Add the shallots, salt, and pepper, and taste. Adjust the salt and pepper.

CHOCOLATE PUDDING

My all-time favorite desserts are chocolate ice cream, too hard to serve a large group, and chocolate pudding, which is easy to serve a crowd. This recipe can be made up to three days in advance. I like it served cold and plain, but add whipped cream, berries, or both, if you like. **SERVES 4-6**

2 cups whole milk	8 large egg yolks
1 cup heavy cream	½ cup raw sugar
8 oz. bittersweet chocolate	2 tsp. vanilla extract
finely chopped (70% cacao	1 tsp. espresso or Kahlúa
works well)	

Scald the milk and cream in a saucepan over medium heat. Remove from the heat and add the chocolate. Stir once and let the chocolate rest to finish melting undisturbed.

Blend the eggs and sugar in a mixing bowl until just mixed.

While warm but not very hot, blend the chocolate and milk in the pan and then slowly add to the egg-sugar mixture and blend until smooth. Add the vanilla and espresso (or Kahlúa), and pour the mixture back in the pot and, stirring continually, cook until the pudding reaches 162 F on an instant-read thermometer. Strain the pudding through a sieve, and pour into individual cups (or a 1-quart soufflé dish). Cover with plastic wrap and refrigerate until cold, about 45 minutes.

NOTES AND VARIATIONS

You may steep spices such as cardamom, cinnamon, mace, chiles, or fennel seed in the milk and cream to flavor the pudding.

Chocolate pudding

SPICY CABBAGE
WITH BROWN MUSTARD SEEDS

I love the popping sensation and pleasantly bitter taste of mustard seeds with soft-cooked cabbage. If you make the cabbage without the lentils or with lentils but no curry seasoning, try adding curry powder to the cabbage. Instead of tofu, you might add sautéed, ground lamb or diced chicken. **SERVES 4-6**

¼ cup vegetable oil
1 Spanish onion, thinly sliced
2 green or red chiles, sliced with seeds for extra heat
½ head green cabbage, thinly sliced
1–2 tbsp. mustard seeds (I like the brown ones)

1 lb. soft tofu, cut into 1-in. dice (optional)
Salt & black pepper
1 lemon (optional)
2 tbsp. chopped cilantro (optional)

Heat the oil in a large saucepan over medium-high heat. When the oil's hot, add the onions and sliced chiles, and cook until they begin to brown and soften. Add the cabbage, stirring as you sauté. (The cabbage will shrink by at least half.) As it begins to deflate, add the mustard seeds. The cabbage is tasty firm with a little bite left or cooked down until soft. Add the optional tofu cubes and heat until the tofu is very warm. Add salt and pepper, taste, and adjust. If you like, you may brighten the taste with a squeeze of lemon juice and serve more wedges on the side. Top with cilantro (if using).

WILD RICE

I buy a good-quality, long-grain wild rice from Minnesota. Usually at the Institute we combine the wild rice with white or brown rice, but at home a small amount of straight wild rice is a special treat. I like to cook it in boiling water like pasta, draining it when it's done as I like it or just when it begins to splay but still has an almost crunchy texture. **SERVES 6-8**

2 qt. water
Pinch salt (optional)

2 cups wild rice

Bring water to boil in a medium pot. Add salt, if desired. Add wild rice, cover, and boil until rice is desired doneness, about 35 to 45 minutes, but check frequently after 25 minutes. Drain, and serve warm, plain, or tossed with butter and salt.

Menu 32, spicy cabbage with brown mustard seeds

CURRIED LENTILS

I like all varieties of lentils. In this recipe the peeled split yellow or red lentils are delicious, but any variety is fine. Yellow and red lentils will fall apart, but the brown or green ones will stay intact.

SERVES 6-8

2 tbsp. mixed seeds, such as fennel, anise, and cumin seeds, all toasted, a few cloves, all ground
1 tsp. turmeric
½ cup vegetable oil
1 large Spanish onion, cut into a 1-in. dice
8 garlic cloves, chopped
6 scallions, thinly sliced or chopped

1-in. piece fresh ginger, peeled and minced
1 bay leaf
4 cups water or vegetable stock
2 cups dried lentils
1 cup peeled and diced tomatoes, (canned is fine; optional)
1 cup unsweetened coconut milk
Salt & black pepper

In a small bowl combine the ground seed mixture with the turmeric and set aside. (You may substitute a premade ground curry blend.)

Heat the oil in soup pot. Add the onions, garlic, scallions, ginger, and bay leaf, and sauté until the onions are soft. Add the water or vegetable stock, lentils, and tomatoes (if using), and simmer for about 30 minutes, stirring occasionally. If the liquid is too thick, add more water or stock. If the lentils are tender but there's too much broth, boil longer to reduce the liquid. When the lentils are tender, add the coconut milk and simmer until the liquid reduces by half. Taste, and add salt and pepper. Remove the bay leaf before serving.

NOTES AND VARIATIONS

If you're serving these lentils alone or very simply with rice, serve fresh cilantro, sliced green chiles, or hot sauce and a lemon wedge on the side. You may also add lamb, chicken, tofu, or top with a soft fried egg (for recipe, see page 226).

LIME AND TOASTED SESAME SEED VINAIGRETTE

For information on greens and instructions on dressing a salad, see page 229. Makes about ¾ cup. **SERVES 4–6**

Juice of 3 limes
2 tsp. rice vinegar
2 tsp. minced garlic
2 tsp. toasted sesame seeds

1 tsp. honey (optional)
Salt & black pepper
½ cup olive oil

Whisk together the lime juice, vinegar, garlic, sesame seeds, honey (if using), salt, and pepper. Whisk in the oil slowly, until emulsified. Taste the dressing and adjust the salt and pepper. If you like a thinner dressing, add a few drops of water.

WALNUT BAR

To make these blondie-like bars, we use the same recipe as our Chocolate Chip Cookies (for recipe, see page 82) but bake the batter in a pan with lots of walnuts. You can use pecans, peanuts, hazelnuts, chocolate chips, coconut, dried fruit, some whole wheat flour, or make your own version. **MAKES 10–12 PIECES**

12 oz. walnut halves or pieces, divided
2½ cups all-purpose, unbleached flour
1¼ teaspoons baking soda
Pinch salt
1 cup (2 sticks) unsalted, room-temperature butter, plus more to grease the pan

⅔ cup granulated sugar
⅔ cup brown sugar
2 eggs
1½ tsp. vanilla extract

Preheat oven to 350 F. Toast half the walnuts and set aside. Butter a square cake pan, about 9 x 9. Mix together the flour, baking soda, and salt, and set aside.

Using a wooden spoon or the paddle attachment of a stand mixer set at medium high, blend the butter and sugar until the butter is creamy and fluffy.

Mix in the eggs until thoroughly incorporated. Lower the

paddle speed and add the flour mixture, little by little, until mixed. Add the toasted walnuts and vanilla, and incorporate.

Spread the batter into the pan. Sprinkle the untoasted walnuts on top, pressing gently into the batter. Bake until golden brown and a thin knife comes out dry when inserted into the center, 18 to 20 minutes. Cool for 5 to 10 minutes and cut into squares. Wrapped in plastic, these bars will last for days and can be frozen.

MENU 33

NOODLE SOUP
WITH SHIITAKES AND SCALLIONS

Normally, the fresh shiitakes I see at the market have fairly thin flesh with smooth caps. They're very good, but recently I've been able to find the thicker variety with cracked tops that previously I have only been able to buy dried. I like both, but the thick variety is especially meaty, fragrant, and has a very silky texture. Try them for a change if you can find them. This is a very simple vegetarian ramen recipe. It calls for familiar, easy-to-find ingredients and comes together in no time. Use it as a base to add different vegetables, fish, fowl, or meat. **SERVES 4-6**

FOR THE BROTH

6 oz. dried shiitakes, soaked for at least 30 minutes in 1 qt. boiling water
Stems from 12 fresh shiitakes (see soup ingredients below)
1 tbsp. vegetable oil
2 onions, cut into 1-in. dice
2 carrots, cut into 1-in. pieces
6 garlic cloves, halved
1 bunch scallions, green part only (Chinese chives are a great substitute, as are Chinese or European leeks)

1-in. piece fresh ginger, peeled and minced
3 tbsp. soy sauce, (see Notes and Variations below)
1 tbsp. mirin
Soft-cooked egg (optional) (see recipe, page 226)

A meal from Menu 33, noodle soup with shiitake and scallions

After soaking the mushrooms and reserving the liquid, remove and discard the stems and rinse the mushrooms of any remaining grit.

Heat oil in a soup pot over medium heat. Add the carrots and onions and cook for a few minutes before adding the garlic, scallions, rinsed reconstituted mushrooms, fresh mushroom stems, and the water from the dried mushrooms. (Make sure not to use the water at the very bottom of the bowl, which might be sandy.) Simmer until the vegetables are fully cooked, 25 to 30 minutes.

Strain the stock, discarding the vegetables, and set to cool (see Notes and Variations below).

FOR THE FINISHED SOUP

2 tbsp. vegetable oil

12 fresh shiitakes (optional, dried shiitakes will also work), stems removed

12 oz. Chinese wheat noodles (any Asian-style noodles or spaghetti will do), cooked according to package directions and drained (see Notes and Variations below)

1 bunch scallions, both white and green parts, cut diagonally into thin slices

Salt & black pepper

Assorted condiments to top soup, such as Japanese seven spice blend, sesame oil, and Sriracha

Heat oil in a saucepan. If you're using smooth-capped shiitakes, leave the caps whole. If you have the thicker, cracked-cap variety, cut them in half or slice them into ½-inch strips. Add the mushrooms, and sauté until tender, for 2 to 3 minutes. Set aside.

Heat the broth.

Divide the cooked noodles in soup bowls or place them in one big bowl. Pour the hot broth over the noodles. Top with the cooked mushroom caps and sliced raw scallion. Taste and add salt and pepper. Serve with the optional condiments and sides in separate bowls along with the sliced pork belly, if you're preparing the whole menu.

NOTES AND VARIATIONS

There is a nearly unlimited choice when it comes to noodle varieties, including those distinctive to China, Korea, and Japan. We don't make noodles from scratch at the Institute, though at some point I would love to try. Sometimes we use a very simple dried Japanese wheat noodle. Sometimes we use fresh Chinese egg noodles. Many of the fresh noodles have food coloring and preservatives added to them, so read the package if that doesn't appeal to you. I avoid the precooked noodles in the refrigerator cases, which I find watery and lacking in flavor. I am still experimenting with all the varieties.

Optional toppings include sautéed greens, Chinese chives, green or yellow or flowering chives in the summer or from an Asian vegetable market, mung bean sprouts, and pickled turnips.

We use a quality basic wheat-free soy sauce at the Institute, but try the various types available at a good Asian market and experiment.

PORK BELLY

Pork belly is used to make bacon, which is usually smoked and cured, as well as pancetta, which is typically cured. One of the nice aspects of this cut (besides the irresistible good taste and texture) is that a little goes a long way. Sometimes we marinate or brine pork belly (see Notes and Variations below), but it isn't necessary. The simple flavor of plain pork with garlic and herbs is delicate and delicious. **SERVES 4–8 (AS A TOPPING FOR SOUP)**

1 lb. pork belly	6 slices fresh ginger
6 garlic cloves, sliced	2 tsp. soy sauce (optional)
3 scallions, chopped	Salt & black pepper

Preheat oven to 250 F.

For a nuttier taste, sear the pork belly on all sides. For a milder flavor try it without searing. Place the pork belly in a baking pan. Toss the garlic, scallions, ginger, and soy sauce (if using), salt, and pepper, coating the pork. Add 2 to 3 cups water to the pan. The water should come about half way up the pork. Cover the dish with foil and roast for 2 hours. After 2 hours, check the pork belly for doneness. It will probably need another hour or so of cooking. When it's done, it will be fatty, but the texture will be soft and jiggly and generally easy to cut. You may leave the pork uncovered for the last hour to brown or keep it covered for a sweet, mild taste that has a steamed quality. (You may cook the pork in advance and reheat it in a pan covered with foil just before serving.) Slice the hot pork belly and serve on a platter or use it to top bowls of noodle soup or steamed rice.

If you choose to brine the pork for a sweet-and-salty cured flavor, I recommend soaking it for at least for 12 hours in a proportion of 1 part salt, 1 part sugar, and 4 parts water with other spices, aromatic vegetables or herbs added to the brine. I like rosemary, garlic, and juniper together. I also like the combination of ginger, garlic, and star anise. You may also marinate the belly, but you'll need, at minimum, 4 hours for the flavors to "stick." Combine ½ cup soy sauce, ¼ cup rice wine, and 3 slices ginger or a simple mix of ¼ cup maple syrup, ¼ cup water, and 4 sliced garlic cloves. You could also try a salt-spice rub with ground black pepper, salt, Sichuan pepper, and crushed star anise.

NAPA CABBAGE SLAW

This recipe is quick, crisp, spicy, and refreshing as a slaw or a topping. Dress shortly before serving as the cabbage releases water after it's dressed. **SERVES 6-8**

1 head Napa cabbage, cut into 1-in. pieces	1 tsp. hot chile oil
3 tbsp. rice wine vinegar (unseasoned)	1 tsp. to 2 tsp. sliced fresh red chile
2 tsp. sesame oil	1 tsp. to 2 tsp. finely minced fresh garlic

Toss the cabbage, rice vinegar, sesame oil, chile oil, red chile and garlic together in a bowl and serve. If the cabbage sits too long it will release water. This will change the texture of the slaw. If you want to make this in advance, you're better off blanching the cabbage and squeezing it to get rid of the extra water before dressing it. It will be less crisp, but the dressing will hold up.

NOTES AND VARIATIONS

In a pinch, simply use 2 tsp. Sambal Oelek in place of the red chile and garlic.

Sassafras turning color. See Menu 13 for a recipe using the leaves and branches with chicken

CIDER-CARDAMOM VINAIGRETTE

For information on greens and instructions on dressing a salad, see page 229. Makes ¾ cup. **SERVES 4-6**

3 tbsp. cider vinegar
1½ tbsp. Dijon mustard
Pinch toasted and ground whole
cardamom seeds,
brown or green

¼ cup grape seed oil
¼ cup olive oil
Salt & black pepper

Whisk together the vinegar, mustard, and cardamom in a bowl. Slowly whisk in the oils until emulsified. Add salt and pepper, taste, and adjust.

PEAR TART

For custard and pastry crust recipes, I turn to Julia Child's *Mastering the Art of French Cooking*. The list of ingredients for pâte brisée here is lifted straight from her book, except I use unrefined sugar instead of white cane sugar. This is a very simple pear tart recipe. **SERVES 6-8**

1 cup all-pupose, unbleached
flour
7 tsp. unsalted butter, cut into
½-in. cubes and kept cold
(European-style, low-moisture
butter works well, a brand such
as Plugras, but there are many)
½ tsp. salt
⅛ tsp. raw sugar plus more for
sprinkling (optional)
1 tsp. to 2 tsp. ice water
(amount varies depending on
how much moisture
is in the flour)

3 to 4 ripe pears, any variety will
do, peeled, cored, and cut into
¼-in. slices
Juice of 1 lemon
2 tbsp. maple syrup or honey
(optional)
1 egg, beaten, or 2 tbsp. heavy
cream to brush on tart edge
before baking (optional)

The key to light, crisp pastry is cold ingredients, very little handling, and as little water as possible. It is convenient to use a food processor, but you must not overwork the flour-and-butter mixture.

Place the flour, butter, salt, and sugar into the bowl of a food processor with the metal mixing blade. Pulse until the butter is distributed throughout, about 20 seconds. Add water 1 teaspoon at a time until the dough just starts to form a ball, another 20 to 30 seconds. Take the still-crumbly mixture out and place it on a clean, dry surface or a large sheet of parchment paper on the counter. Using the heel of your hand, spread a bit of the mixture across the surface to blend, mixing each bit only once. When you're finished with this process gather the still somewhat-crumbly dough into a ball, barely handling it. Wrap the dough in plastic wrap and form and flatten the dough through the plastic into a smooth disk for easier rolling. For the flakiest crust, the butter should be noticeably marbled throughout, not fully incorporated into the flour. Refrigerate the dough for at least 1 hour or overnight.

Remove the dough from the refrigerator about 10 minutes before you're ready to roll the tart, as cold butter is rock solid. Roll the disk about ⅛ inch thick and place on a baking sheet lined with parchment or brushed with butter. Cut out the biggest circle you can and bake the scraps plain or sprinkled with sugar for a kitchen nibble.

Preheat oven to 400 F. Toss pear slices with lemon juice and maple syrup or honey (if using). Distribute the pear slices evenly over the dough, leaving about 2 inches uncovered, around the edge. Entire sliced halves of pears can be placed on the dough with the slices fanned like dominos, or the individual slices can be arranged in concentric circles, as you wish. Turn the crust edges inward covering some of the pear. Brush the folded-over edge of the crust with beaten egg or heavy cream if you want a shiny crust and to help make the coarse, unrefined sugar stick. Refrigerate the raw tart until set, at least 10 minutes. Place the tart in the hot oven, checking and turning in 10-minute intervals to be sure the tart is cooking evenly. Bake until the crust is golden brown, about 30 to 40 minutes. If the sugar is getting dark, and the dough needs to bake longer, lower the oven to 350 F. Allow it to cool a few minutes on the counter before cutting and serving. It can be eaten hot or at room temperature, plain or with custard, ice cream, or whipped cream.

A December snowfall

DECEMBER MENUS

34

35

36

SPLIT PEA SOUP WITH PORK SHOULDER

This split pea soup is made with a whole pork shoulder rather than cured ham. It makes a hearty winter meal. In summer, when you want something lighter, or if you don't eat meat, make the vegetarian version. You may also choose to use less meat, perhaps in the form of a smoked hock or bacon more for a meaty flavor than for the sake of the meat itself. **SERVES 6–8**

FOR THE PORK SHOULDER

1 3 lb. to 4 lb. piece pork shoulder, boneless or bone in	1 quartered onion
Salt	2 celery stalks, cut into 2-in pieces
Assorted aromatic vegetables and spices, such as:	1 celery root, peeled and cut into 2-in. pieces
4 sprigs dill	1 turnip, peeled and quartered
1 bunch parsley	1 bay leaf
1 to 2 peeled carrots, cut into 2-in. pieces	A few cloves
	A few juniper berries

You may prepare the pork a day in advance. Place the meat in a large stock pot, cover with water, add a pinch or two of salt and simmer over medium-low heat for 40 to 50 minutes. Add an assortment of aromatic vegetables. The pork is done when it's fully cooked but still quite tough. Drain the pork stock into a bowl and set aside. Cool the meat and cut it into 2-inch cubes. Leave the fat on if you like the flavor; it will soften and be delicious in the soup. (Any fat you trim can be reserved and rendered for another use.) Set the meat aside along with the bone, if you have one.

FOR THE SOUP

2 tsp. vegetable oil	yellow (see Notes and Variations below)
1 Spanish onion, diced	Salt & black pepper
3 garlic cloves, minced	½ cup chopped parsley (optional)
4 large carrots, peeled and cut into 1-in. pieces	¼ cup chopped dill (optional)
4 celery stalks, cut into 1-in. pieces	3 tbsp. olive oil (optional)
1 bay leaf	2 lemons, cut into wedges (optional)
2 cups dried split peas, green or	

Menu 34, split pea soup with pork shoulder on the side

Heat the oil in the stock pot, add the onions and garlic, and sauté over medium heat until soft, about 5 minutes. Add the carrots, celery, and bay leaf, and cook 2 or 3 minutes more. Add 1 quart of the pork stock (stretch with water or vegetable stock if necessary), the pork cubes, bone (if you have one), and the split peas. Simmer over medium-low heat until the split peas are falling apart and the carrots are tender, 30 to 40 minutes. Remove bay leaf. Add salt and pepper, taste, and adjust, and serve in bowls topped with parsley, dill, and, if you like, a drizzle of olive oil. I like lemon wedges on the side.

CELERY ROOT RÉMOULADE

This is a crunchy, not-too-rich version of the classic French salad. There are many celery root rémoulade recipes in which the julienne-cut root is blanched before it's dressed. This produces a milder, tender salad that's also good. At the Institute we usually make celery root rémoulade with raw root. We also make celery root slaw without the mayo and mixed with other root vegetables such as beets and carrots for a colorful refreshing slaw.

SERVES 6-8

2 large celery roots, peeled (or the equivalent to yield roughly 1 qt. shredded)

2 tsp. to 3 tsp. lemon juice, divided

1 cup mayonnaise, homemade (see recipe, page 205) or store bought, divided

1 tbsp. whole-grain mustard

1 tbsp. finely chopped parsley

1 tbsp. finely chopped shallots (substitute red onion)

Salt & black pepper

Some optional but very tasty additions:

1 tbsp. Dijon mustard

1 tbsp. minced cornichons

1½ tsp. chopped salted capers, rinsed and drained

1 tbsp. snipped chives

If you're using the shredder blade of a food processor, cut the root into approximately 2-inch pieces, and toss with 2 teaspoons lemon juice. If you're using the julienne blade of a mandoline or a box grater, cut the root into larger pieces for easy handling, but still toss them in lemon juice as the root will brown as quickly as a potato when exposed to the air.

Place the shredded root in a mixing bowl. Mix in ½ cup of the mayonnaise, grain mustard, and parsley. Add as much of the rest of the mayonnaise as you like (or use less, as you like), tasting and adjusting for acidity while also adding part or all of the remaining lemon juice along with the shallots. Taste and add salt and pepper. Serve right away or keep covered in the refrigerator until the next day.

MAYONNAISE

4 egg yolks
1 tsp. Dijon mustard
¼ tsp. salt to start,
adjust to taste

⅛ tsp. black pepper
1 cup vegetable oil, divided
1 tsp. lemon juice

Place the egg yolks, mustard, salt, and pepper in the bowl of a food processor and blend until pale yellow and smooth. While the processor is running, slowly drizzle in half the oil. Add the lemon juice and continue slowly adding the rest of the oil until the sauce is thick. Add a few drops of water if you want a thinner sauce. If the sauce breaks, empty the food processor bowl, wash it and dry it, add a new egg yolk and while the processor is running, slowly add the broken sauce to re-emulsify.

ROASTED CAULIFLOWER
WITH JUNIPER AND BLACK PEPPER

When cauliflower is roasted is becomes pleasantly sweet and browns into a crispy snack-like treat. It's one of the vegetables that disappears fastest from the baking sheets in kitchen because folks want a nibble each time they pass by. **SERVES 4-6**

1 large head cauliflower, cut into
small or medium florets
½ cup olive oil or grape seed oil
¼ tsp salt

⅛ to ¼ tsp. black pepper
⅛ tsp. ground juniper berries
1 lemon, cut into wedges

Preheat oven to 400 F. Toss the cauliflower in a bowl with the oil, salt, pepper, and juniper. Spread the florets on a baking sheet and roast until they're brown on the edges and tender when tested with a knife, 20 to 30 minutes. Taste a piece. You might like them firmer, with a little bite (cook for about 20 minutes) or very caramelized, soft, and sweet (cook for about 35 minutes). Serve either piping hot from the oven, at room temperature, or cold with lemon wedges.

CIDER-APPLE VINAIGRETTE

For information on greens and instructions on dressing a salad, see page 229. Makes about 1 cup. **SERVES 4-6**

1 raw apple, peeled and cut into chunks
¼ cup olive oil or hazelnut oil
¼ cup grape seed oil
3 tbsp. French (or good-quality domestic) cider vinegar or white wine vinegar

1 tbsp. Dijon mustard
Salt & black pepper

Place all ingredients in the bowl of a food processor and puree until smooth. Taste and adjust salt and pepper.

HAZELNUT KEEPING CAKE

I offer two recipes here. Both cakes keep well, but one is more like a dense pound cake while the other is closer to a thick, rich, yet drier and toasty shortcake (something like a gâteau Breton). Both are buttery and nutty.

POUND CAKE STYLE

MAKES 2 LOAVES

2¼ cups (5 sticks) unsalted, room-temperature butter, divided
2 cups raw sugar or maple sugar
3½ cups all-purpose, unbleached flour

1 cup whole wheat flour
12 egg yolks
1 cup lightly toasted, ground hazelnuts
2 tsp. brandy or rum
1 tbsp. vanilla extract

Preheat oven to 300 F. Butter 2 9 x 5 loaf pans.

Cream 4 sticks of the butter and sugar using the paddle attachment of a stand mixer or with a hand mixer in a bowl. Add the flour, one cup at a time, then add the egg yolks, a few at a time, incorporating after each addition. Add the hazelnuts and mix before mixing in the brandy and vanilla. Divide the batter into each of the 2 loaf pans.

Bake until the cake is golden brown and a thin knife comes out clean when inserted into the center of the cake, 55 to 65 minutes. Turn cakes out onto a cooling rack after they sit for 5 minutes. Slice and serve once the cakes are completely cool.

Hazelnut keeping cake, pound cake style, made in the summer, garnished with currants and gooseberries

GÂTEAU BRETON STYLE

MAKES 2 LOAVES

3½ sticks unsalted room-temperature butter, divided
1⅓ cups raw sugar or maple sugar
2⅓ cups all-purpose, unbleached flour

⅓ cup whole wheat flour
8 egg yolks
3 cups lightly toasted, ground hazelnuts
1 tbsp. vanilla extract
2 tsp. brandy or rum

Preheat oven to 300 F. Butter 3 7 x 2 round cake pans

Cream 3 sticks of the butter and sugar using the paddle attachment of a stand mixer or with a hand mixer in a bowl. Combine the flours and add one cup at a time, then add the egg yolks, a few at a time, incorporating after each addition. Add the hazelnuts and mix before mixing in the vanilla and brandy. This batter will be very stiff, more like cookie dough. Divide the batter into each of the 3 round pans. Press to distribute the batter evenly in each pan.

Bake until the cake is golden brown and a thin knife comes out clean when inserted into the center of the cake, about 90 to 120 minutes. Turn cakes out onto a cooling rack after they sit for 5 minutes. Cut and serve in small slices once the cakes are completely cool. This cake will keep for a week at least, wrapped in plastic or in a tin.

Hazelnut keeping cake, gâteau Breton style

MENU 35

BEAN CAKES, TWO WAYS

At the Institute, we vacillate between chickpea cakes that are super simple and bean cakes with lots of ingredients that taste more like what most people think of as a veggie burger. In either case, because I care more about flavor than creating a sturdy "burger," I would avoid grilling these as they may not hold together well enough to flip. At the Institute we bake them because we make so many, but at home you can sauté them in a little oil or butter for a crustier outside. These burgers are good on a bun with traditional hamburger condiments or on a plate with sides, as in this winter menu. The recipe is very flexible; once you try it a few times, you can experiment with all kinds of nuts, vegetables, and grains. **SERVES 8**

BLACK BEAN BURGERS WITH AIOLI

Up to 1 cup olive oil (any vegetable oil will work), divided
½ lb. mushrooms, pulsed in food processor until finely chopped
2 large Spanish onions, cut into ¼-in. dice
2 celery stalks, cut into ¼-in. dice
½ cup cooked brown rice (see recipe, page 91)
¼ cup chopped parsley
2 cups cooked black beans or 1 15-oz. can black beans (see Notes and Variations below)
1 cup walnuts
½ cup whole plum tomatoes (canned is fine), cut in half and roasted for 5 minutes to char and soften

8 garlic cloves
½ tsp. salt
¼ tsp. black pepper
1 tsp. cayenne pepper or smoked paprika (optional)
½ cup cooked lentils, brown, green or black (see Notes and Variations below)
½ cup cooked red kidney beans or ½ cup canned beans (see Notes and Variations below)
1 tsp. to 1 tbsp. lemon juice or red wine vinegar

Preheat oven to 400 F. Heat 1 tablespoon of the oil in a saucepan over medium heat, and sauté the mushrooms, onions, and celery until they reabsorb the liquid they release and the mixture is thick and soft, 20 to 25 minutes. Transfer the cooked vegetables to a mixing bowl and stir in the rice and parsley.

In the bowl of a food processor start by pulsing a little of each of the black beans, walnuts, tomatoes, and garlic. Add up to half the remaining oil to help the processor work. Use the pulse button to prevent overworking the mixture; it should have some texture. If it's too stiff or dry, you may add a little water in addition to oil or bean-cooking liquid. The idea is to have a coarse, thick paste the consistency of ground beef.

Add this paste to the rice and vegetable mixture as you work. Mix thoroughly and add salt, pepper, and cayenne or paprika (if using). Add the lentils and kidney beans. Taste and adjust the salt, pepper, spices, and lemon juice or vinegar if your mixture tastes too sweet.

The patties are easier to form if you refrigerate the mixture for 20 minutes, but it's not necessary. Wet your hands slightly and form patties of any size or shape. This recipe should make about 8 7-ounce patties. If baking, brush a baking sheet with oil, place the patties on the sheet, and brush the tops of the patties with oil. Bake until very hot and slightly crisp on the outside, 10 to 12 minutes. If you're sautéing, heat the oil in a large saucepan and cook the burgers over medium-high heat until they're brown on one side. Carefully flip them and brown the other side, cooking 3 to 4 minutes per side. You may form the patties the day before and cook just before serving. They will also hold nicely once cooked in a warm oven; they're soft and a bit fragile when they're very hot. Serve with aioli on the side (see recipe, page 210) or tahini sauce, plain mayonnaise, mustard, roasted pepper purée, salsa, relish, or chutney.

NOTES AND VARIATIONS

If you're using dried beans, soak them the night before or use the quick-cook method (see page 21) and reserve some of the cooking liquid.

If you're using canned beans, drain the liquid and rinse the beans. A good compromise is to use dried black beans and canned kidneys beans since you're using less of the kidneys. The lentils don't need soaking before cooking but may be made the night before, or allow up to an hour for them to cook depending on the variety you choose. (We use regular brown lentils or French green ones.)

AIOLI

This is a classic garlicky, olive oil mayonnaise. **MAKES 1¼ CUPS**

6 garlic cloves, mashed to a smooth paste with a pinch of sea salt	4 egg yolks
	1 cup fruity olive oil
	Salt & black pepper
¼ teaspoon sea salt	

Put mashed garlic cloves, ¼ teaspoon salt, and egg yolks in the bowl of a food processor and blend until the mixture is thick and pale yellow, about 1 minute. While the processor is running, slowly drizzle in the oil until the sauce is thick and emulsified. If it's too thick, add a little water (see Notes and Variations below). Taste and add salt and pepper.

If the sauce breaks, remove the mixture from the processor bowl, clean and dry the bowl, add another egg yolk and start again buy slowly adding the broken sauce to the new egg yolk while the processor is running.

CHICKPEA CAKES WITH TAHINI SAUCE

These are simpler to make than the black bean burgers but are also delicious. **SERVES 8**

Up to 1 cup olive oil (any vegetable oil will work), divided
2 large Spanish onions, cut into ¼-in. dice
4 cups cooked chickpeas (you may substitute 2 15-oz. cans)
1 cup walnuts
8 garlic cloves

Up to 1 tbsp. lemon juice or vinegar, to taste
¼ cup chopped parsley
Salt & black pepper
1 tsp. cayenne pepper or smoked paprika (optional)
1 tsp. toasted, ground cumin seed

Sauté the onions in 1 tablespoon of the olive oil over medium heat until just softened, 5 to 6 minutes. Set aside.

If you're using canned chickpeas, spread them on a baking sheet and bake in a 400 F oven for about 5 minutes to dry them out for a drier cake.

In the bowl of a food processor pulse the chickpeas, walnuts, and garlic. Use up to about ½ cup olive oil, lemon juice, and, if necessary, a little water to achieve a thick, coarse paste. Add the cooked onions, chopped parsley, and either cayenne or paprika and cumin (if using).

The method of forming and cooking patties is the same one used with the black bean patties, but I tend to form these cakes into ovals. The patties will be easier to form if you refrigerate the mixture for 20 minutes, but it's not necessary. Wet your hands slightly and form patties into any size or shape. This recipe should make about 8 7-ounce cakes. To bake, brush a baking sheet with oil, place the patties on the sheet, and brush the tops of the patties with a little oil. Bake for 10 to 12 minutes. They just need to get very hot through and through. They don't become crispy in the oven. If sautéing, heat the oil in a large saucepan and cook the burgers over medium-high heat until they're brown on one side, 3 to 4 minutes. Carefully flip them and brown the other side, cooking 3 to 4 minutes more. You may make the patties the day before and cook before serving. They hold nicely in a warm oven; they're soft and a bit fragile when they're very hot. Serve the tahini sauce (see below) on the side. If you prefer, yogurt plain or with mint or any herb is a great topping for these cakes. We serve hot sauce on the side as well.

TAHINI SAUCE

This is a classic sesame-flavored, vinaigrette-type sauce.
SERVES 6-8

½ cup well-mixed tahini paste
½ cup water
4 tbsp. to 5 tbsp. lemon juice
1 finely minced garlic clove
(optional)

¼ cup olive oil
Salt & black pepper

Combine tahini, water, lemon juice, and garlic (if using) in blender or food processor and puree until smooth. Slowly add the olive oil, then a pinch of salt and some black pepper. I like the sauce on the thin side, like a mustard vinaigrette, but use less water if you like a sauce with the consistency closer to a sour cream salad dressing.

COUSCOUS SALAD WITH ALMONDS, ORANGE, OLIVES, FENNEL SEED, AND CURRANTS

This recipe was inspired by Janet Murff, a great cook and friend. Depending on what you have on hand, it's easily adapted and equally good with all or some of the ingredients I've listed here. Look for whole wheat couscous for your salad; it holds up nicely and has a pleasant grainy texture. This quick method of preparing couscous for a salad works well, but be sure not to use too much water or even the whole wheat variety will be mushy. Whole wheat berries of any variety, quinoa, barley, or other grains may be substituted for the couscous. **SERVES 6-8**

2 cups couscous, whole wheat or traditional, but preferably not instant

½ cup currants, soaked in warm water for 10 minutes to plump and soften (substitute golden or black raisins)

½ cup finely chopped almonds, toasted (blanched or skin on are fine)

¼ cup chopped, pitted olives, niçoise, picholine, oil-cured, or any variety you like

½ red onion, thinly sliced, or minced

4 scallions, thinly sliced

1 tbsp. fruity olive oil

Up to 1 tbsp. red wine vinegar (see Notes and Variations below)

1 tsp. Dijon mustard

1 tsp. minced fresh ginger

1 tsp. coriander seeds (see Notes and Variations below)

¼ tsp. ground cinnamon

Salt & black pepper

½ tsp. orange zest or lemon zest

Cook the couscous according to the recipe on page 175.

In a separate mixing bowl combine the rest of the ingredients. Mix in the couscous, taste, and adjust the salt and pepper.

NOTES AND VARIATIONS

I have grown tired of sweet commercial balsamic vinegar, but in this recipe the sweet, rich taste is good in place of all or part of the red wine vinegar.

The coriander seeds can be used whole or coarsely ground. You may toast them lightly first in a skillet for a stronger flavor. In place of the coriander seeds you might try fennel seeds, cumin, anise, or caraway. Toast the seeds and coarsely grind them or simply use them whole.

An extra step that's tasty but not necessary is to toast the couscous briefly in the oven before adding the hot water. It adds an extra nutty taste to the salad.

You can add fresh chopped parsley, dill, mint, or cilantro to this salad as well as diced celery or fennel.

ROASTED BEETS WITH PINK GRAPEFRUIT AND WATERCRESS

At the Institute when we use citrus in a salad we generally peel the fruit with a knife and then simply slice the fruit "across the equator" so that the slices look like wagon wheels. At home I make supremes by peeling the fruit the same way but by using a paring knife on either side of the membrane, slipping out the sections of fruit so that they're completely peeled. This is not necessary and the fiber is good for you, but I prefer the soft fruit plain.

This is one variation of the many ways we serve cold roasted beets. This salad can be sliced and arranged on a platter or cut into chunks and tossed in a bowl. **SERVES 6–8**

3 beets, roasted (see recipe, page 176), sliced, or cut into bite-size chunks
2 pink grapefruits, cut into supremes (see headnote above)
1 bunch watercress

2 tsp. olive oil
Salt & black pepper
2 tsp. your favorite vinegar (optional)
1 tsp. freshly ground coriander seeds (optional)

Toss the beets into a bowl with the grapefruit. If you like the watercress stems and all, simply cut the bunch into 1-inch or 2-inch pieces. If you prefer the tender parts, then snip or pinch off the thick stems and use the sprigs. Add the watercress, olive oil, and a pinch of salt and pepper to the beets and grapefruit, and toss gently. Add a bit of your favorite vinegar if you want a little extra tang and a spice such as coriander seed for additional flavor.

SHERRY VINAIGRETTE

For information on greens and instructions on dressing a salad, see page 229. Makes a generous cup. **SERVES 6–8**

¼ cup sherry vinegar
2 tbsp. Dijon mustard
Juice of 1 orange

Salt & black pepper
¾ cup grape seed oil

Whisk together the vinegar, mustard, orange juice, salt, and pepper in a bowl. Slowly whisk in the oil until emulsified. Taste and adjust salt and pepper.

TRIPLE-CHOCOLATE COOKIES WITH SEA SALT

These rich chocolate chip cookies have cocoa in the dough and white and semisweet chips added. We sprinkle them with a bit of sea salt and, no matter how many we bake, they all seem to disappear from the tray. **MAKES 24 TO 30 COOKIES**

2 cups all-purpose, unbleached flour
½ cup cocoa
1¼ teaspoons baking soda
Pinch salt
1 cup (2 sticks) unsalted, room-temperature butter
⅔ cup granulated sugar
⅔ cup brown sugar
2 eggs, beaten

1½ tsp. vanilla extract
¾ cup white chocolate, chopped into ½-in. pieces, or use chips
¾ cup semisweet chocolate chips
¾ cup toasted, chopped hazelnuts (optional)
Coarse sea salt for sprinkling
Raw sugar for sprinkling (optional)

Preheat oven to 350 F. Mix the flour, cocoa, baking soda, and salt in a bowl. Set aside.

Using the paddle attachment of a stand mixer on medium high or a wooden spoon if working by hand, beat the butter and sugars until the mixture is light and fluffy.

Add the eggs and blend. Using the low speed on the mixer, add ¼ of the dry mixture at a time. Add the vanilla, the white chocolate, semisweet chocolate, and hazelnuts (if using) and combine. Refrigerate the dough for at least 30 minutes.

Scoop the cookies with a tablespoon and roll into balls 1¼ inches to 1½ inches in diameter. (You may freeze these balls to bake whenever you want them.)

Either grease a baking sheet or cover with a piece of parchment. Space the cookie-dough balls about 2 inches apart; they will spread. Bake for 10 minutes. Rotate the pan in the oven and, if you like, sprinkle a little coarse seat salt and sugar (if using) on each cookie and bake for another 10 minutes. They will have flattened and have cracks and crevices on top but will still be soft when done. We bake these for a little less time than regular chocolate chip cookies because the cocoa isn't so good when it's overdone. Transfer to a cooling rack or eat piping hot and gooey.

POTATO PANCAKES (OR KUGEL)
WITH YOGURT

Potato pancakes take a while to fry. For large groups at the Institute we bake the mixture in the oven and make a kugel (pudding) served with applesauce and yogurt (or sour cream) on the side. This is close to my family recipe, though my father was insistent we use a box grater, and I have moved on to the food processor. Draining the potatoes is a tip I learned from Mimi Sheraton. It really helps reduce hot oil from spattering and keeps the pancakes from sticking to the pan.

MAKES ABOUT 12 TO 16 PANCAKES

6 large russet potatoes, cut into 1-in. or 2-in. chunks (any variety will do although each variety will make a different sort of pancake; there is no need to peel the potatoes, just scrub them clean)
1 very large Spanish onion or 2 medium onions, cut into 1-in. to 2-in. chunks

2 eggs, beaten
3 tbsp. to 4 tbsp. matzo meal
Salt & black pepper
1 qt. vegetable oil
1 cup plain yogurt, any variety (substitute sour cream)

Combine about a third of the potatoes and onions in the bowl of a food processor with the metal blade, and process until the mixture is smooth. Pour the mixture into a fine mesh sieve over a mixing bowl and let it drain while you blend the next third of the potatoes and onions. Empty the sieve into another mixing bowl and drain the next batch of mixture from the processor. Repeat a third time until all the potatoes and onions have been processed and drained.

Pouring the water out that has drained off the shredded potatoes, but reserve the starch at the bottom. Scrape this white paste-like mixture into the bowl with the potatoes.

Add the eggs, matzo meal, salt, and pepper. Too much matzo meal will make the pancakes dry and bland, but a little is good to help hold them together.

Pour the vegetable oil about ¼-inch deep into a large skillet over high heat. When the oil is hot but not smoking, use a serving spoon to add about ½ cup of batter to the hot oil. Repeat, leaving enough room around each pancake so that you can flip them with a spatula. The pancakes are ready to flip when they're brown on the underside. Place the pancakes on a wire rack or paper towel–lined plate. Add oil, as needed, as you work. Use a slotted spoon to remove brown bits that stay in the pan to avoid a burnt-potato taste. If you're making a large batch you might want to discard the oil after four or more batches and add fresh oil. Serve the pancakes as soon after cooking as you can; if not, keep them warm in the oven at a low temperature. Serve with applesauce and sour cream.

TO MAKE KUGEL

Preheat oven to 350 F. Generously oil a 13 x 9 baking pan. Pour in the pancake batter. Bake until the top of the kugel is brown and a thin knife inserted comes out clean, about 45 to 50 minutes. Serve hot from the pan. **SERVES 6-8**

NOTES AND VARIATIONS

Mimi Sheraton goes on to separate the eggs, and whips the whites for very light, crisp pancakes. It's a very nice touch, which if I have time for I like, but it's a step I usually skip. You might also try the shredder blade of your processor for hash brown–style crispiness.

APPLESAUCE

I grew up with applesauce that was unsweetened, but my boys like me to add a little sugar when I make it at home, especially when I use tart apples. I also like to add a cinnamon stick or a little cardamom and serve it cold. A friend of mine uses red apples and doesn't peel them. When the apples are soft and cooked she puts the mixture through a food mill for pretty pink applesauce. In the Hudson Valley we are lucky to be able to choose from a wide variety of apples. **SERVES 6-8**

6 apples, peeled, cored, and cut into chunks (any variety, but each will produce a slightly different flavor)

Optional: sugar, maple syrup, cinnamon, and nutmeg

Menu 36, potato kugel with yogurt on the side

Place the apple chunks in a saucepan with ½ cup water over medium heat. As the apples cooks you will notice whether they're giving off a lot of water or if they're dry and starting to stick to the bottom of the pan. If they stick, add a little water. Mash the apples in the pot as they cook. I don't mind lumps but, if you prefer, you can put the cooked apples in a food processor for a smother sauce. Taste the apples as they cook and decide if you want to sweeten the sauce, spice it, or do both. Start with a small amount of sweetener and a pinch of spice and gradually add more until it tastes right.

BLACK RADISHES

We buy black radishes well into the winter from local farms that store them. We often serve them raw. Last year we started getting watermelon radishes (whitish green on the outside, vibrant pink inside). Mixed in a salad with thinly sliced black radishes, the combination makes a dramatic platter. **SERVES 6-8**

6 black radishes, thinly sliced (see Notes and Variations below)	Juice of 1 lemon 3 tbsp. olive oil Salt & black pepper

Place the radishes in a mixing bowl and, just before serving, toss with lemon juice, olive oil, salt, and pepper.

NOTES AND VARIATIONS

To get the thinnest slices, a mandoline comes in handy. The inexpensive Japanese mandolines work well (use the guard please). Black radishes are woodier than small red ones, so it's important to slice them as thin as possible.

RUSSIAN DRESSING

It's very rare for us to serve a rich dressing such as this at the Institute, but we make it in winter, once in a while. It is a popular treat and with fewer varieties of fresh ingredients in the winter it is a good time to pull out exotic or rich foods. For information on greens and instructions on dressing a salad, see page 229. Makes 2½ cups. **SERVES 10-12**

2 cups mayonnaise (store bought or homemade, see page 205)	2 tbsp. horseradish
	2 tsp. Worcestershire sauce
	Juice of 1 lemon
½ cup ketchup	Salt & black pepper

Whisk mayonnaise, ketchup, horseradish, and Worcestershire together. Add lemon juice, salt, and pepper. Taste and adjust salt and pepper.

FLOURLESS CHOCOLATE CAKE

This is a very simple recipe for a cake that looks fancy. This isn't a soft-in-the-middle cake; it bakes all the way through. First it rises like a soufflé, then it settles a bit. The texture is soft and delicate, but it's forgiving and lasts for days. It keeps best when left unrefrigerated. **SERVES 8-10**

12 oz. bittersweet chocolate, broken into approximately 1-in. to 2-in. chunks	¾ cup granulated sugar, divided
	8 eggs, separated
12 tbsp. unsalted, room-temperature butter plus more for the pan	

Chocolate soufflé cake made in the early summer, garnished with cherries

Preheat oven to 325 F. Butter a 9-inch springform pan.

In a mixing bowl combine the chocolate, butter, and ½ cup sugar.

Place the bowl over a pot of boiling water (or in the top of a double boiler) taking care that the underside of the bowl does not touch the water. Heat until the chocolate is melted, 10 to 15 minutes. When it's melted, using a rubber spatula, blend the chocolate, butter, and sugar until mixed and set aside. You want the chocolate to be warm but not hot as you add the mixture to the eggs.

In another bowl, mix the egg yolks with the remaining ¼ cup sugar. Blend the chocolate mixture into the egg mixture using the spatula and set aside.

Beat the egg whites with a whisk or the whisk attachment of a standing mixer until medium peaks form (not too stiff and dry). Fold a little of the egg whites into the chocolate mixture to loosen it, then fold the rest of the chocolate into the egg whites.

Gently pour the thick batter into the prepared cake pan and bake for about 35 to 45 minutes. The cake should rise all the way across but not so much it cracks. It's better to slightly underbake than to overbake.

Allow the cake to cool. Remove from the pan, cut, and serve.

NOTES AND VARIATIONS

This cake is pretty dusted with powdered sugar. You may also serve with whipped cream, berries, or both.

Adding a ¼ cup of ground toasted almonds and 1 teaspoon of cinnamon to the batter is good and adds a little Mexican flavor. You can also add a pinch or two of cayenne if you like spicy chocolate.

CHAPTER 13

OUR BREAKFAST BUFFET WITH RECIPES

Our breakfast buffet at the Institute is pretty similar from day to day. We try to have something for everyone with choices of granola, yogurt, scones, egg dishes, sliced fruit, breakfast breads and muffins, steel-cut oatmeal, butter, jam, peanut butter, brown sugar, and maple syrup. In addition, when groups are with us for longer stretches we prepare specials such as grits and baked French toast and various scrambled-egg dishes.

WALNUT, RAISIN, SESAME, HONEY GRANOLA

CHERRY, LEMON ZEST, HAZELNUT, AND MAPLE SYRUP GRANOLA

CHEDDAR-FENNEL SCONES

CRANBERRY-GINGER SCONES

MRS. LEWIS'S BLUEBERRY MUFFINS

OATMEAL

CHEESE GRITS

EGGS FOUR WAYS:
—HARD-BOILED
—SOFT-BOILED
—OVER-EASY
—SCRAMBLED

EGG SALAD

SCALLION EGGS

BROWN ONIONS AND EGGS

BAKED FRENCH TOAST

WALNUT, RAISIN, SESAME, HONEY GRANOLA

There are, of course, endless varieties of granola. You can follow the basic recipe but add dried coconut, any nuts, spices, or seeds you like. Remember to add the dried fruit to the finished, cooled granola. Fruit will burn and/or dry out baked in with the oats. **SERVES 8–12**

4 cups rolled oats
1½ cups walnuts
6 tbsp. mild olive oil, grape seed, or coconut oil
⅓ cup honey

2 tbsp. sesame seeds
1 tsp. cinnamon
½ tsp. salt
1 cup raisins or dried cranberries

Preheat oven to 250 F. Line a baking sheet with parchment. In a mixing bowl, toss together all ingredients except the raisins. Spread the mixture on to the baking sheet and bake for 15 minutes. Look at it, and if the edges have begun to brown before the middle, fold the mixture in from the sides to the center, spread flat so that the granola cooks evenly. Put the granola back into the oven and continue to check its progress every 15 minutes or so. It takes 40 to 50 minutes to bake completely. It will be lightly browned.

When it's finished, allow the granola to cool in the pan, break it up into bite-size pieces as necessary, and add the dried fruit. Granola may be stored in a jar or a sealed bag for a few weeks. Serve with milk, yogurt, or as a snack plain or over ice cream.

CHERRY, LEMON ZEST, HAZELNUT, AND MAPLE SYRUP GRANOLA

Here is another, slightly fancier, version of granola. **SERVES 8–12**

4 cups rolled oats
1½ cups hazelnuts
6 tbsp. mild olive oil (substitute grape seed oil or coconut oil)
⅓ cup maple syrup
2 tbsp. sesame seeds
2 tbsp. pumpkin seeds (substitute sunflower seeds)
1 tsp. nutmeg
½ tsp. salt
1 cup dried cherries
1 tbsp. candied ginger (optional)
1 tbsp. lemon zest (optional)
1 tsp. fennel seed (optional)

Prepare in the same way as Walnut, Raisin, Sesame, and Honey Granola.

CHEDDAR-FENNEL SCONES

Our base scone recipe works with savory and sweet flavorings. For a simple scone leave out all the flavorings and add raisins or currants and a teaspoon of lemon zest. **MAKES 12 SCONES**

2 cups all-purpose, unbleached flour
1 tbsp. baking powder
1 tsp. salt
1 tsp. cayenne (optional)
½ tsp. granulated sugar
4 tbsp. cold, unsalted butter
1 cup shredded sharp cheddar cheese
½ cup half-and-half or cream
1 egg, beaten
¼ cup heavy cream for brushing tops
2 tsp. coarsely ground fennel seed, or whole seeds if you prefer
2 tsp. coarse sea salt, such as Maldon

Preheat oven to 450 F. Mix the dry ingredients together. Cut the butter into the dry ingredients, using a pastry blender, or two butter knives in a crisscross manner, or use your hands to blend the butter between your fingers. Add the cheese. Mix the half-and-half with the beaten egg and stir into the flour mixture. Use a fork to combine, but do not overmix. Knead as little as possible to form into a dough. Divide the dough into three balls and pat each out into a ½-inch-thick circle. Using a knife, cut each flattened dough ball into four triangular scones. Place on a parchment-lined baking sheet. Brush the tops with heavy cream and sprinkle with salt and fennel seed. Bake until golden brown, about 12 minutes.

CRANBERRY-GINGER SCONES

MAKES 12 SCONES

3 cups all-purpose, unbleached flour
1 tbsp. baking powder
Pinch salt
2 sticks cold, unsalted butter
⅔ cup heavy cream
1 egg, beaten
½ cup dried cranberries (substitute dried cherries)
1 tbsp. chopped candied ginger
½ cup chopped pecans, lightly toasted
¼ cup heavy cream for brushing tops
2 tbsp. raw sugar

Preheat oven to 400 F. Mix the dry ingredients together. Cut the butter into the dry ingredients, using a pastry blender, or two butter knives in a crisscross manner, or use your hands to blend the butter between your fingers. Mix the cream with the beaten egg and stir into the flour mixture. Use a fork, but do not overmix. Add the dried fruit, ginger, and pecans. Divide the dough into three balls and pat each out into a ½-inch-thick circle. Cut each into four triangular scones. Place on a parchment-lined baking sheet. Brush the tops with heavy cream and sprinkle with raw sugar. Bake until golden brown, about 15 to 18 minutes.

MRS. LEWIS'S BLUEBERRY MUFFINS

Shirley Lewis, my late-mother-in-law, made great muffins. Not too big or too sweet with just the right amount of blueberries. My sister-in-law recorded this recipe, and it's what we use at the Institute. **MAKES 12 MUFFINS**

1½ cups flour (use part whole wheat if you like)
½ cup sugar (I use raw sugar)
2½ tsp. baking powder
½ tsp. salt
½ cup whole milk
4 tbsp. unsalted, room-temperature butter
1 egg, lightly beaten
½ tsp. vanilla extract
1 cup fresh blueberries, (substitute frozen berries)
1½ tbsp. cinnamon sugar, use a proportion of 2 to 1 sugar to cinnamon, for sprinkling

Preheat oven to 400 F.
Grease a 12-cup muffin pan or fill with paper liners.
Mix the flour, sugar, baking powder, and salt in a bowl. Add the milk, butter, egg, and vanilla. Cut in the liquid ingredients with a pastry blender, or do this gently using the paddle attachment of a stand mixer.
Carefully fold in the blueberries.
Distribute the batter evenly in the muffin tin. Sprinkle the top of each uncooked muffin with cinnamon sugar and bake until the muffin springs back when you press on it or a thin knife inserted into the center of a muffin comes out clean, 15 to 20 minutes.

OATMEAL

We serve Irish, or steel-cut, oats at the Institute almost every morning. They're the only kind of hot cooked oats I enjoy. Coarsely cut, not rolled, they're nutty and a bit crunchy, depending on how much water you use and how long you cook them. We serve various toppings on the side. In many stores you can find McCann's brand or find steel-cut oats in bulk at health food stores. **SERVES 6–8**

We use a rice cooker to cook oatmeal. The basic proportion in a rice cooker is between 2½ to 3 parts water to 1 part oats. If you're cooking in a pot on the stove, the ratio is more like 4½ cups water to 1 cup oatmeal. I like my oats thick, sticky, and a tiny bit crunchy. More water and more time yields creamier, softer oats. I like a little maple syrup on top, but you can serve brown sugar, dried fruit or nuts, warm milk, butter, honey, or berries. Depending on the amount you make it can take between 20 to 30 minutes to prepare.

CHEESE GRITS

Grits are a hot-breakfast alternative to oatmeal at the Institute. I was introduced to grits by my Southern roommates when I lived in New York City. They were from Georgia and growing up mostly ate white grits. When we could spend the extra money, we bought whole grits with "specs" of husk, which are very tasty. Sometimes we added an egg yolk at the end of the cooking, sometimes just butter, sometimes cheese. At the Institute we serve grits soft from a soup cauldron to be eaten sweet or savory depending on how guests choose to top them. Sometimes we serve them with lots of cheese baked in a hotel pan. Instead of eating them at breakfast you might serve these cheese grits as part of a lunch or supper buffet. **SERVES 8–10**

1 cup coarse grits	1 cup to 3 cups grated cheddar,
4 cups water	Gruyère, local hard cheeses, or
Salt	Parmesan in any combination
2 tbsp. to 4 tbsp. butter	(optional)
(optional)	1 cup maple syrup (optional)

Prepare grits per the package directions. If you buy grits in bulk, depending on the coarseness, cook grits with the ratio of about 4 parts water to 1 part grits for medium and coarse grinds. The ratio for finer grinds is 2 parts water to 1 part grits. If after cooking, your grits are tender but too watery you can gently boil them until the water evaporates. If you need more water, simply add it. Add a pinch of salt to bring out the flavor. Serve plain or with optional butter. Serve cheese or maple syrup or both on the side.

To bake the grits, prepare enough grits to yield 2 quarts cooked, soft grits. Add anywhere from 1 cup to 3 cups cheese and spread the cheesy grits into the buttered ovenproof pan and bake in a preheated 375 F oven until the top is golden brown, about 20 to 25 minutes.

EGGS FOUR WAYS

These recipes may seem self-evident, but I always like to read about the quirky, personal ways other people cook and eat their eggs. At home, for all eggs except boiled, I use a cast-iron skillet or a seasoned black steel pan. In a pinch, I will use an enameled cast-iron pan; stainless steel isn't very good for eggs.

HARD-BOILED

Place however many eggs you want to make in a saucepan that holds them comfortably but is not too big, cover with cold water, and bring to a boil. When the water boils, immediately cover the pot, turn off the heat and leave the pot on the burner for 10 to 12 minutes. I used to swear by 10 minutes, but frequently the center of the yolk was slightly chewy. I like the yolk cooked through, even if it means risking having it slightly overcooked. I think of the texture of a perfectly hard-boiled egg yolk as pleasantly dusty.

SOFT-BOILED

I love David Chang's poached-in-the-shell, soft-cooked egg recipe from his Momofuku cookbook. He puts eggs in a 140 F bath for about 45 minutes. The result is amazing: the eggs slip out of their shell, creamy soft, the yolk runny. Practically speaking, I'm not usually in a position to take 45 minutes to soft boil an egg. My recipe was to add cold eggs to boiling water and remove them after 4 minutes, always suffering a little loose white for a running yolk, then I was introduced to the David Chang quick method. He also adds the eggs to boiling water, but cooks them for exactly 5 minutes and 10 seconds, and they are perfect. If you don't want to eat the eggs immediately, place them in ice water to stop the cooking. Simply heat them in warm water for a minute to take off the chill before serving.

OVER-EASY

I don't like broken fried eggs, almost to the point of neurosis. Let's just say I would have to be really hungry to eat an egg that breaks in the pan. I try to find a taker when it happens, and when I can't, my dog Jones gets lucky. I use butter to fry eggs, when I try safflower, grape seed, or olive oil the eggs often stick to the pan. When the butter is medium hot, just beginning to bubble, I crack the egg into the pan. After about 20 seconds I use a very thin, very flexible spatula to gently lift the egg and turn it over. My goal is to cook the white through and have the runniest-possible yolk. After I turn the egg I gently poke the white in a few places so that some of the white runs out, hits the pan, and cooks. I flip the egg again so that the loose egg white cooks; the white surrounding the yolk is thin and fragile. I might do this a few times making sure the yolk is still soft. I remove the egg from the pan to top vegetables, toast, rice, noodles, or just to eat plain.

SCRAMBLED

When I make scrambled eggs, I mix them well. I use a type of small whisk that's more like a spring. Growing up my kids called it the "boinger." Another neurosis of mine: No white can show. I make scrambled eggs for my family the way my mother-in-law cooked them: I melt butter in a saucepan, and when it's hot, I add the eggs, constantly lifting them with a fork like an omelet so that the egg doesn't overcook. I stop them when they're quite soft. When I lift the eggs onto the plate I make sure the wet part stays on top so the eggs remain creamy. When the boys have friends over, I usually turn their eggs over into the pan once so that they aren't so soft.

My mother added milk to our scrambled eggs, probably to stretch them. Because I grew up with milk added, eggs cooked this way remain one of my ultimate comfort foods. I add about 1 teaspoon of milk per egg, but I'm never precise. I then pour the mixed eggs into the buttered pan and stir slowly to keep the curds large. When the eggs hit the plate, tasty water releases and the overall flavor is wonderfully mild.

Fankuchen translates literally as pancake, and that's what my father called his favorite eggs for a sandwich. This is made from beaten eggs that weren't scrambled, but were cooked like a pancake or a flat omelet and eaten with lots of salt and pepper on a buttered Kaiser roll or buttered rye toast. We use the same method at the Institute when making our version of egg foo yong. We add filling to the pan, scallions or pork, not unlike a frittata, but even thinner, so it can be easily flipped. We make these egg pancakes when we add egg to fried rice. To both of these I might mix in a bit of sesame oil.

EGG SALAD

We serve hard-boiled eggs every day as part of the breakfast buffet at the Institute, which means we're always prepared to make egg salad. We usually use Hellman's mayonnaise. I love homemade mayonnaise and think it's worth making if you have good eggs and a little time. Mayonnaise, salt, pepper, and chopped eggs are all you really need. Chopped chives are good if you use enough to allow the flavor to come through. Sometimes we add toasted curry powder. Egg salad sandwiches are particularly good with lots of watercress or arugula on brioche or pumpernickel bread.

SCALLION EGGS

This is another Dad recipe. I thought of this as Green Eggs growing up. The dish was a little smelly, with many scallions and hard-boiled eggs—not exactly a child's dream. I now find it snappy and tasty. We don't make this too often at the Institute for breakfast because it's so rich and spicy, but on multigrain bread it makes a good snack. The recipe is like egg salad made with butter instead of mayo. **SERVES 6-8**

8 fresh eggs, hard-boiled (see recipe, page 226)
2 bunches scallions, cut into ¼-in.slices (use the whole scallion)
4 tbsp. unsalted butter, cut into small chunks

Salt & black pepper
4 slices rye or your favorite bread, matzo, cracker, or rolls

Chop the hard-boiled eggs as you would for egg salad and place in a mixing bowl. Add the scallions and the butter and with a wooden spoon combine until mixed through and the butter is evenly distributed. Add a generous amount of salt and pepper, taste and adjust, and serve. It's best not to refrigerate as the butter will get very cold and hard. Serve with toast, rye bread, or on a Kaiser roll.

BROWN ONIONS AND EGGS

These are scrambled eggs with lots and lots of onions in them. It's one of a few recipes my father made for us growing up. He clearly liked eggs. **SERVES 4–6**

4 tbsp. unsalted butter
3 large Spanish onions, cut into
½-in. dice

Salt & black pepper
6 to 8 eggs, beaten

Melt the butter into a saucepan over medium-low heat. Add the onions, salt and pepper and cook, stirring occasionally, until the onions are light brown. This takes as long as 15 to 20 minutes. When the onions are the color you like, add the eggs and scramble until just set. There will be more onion than egg. A generous amount of salt in this dish balances the sweet onion flavor. Serve with buttered toast.

BAKED FRENCH TOAST

This is our way of making French toast for a big group without facing the challenge of making it to order. It's cross between traditional French toast and bread pudding, and we serve this with maple syrup on the side. **SERVES 6–8**

3 cups whole milk
5 large eggs
1 tsp. vanilla extract
Freshly grated nutmeg or ground
cinnamon (optional)
8 to 12 slices of bread, enough to fill ¾

of a 13 x 9 baking dish (I love sourdough bread, but any type will do including brioche, baguette, raisin bread, white, or wheat)
Maple syrup to pour on top just before eating

Preheat oven to 350 F. Beat together the milk, eggs, and vanilla in a mixing bowl. Add the nutmeg or cinnamon (if using).

Place the bread in the baking dish and cover with the milk-egg mixture, moving the bread around and flipping the slices so that the bread is evenly soaked. (You can do this the night before and let it sit in the refrigerator overnight.)

Bake until the bread is set, about 45 to 50 minutes. An instant-read thermometer should reach 160 F. Serve warm from the oven, as you would French toast with maple syrup on the side.

CHAPTER 14
SALAD

At every lunch and dinner at the Institute we serve a big bowl of greens with vinaigrette on the side. At home you might do the same, or toss your greens lightly with vinaigrette before serving. At our home we often dress our salads in what I think of as the Italian way. First the oil, toss, then vinegar or lemon (using a third or half the amount as the oil), salt and black pepper, toss again. I tend to like my salad dressed with a little more acid (vinegar or lemon usually) than most people. I much prefer sea salt, but kosher salt will do and I like to freshly grind my pepper. A portion of salad is anywhere from ½ cup to 2 cups per person. A tablespoon or 2 of dressing per person is plenty. Every menu in this book has a vinaigrette or salad-dressing recipe, but there is no mention of the greens. Any greens will do, depending on the time of year, what you like, and what's available to you.

There are a few farms that grow salad greens all year, either outside in hoop houses or in greenhouses, traditionally or hydroponically. In winter these salad mixes are a little pricey so we also keep romaine hearts on hand. We buy other individual salad greens as well: watercress, arugula, young spinach, Bibb and red-leaf lettuces, and occasionally radicchio, endive, and frisée, which tend to be more expensive.

In the spring, young salad greens are potent, crisp, and tender. In the summer, they are strong flavored, spicy, and more toothsome, and in the fall, bitter and slightly, pleasantly tough. Over the winter, the lettuces that grow outside in hoops or hydroponically are somewhat mild in flavor and gentle in texture.

At various times in addition to lettuce, our greens mix includes: dandelion, amaranth, chard, kale, mustard greens, tatsoi, assorted leafy herbs, and other small braising greens. There are also foraged wild greens, some of which to me are weedy and I am not too fond of, such as purslane or lamb's-quarter, though they're reasonably popular with other folks.

See Pantry (page 230) for information on oil and vinegar.

Summer leaf lettuces

CHAPTER 15

THE PANTRY

The strongest piece of cooking advice I can give is about ingredients. Know them. Look carefully. Smell and taste them—even bitter, dry herbs, vinegars, and plain fats. If something isn't very good or you don't like the smell or taste, get rid of it. While it is good to continue to experiment with new flavors, if you don't like the ingredients you're using, it's hard to make something that tastes good to you, much less to anyone else. If you don't like honey in a recipe, use maple syrup. If you don't like lamb, use chicken or beef. If you don't like cooked tomatoes, leave them out and add a little water or stock instead. Make food you like while considering the tastes of the people you're cooking for and the results will be consistently gratifying.

This pantry chapter is a personal inventory of the ingredients I like to have around at home, and at the Institute. I'll include what I use most often, items I put on a list to replace when I am running low. And I will provide a bigger assortment of ingredients I buy, ranging from frequently to from-time-to-time. I suggest buying the best ingredients you can afford. Some of the items on my list will be special treats and cost a lot, others are quite basic. Some can be found in any supermarket, others at specialty food stores, farmers' markets, your garden or fire escape, or online. I will note brands if I think it is very important, but the only way to know what you like is to experiment, and brands and availability will vary from state to state, and certainly around the world. I am a product of metro-New York and my pantry reflects my experience and history.

I have grouped items the way I think about them so while I know a peanut is a legume it is on the nut list, couscous is listed with grains, wild rice with rice, and categories overlap. These lists are meant as an example and a starter guide.

SPICES

Reading about food, traveling and eating, has taught me that there are unexpected similarities between world cuisines. While making burritos with my son one day, he noticed the ingredients on the counter and realized they weren't much different from the ingredients we had used to make rotis a few weeks earlier. I realized the texture combinations were similar as well. I traded yogurt and lemon for avocado and lime, tortillas for flatbread, dried ancho chiles-flavored beef for curry-flavored lamb. But the cilantro, cumin, coriander seeds, onion, tomato, and green chiles were common to both, as was the assembly. Spices have traveled all over the world, but specific combinations are very local to a place, in our case the cosmopolitan kitchens of New York, where we feel comfortable with the influences of many cuisines. I frequently buy whole spices and grind them, often from Penzey's in Wisconsin, ordered online.

My basic spice list includes black pepper, always freshly ground. Pre-ground pepper gets stale very quickly. Try Tellicherry peppercorns if you see them. Pre-ground cinnamon is my basic go-to variety; if I am ordering, I choose Chinese (for savory applications) and Vietnamese for sweets. I like cinnamon sticks for braises and for steeping in cream. Fennel seeds, vanilla extract (I am very happy if I have a vanilla bean for baking, but I usually don't remember to buy them), saffron (the expensive threads make rice, eggs, and soups very special, try a Spanish brand), star anise, nutmeg (I only buy whole and grate as needed), red chiles (I like at least one on hand even if all I have are red pepper flakes, see below for a bigger list I choose from), bay leaves, brown mustard seeds, brown cardamom, and caraway.

Other spices I frequently keep on hand, not necessarily all at one time, include cumin seeds, assorted chiles (whole pasilla, guajillo, arbol, pequin ancho and chipotle, ground cayenne, ground paprika, sweet and hot, ground ancho), dried oregano, juniper berries, mace blades, anise seeds, ground turmeric, whole cloves, green cardamom, and white pepper.

Salt can be a dilemma for many cooks. People who don't cook a lot don't realize how much salt affects the flavor of food. Saltiness is a personal preference, but when cooking for others it is worth noticing how often food is under salted, and over salted. Salt does make food taste better to most people, but cooks get salt fatigue and add more and more. Too much salt, for example, can mask the subtle taste of a fresh soft egg yolk. After cutting back on salt, I noticed it is easier than one might think to get used to lower amounts. Sea salt is less "salty" than iodized table salt and it has a crunchy texture and subtle mineral flavor. I keep kosher salt, Maldon sea salt, and "Fleur de sel" on hand. I use kosher salt for salting pasta water, making pickles, and when I am feeling frugal, but as much as I can I use sea salt for most everything else.

HERBS

When I was growing up, fresh herbs meant dill and parsley. My mother, on occasion and by mistake, bought (much to our dismay) Chinese parsley (cilantro). My experience is that one can develop a love of cilantro and that the so-called genetic offense people take is learned. By the time I moved to the city, fresh tarragon was showing up in chicken salad, fresh thyme with roasted chicken. My mother switched from dried rosemary on lamb chops to fresh. She bought fresh basil for pesto. She also started buying fresh herbs to experiment with their medical properties, an interest I have never developed. But the simpler my food has gotten, the more I make use of fresh herbs. I love them. I always have flat-leaf Italian parsley and cilantro.

At the Institute we have a small garden that is really an herb garden where we try to grow things that are cut and come back with a few other high-producing plants for variety. We have a short growing season and limited space, so we plant small vegetables that grow in abundance on each plant, like chiles and cherry tomatoes, or special items that would be too expensive for us to buy, like squash blossoms.

We grow brown cherry tomatoes, assorted spicy chiles, and all our favorite herbs: thyme, sorrel, tarragon, sage, chives, garlic chives, parsley, marjoram, lemongrass, shiso (I prefer the Japanese varieties—green and red), dill, cilantro, chervil, bronze fennel, basil (Thai and Italian), rosemary in pots, lemon verbena, spearmint, and black peppermint. We have a small asparagus bed, rhubarb, and a berry patch (for the birds).

MEAT, POULTRY, AND EGGS

At home and at the Institute I buy as little conventionally raised meat as possible (with the exception of skirt steak). Clearly I am not a vegetarian, but the state of conventional animal husbandry matters to me a lot. We do our best at the Institute to buy local meat from farms that treat their animals in as humane a manner as possible, given that they're farms raising livestock for slaughter. We buy beef from Padgett Farm in Upstate New York and through a co-op, Hudson Valley Farms, which buys from a group of local farms. We have access to lot of great local meat in the Hudson Valley, ducks, whole chickens, lamb (shanks shoulder chops and merguez are favorites at home), and pork (spare ribs, ground pork, bacon, shoulders, hot dogs, and various sausage are our favorites). For special occasions, I buy items from D'Artagnan like quail and rabbit, and I especially like squab.

We can also get local eggs easily. We typically buy from Featherstone, but when we can, we get eggs from nearby Glynwood Farm: blue eggs with orange yolks and amazing flavor.

FISH

I could give up meat for fish, but our oceans are in sad shape and the price of good fish makes it a special-occasion meal at the Institute. At home I serve whole fish, skate, blowfish when I see them, sardines, bluefish, flounder, blackfish, monkfish, plus shellfish like clams (hard and soft shelled) and oysters, raw and cooked, scallops, crabs (hard and soft shelled), and lobster. At the Institute, where we have to please larger groups and bone-in fish aren't an option, we stick to simpler varieties. Arctic char, though farmed, remains high on the recommended Seafood Watch list and has good taste, unlike many farmed fish with their bland or muddy taste, like farmed striped bass or catfish. We serve hake and wild striped bass (occasionally, so good, and fairly well protected, but expensive).

OILS AND FATS

At home I usually use grape seed or peanut oil for cooking, but sometimes I use olive oil as well. In general, olive oil and grape seed oil should be greenish in color. If they're yellow-golden or brownish, don't buy them, as they are likely rancid. Oils don't have as long a shelf life as people assume. Try to use them within a few months of purchase. I buy a good quality Spanish extra-virgin olive oil for basic vinaigrettes and some cooking, but I try to keep a good finishing oil around as well. My go-to fancy oil these days is Frantoia from Sicily. If I find it when it is unfiltered (cloudy) I grab a bottle as it is very flavorful. I don't cook with cold-pressed extra virgin olive oil that is of very high quality as the heat will destroy the flavor and it is waste of a lot of money. I love Tuscan olive oils, but they are so expensive and the best Sicilian ones are quite good. I prefer Italian olive oil to those from France and California, but that is totally subjective. There are great oils from all over, including Greece and Turkey, and it is worth experimenting. I like coconut oil a lot, but it has a noticeable flavor that needs to be considered and it's also expensive. Nut oils are especially volatile. I love LeBlanc brand toasted nut oils, especially hazelnut and walnut, and store those in the refrigerator. I keep toasted sesame oil on hand.

I love to cook with butter. Usually I use whole butter. There is nothing better than to fry an egg with than whole butter in a cast iron or rolled-steel pan. I like whole unsalted butter for baking, on top of vegetables, on bread, and at home we like a little whole butter added to most pasta recipes. Butter is typical in Moroccan cuisine to start the vegetable base of stews. I had a roommate who introduced me to peanut butter and jelly and butter, and it was good. I use clarified butter at high temperatures for things like crepes. Toasted clarified butter (ghee) is typical of Indian cuisine.

I also like to use rendered duck fat if I have it, especially scented with garlic. Growing up, my mother used chicken fat until we were told it was "bad." There isn't an area more contentious than "fat advice." Somehow my mother avoided buying into margarine as a butter substitute. (She had amazing good sense, but also good taste, and who really prefers the taste of margarine to butter?) She gave up shortening (Crisco) and something called Nyafat, which was a chicken-fat substitute that I kind of liked, though it is straight trans fat, something that actually does seem bad, along with highly refined oils. We weren't raised using lard, but I have used it since and, like coconut oil, rendered meat fats (when melted) are very thin, in a good way; a little goes a long way. Overall I tend towards vegetable fats for day-to-day cooking, but I think the world of butter and meat fats as great alternatives, depending on your recipe.

DAIRY

We have good local dairies in the Hudson Valley producing milk (Hudson Valley Fresh is a local dairy cooperative, and we have Ronnybrook Dairy) and a variety of cheeses. For a long time imported cheeses were way better than all but a few American cheeses (cheddar to name one), but as time has gone by, New York, Vermont, Massachusetts, California, Michigan, and many other states are producing very good cheese. We use a mix of local and imported cheeses at home and at the Institute for flavor due to budget.

We use, on a regular basis, imported Gruyére, Stilton, aged Gouda, New York State cheddar, and local cheeses from Amazing Real Live Cheese Company (I like their Camembert and Gruyére types), Old Chatham Sheepherding Company, and Sprout Creek Farm, along with a variety of other local and more specialty imported cheese from time to time. For pasta we usually use Grana Padano, but sometimes Reggiano-Parmigiano. We have two good local makers of mozzarella and ricotta. At the Institute we serve whole milk, skim, rice, or soy milk with granola and coffee. We serve and cook with sour cream, yogurt, and heavy cream. Look for NOT ultra-pasteurized heavy cream; whether or not it is organic, it is over heated and chalky tasting.

BEANS

At home I usually have dried and canned chickpeas and black beans and dried lentils, green, brown, and red. I also use at home red kidney beans, split peas, flageolet, cannellini, great northern, fancy unusual beans like Jacob cattle beans, appaloosa, Italian small chickpeas, and unpeeled black chickpeas.

At the Institute beans are a major source of protein. Generally I like to eat and cook one variety of bean at a time. Cooking them separately helps focus each flavor and by keeping them separate, there is more variety to our meals. I try to buy "fresh" dried beans from a good source like Cayuga in upstate New York, but the basic varieties from the supermarket work fine. For some people it takes a little time to get used to digesting beans. Occasionally, we get complaints from folks who aren't too fond of them. Navy beans baked with maple syrup, black beans with chiles, lentil soup, and chickpeas, plain and in hummus, are the most popular, and a good place to start when preparing beans for a family.

Typically, I soak dried beans overnight. Alternatively, I use the quick-soak method by bringing them to a boil in a big pot of water, draining, and starting with fresh water. I find beans break apart if you rush them, but sometimes you need to rush. I usually salt beans from the get-go, which may make them take longer to cook but results in a more evenly seasoned dish at the end since whole beans cooked with no salt will always be a little under-salted even after they are dressed. While we usually use dried beans the Institute, we sometimes use canned chickpeas and canned red kidney beans as well as a fancy brand of giant white, Greek-style beans, which are hard to find dried. Canned beans are consistent and taste good, if a little salty and mushier. We use frozen edamame in rice and soup and tofu.

PASTA, NOODLES, AND GRAINS

In America, we often eat pasta as a main course. In Italy, pasta is sauced lightly and makes up only one small course at dinner. When I serve pasta at the Institute I like to have about half the ingredients of the dish be pasta and the other half vegetables and sauce.

Spaghetti is my all-time favorite, my kids love rigatoni and penne, but for large groups I like orrechiette as it keeps its bite. Unless I see a very special locally-made brand of pasta, I love good-quality Italian durum wheat pasta. My basic brand is De Cecco, but the rough bronze dye-cut "artisanal" are worth trying. I love my pasta quite firm. I have learned to enjoy whole wheat pasta (it really can't be overcooked), but my family, not so much. In addition to classic wheat pasta, we serve lots of rice noodles, cello noodles, rice paper, couscous (North African-style, Israeli, and Sardinian [fregola]), freekeh, and corn pasta (an alternative for folks who want to avoid gluten).

We also serve a lot of grains at the Institute. We serve polenta from Wild Hive, white rice (jasmine, arborio, and basmati), haiga rice, which is partially polished and a favorite of mine, short-grained brown rice, wild rice, farro, a wide variety of wheat berries, barley (pearled, whole, and purple), quinoa (red and white), posole (small dried, blue variety, when possible), steel-cut oats, and kasha, to name most. We use a rice cooker for rice and often for other grains when we're serving them plain. It not only frees up stove-top space, but does a great job.

I like egg noodles, Chinese and Eastern European style, thin and wide (the thin precooked variety found at Chinese markets are great for pan-fried noodles (the recipe is not included here as it is not great for very large groups, but it's easy to find online), rice noodles, Korean rice cakes (ovalettes), mung bean or cello noodles, soba noodles (these vary a lot depending on where you buy them, sometimes made from all or part buckwheat, fresh and dried), and udon noodles, fresh or frozen.

We buy bread from Eli's in New York City and from Bread Alone in the Catskills. We alternate their many varieties; sourdough and rye are my favorites. We have made our own and kept a starter going, but we don't really have the space to bake our own bread for as many people as we need to feed. We order our tortillas, flour, and corn from Harbar in Boston. Their flour tortillas are made without preservatives and are consequently less gummy than more commercial varieties. Still, we always heat them on the flattop griddle to lightly char and slightly dry out the bread.

VINEGAR

I'll list lemon here as it falls into the same category as vinegar for me much of the time, as does all citrus. I love lemon on many things: salad, hummus, meats, greens, and fish. I always freshly squeeze lemons as the bright acid taste fades quickly. I usually have a few vinegars on hand. I love sherry vinegar and most brands are good; the older ones have a developed flavor, cost a little more, but I wouldn't say are better, just different. I like French red wine and white wine vinegars, but prefer red. I keep rice vinegar (unseasoned) around for a mild, low-acid taste. At the Institute we use a basic cider vinegar to make pickles and a nice French one for vinaigrettes. I am a bit tired of the sweet taste of balsamic (we don't buy the fancy authentic versions), but combined with lemon juice it is good on bitter, winter salads.

SAVORY CONDIMENTS

Maille is my favorite commercial-brand Dijon mustard. It is robust and spicy. Maille makes a good grain mustard as well. It is a true sauce in a jar, good on canned sardines, with meat, generously basted on a roasted chicken, in vinaigrettes.

I always have a few premade hot sauces around. While I like to purée fresh chiles in a blender with vinegar and salt, it is easy and fun to take out a bottle for folks to use and it usually starts a conversation. Phillip likes Frank's original, your basic wings sauce; Matt prefers Tabasco or Asian sauces like Schriracha, Sambal Oelek, hot sesame chile oil, or chile paste.

We always have a basic soy sauce and a few unusual varieties if I have been to Chinatown, Vietnamese fish sauce, Worcestershire sauce, and sometimes, Vietnamese sweet chile sauce. I like salted capers; the ones in vinegar taste like cheap vinegar to me. We often have anchovies from a simple affordable jar with oil to filets packed in salt to very fancy Spanish ones we had once that were creamy, not too salty, really expensive and delicious, bought at Despana in New York City.

I typically buy Heinz ketchup. I like tomato paste for sauce bases. Peanut butter, smooth and natural at all times, sesame paste after a visit to Chinatown or H-mart. At the Institute and at home we have yuzu, tahini, chile paste for a quick curry, various olives, Hellman's mayo. We have honey (I love Italian chestnut honey and local wildflower) and maple syrup for sweet and savory applications.

BAKING

We use a variety of flour, but our basic flour is King Arthur's unbleached white. We buy whole wheat flour from a local mill called Wild Hive that also sells some of the best polenta I have ever had. We use chickpea flour, hazelnut flour, masa harina, buckwheat flour, and rye. We have on hand baking soda, baking powder, corn starch (my nephew suggests mung bean starch, but I haven't tried it yet), gelatin and agar, and Paul, our new chef, has been introducing the kitchen to various elements used in molecular gastronomy, which has been fun. We use Valrona cocoa, Belgian chocolate, nuts (see separate listing), and dried fruits such as cranberries, cherries, dates, and apricots (I try, but it is hard to find these unsulphured in bulk). We have rolled oats for granola and cookies, molasses, coconut (sweetened and unsweetened), raw sugar, and granulated sugar.

NUTS

At home I always have peanuts, almonds, and walnuts. As treats and for baking, I buy pecans and hazelnuts. I also love cashews, pistachios, chestnuts in season, and sunflower seeds. Nuts are like meat in vegetarian cooking, almost as important as onions. At the Institute we use the same varieties mentioned above in sauces and bean patties. Shelled pumpkin seeds make a great snack when we toss them lightly with vegetable oil, lemon, and sea salt, and roast them until just golden.

VEGETABLES AND FRUIT

This is the area that is really most seasonal. We use so many vegetables and, to a lesser extent, fruit, that it is easier to list the ones I hardly buy, either because they just aren't my favorites (okra comes to mind, though crispy, pickled, or fried okra isn't bad), expensive (like endive) or very labor intensive (like artichokes, cardoons, peas, and beans in the pod), currants, and quince. All the rest are in and out of the kitchen in great abundance.

Onions galore! We can't get enough Spanish onions, red onions, spring onions, scallions, ramps, leeks, chives, garlic chives, garlic chive blossoms, conventional garlic and new garlic, and hardened-off local garlic and shallots.

In spring we grow a few and buy locally lots of asparagus. We can get spinach, lettuces, kale, dandelion, all greens, carrots, strawberries, rhubarb, mushrooms, the spring onion family, and foraged sassafras.

At the height of summer we get amazing tomatoes from Four Winds Farm, greens from Blooming Hill farm, string beans, summer squash, lots and lots of greens, turnips, corn, eggplant, parsnips, potatoes, peppers, fennel, melon, peaches, nectarines, plums, berries, and onions.

In the fall, Concord grapes, winter squash (I love sweet dumpling, golden nugget, butternut, and kabocha), still greens, cauliflower, broccoli, cabbage, celery root, apples, pears, quince, Jerusalem artichokes, potatoes, and onions.

Conventionally, and through the winter, we buy carrots, leeks, herbs, greens, lemon, limes, oranges, grapefruit, pineapple, melon, sweet potatoes, potatoes, avocadoes, cabbage, broccoli, and onions.

A STARTER LARDER (WITH EQUIPMENT)

If I had to set up a first, limited kitchen for myself (this would work even in a shared dorm kitchen), I could cook and eat well for a long time with the following basics:

SHELF

Olive oil	Sea salt	Chickpeas, dry
Red wine vinegar	Pepper in a mill	Black beans, dry
Soy sauce	Hot sauce	Canned plum tomatoes
Sesame oil	Jasmine rice	Canned chicken broth
Peanut butter	Spaghetti or penne	
Honey	Finn crisp crackers	

FRESH

Lemon	Eggs	Greens
Butter	Parsley	Ginger
Fresh garlic	Cilantro	Flour or corn tortillas
Bacon or sausage	Scallion	Avocadoes (a treat)
Parmesan cheese	Onion	
Cheddar cheese	Carrots	

EQUIPMENT

Rice cooker	Kitchen scissors	6 each–plates, mugs,
Pasta pot	Vegetable peeler	soup bowls, forks,
Colander	Wooden spoon	spoons, knives, cloth,
Small saucepan	Cutting board	napkins
10" cast-iron skillet	Thin, flexible metal	8 drinking glasses
1 paring knife	spatula	Church key
8" chef knife	3 sizes mixing bowls	Wine opener

CAN'T LIVE WITHOUT

Coffee beans, simple spice grinder–type coffee grinder, Bialetti stovetop coffee maker, whole milk, chocolate bar. A microwave, a toaster oven, and a 12" skillet would be my next purchases.

INDEX

ABOUT

SHELLEY BORIS

is the chef at the Garrison Institute and is a partner at Fresh Company, where she is the creative director and executive chef. She is inspired by a diversity of regional cooking styles from around the world. In the kitchen, Shelley's warm, relaxed sensibility is an extension of her love of a leisurely stay at the table and her belief in the elemental value of eating and drinking well. A board member emerita of Cold Spring's Farmers' Market, Shelley has long worked to support sustainable agriculture in the Hudson Valley. She lives in Garrison, New York, with her husband and two sons.

THE GARRISON INSTITUTE

explores the intersection between contemplation and engaged action in the world, applying contemplative wisdom to social and environmental change. Its program initiatives on education, environment and trauma care are complemented and enriched by the diverse teachers from around the world who lead retreats there, and whose teachings are conducive to personal and social transformation.